Come to the Water

The Diocese of Springfield in Illinois
1853-2003

A Sesquicentennial History

by

Susan Karina Dickey, O.P.

Jubilee 2003

Catholic Diocese of Springfield in Illinois • 150 Years

The writing of *Come to the Water: The Diocese of Springfield in Illinois, 1853-2003*
was made possible, in part, through the Annual Catholice Services Appeal.

ANNUAL
CATHOLIC SERVICES APPEAL
OFFICE OF THE CHANCELLOR/
PLANNING COORDINATOR

Contemporary photographs by Frantisek Zvardon and Dolce Design

Historical photographs are from the Archives of the Diocese of Springfield in Illinois, *Catholic Times*
and from parish histories except when noted otherwise

Publishing Director: Christian Riehl

Design and Layout: Dolce Design, Springfield, Illinois

Director of Publication: Dr. Claude-Bernard Costecalde

Cover Illustration: Mississippi River, Calhoun County

Published by Editions du Signe
1, rue Alfred Kastler
67038 Strasbourg, Cedex 2 - France
Tel. (33) 88 78 91 91 / Fax (33) 88 78 91 99

ISBN: 2-7468-0777-7
Printed in Italy by Arti Grafiche

ÉDITIONS
DU SIGNE

Table of Contents

Dear Friends,

It is a privilege for me to present this beautiful history of the Diocese of Springfield in Illinois as we celebrate 150 years since the founding of the diocese. During this sesquicentennial celebration, we give thanks to God for the lives of all who have gone before us in southern and central Illinois, who have been marked with the sign of faith.

Our see city has been changed twice, from Quincy to Alton and from Alton to Springfield. However, the journey described in these pages is the journey of God's pilgrim people on their way to full life in God's kingdom. Two things are evident to me as I read the story of their journey. The gifts of the Holy Spirit have been given us in abundance, and individual Catholics have cooperated with grace to build up the Body of Christ with the gifts they have been given.

Our diocesan crest pictures a "field of springs," a reference, of course, to the name Springfield. Throughout our history, in farm fields and coal fields, in towns and cities, we have been enlivened by the sacramental springs of God's grace. At this time of diocesan jubilee, we come again to that life-giving water to drink from our rich Catholic heritage and to be refreshed with hope to continue our pilgrimage of faith.

May God bless us all, laity, religious and clergy, with every grace we need to remain faithful.

Sincerely in Christ,

+ George J. Lucas

Most Reverend George J. Lucas
Bishop of Springfield in Illinois

Preface

"Gather up the crusts that are leftover so that nothing will go to waste."
John 6:12

After Jesus fed the multitudes the disciples gathered up the leftover loaves. Historical research is something like that. Church historians gather up fragments—in the form of documents, photographs, and artifacts—left by our ancestors in the faith. For the past two-and-one-half years it has been my privilege to gather up these bits and pieces to write the sesquicentennial history of the Diocese of Springfield in Illinois. Just as food nourishes the body, history nourishes the mind. So I hope that readers will find this book to be educational, entertaining, and most of all, edifying.

No history of this type can be all things to all people. Some will be disappointed that the stories of individual parishes are not included. Early on, the Diocesan Sesquicentennial Steering Committee decided that compiling such histories would result in an entirely different kind of book. Nor was it possible to include every story I collected. Our aim was to tell the overall history of the diocese so as to better understand our role as Catholics who are part of the universal Church who live, work, and worship in our particular diocese.

Photographs, however, of each active parish church, as of February 1, 2002, will be found in the special portfolio. These images are arranged chronologically by the year of founding. The names of parishes that formerly existed, but were later suppressed, are included and appear on the timeline with events of state, national, and ecclesiastical importance.

All historians stand on the shoulders of their predecessors and colleagues. I am indebted to the late Joseph J. Thompson, the editor of *The Diocese of Springfield in Illinois, Diamond Jubilee, 1853-1928*. This monumental work was an invaluable reference in ascertaining the temporal and spiritual condition of our diocese in the nineteenth and early twentieth centuries. I also wish to thank James E. Davis, Professor of History, Illinois College, Jacksonville, Illinois, and Monsignor Robert F. Trisco, editor of *The Catholic Historical Review* and Professor Emeritus of Church History, The Catholic University of America, Washington, D.C. Their criticism and encouragement were most helpful. As the author, however, I assume responsibility for any errors that remain.

A few words about stylistic conventions are in order. Readers will notice, for example, that the word "Saint" is sometimes spelled out and other times abbreviated. I deferred to the usage preferred by the church or institution involved. The same rule applied to the use of the possessive in a saint's name. Thus, for example, you will see "St. John's Hospital," but St. Teresa High School." Regarding the identity of persons in the photographs, names were provided when known.

Numerous individuals and institutions helped to bring this project to completion. They are listed at the end of the book, but a few deserve special mention. Sister Mary Bernardine Kapusta, O.P., examined back issues of *The Western Catholic, Time & Eternity,* and the *Catholic Times* newspapers to extract information about the history of the diocese. I also wish to thank Father J. Michael Jenkins of St. Mary, Pittsfield. He provided detailed information about the history of the Catholics in Pike County and responded generously to every call for help.

I am also grateful to the other members of the Diocesan Sesquicentennial Steering Committee. Sadly, we were deprived of the presence of Sister Mary Matthias Clarke, diocesan archivist, due to her untimely death in January 2002. The remaining members are Very Reverend John Renken, V.G. (Chair); Reverend Thom Dennis; Eliot Kapitan; Patrick Fitzgerald; Marlene Mulford; Kathie Sass; Brother Patrick Shea, O.F.M.; and Monsignor Paul Sheridan. The sisters of my local community, St. Rose Convent, Springfield, also merit a word of praise. Their patience, good humor, and support are most appreciated.

May God bless you all.

Yours in Christ,

Susan Karina Dickey, O.P., Ph.D.
Archivist and Diocesan Historian

The Church Comes to Illinois

1663 to 1853

"Go therefore and make disciples of all nations, baptizing them in the name of the Father, and of the Son and of the Holy Spirit, and teaching them to obey everything that I have commanded you. And remember, I am with you always, to the end of the age."

Matthew 28:19-20

CHAPTER ONE
French Beginnings

Jesus' words have inspired generations of missionaries including the Jesuits who planted the seeds of Christianity in Illinois. The mandate to baptize and teach spurred them to extraordinary feats of endurance, but their efforts were simply one part of a larger movement. During the Age of Discovery, Europeans extended their influence to parts of Africa, East Asia, and the New World. Missionary activity went hand in hand with the business of exploration and trade because Christians took to heart the commission to baptize and teach.

At the risk of oversimplifying, the missionaries labored for the glory of God and the explorers for the glory of king and country. In reality, these motivations overlapped. Winning converts brought honor to the king, and missionaries took pride in helping to advance the prestige of their homelands. Both zeal for the faith and a taste for adventure attracted young men, men like Jacques Marquette, into the missionary orders.

Father Jacques Marquette, S.J., first missionary to the Illinois County.
Photo courtesy of the Midwest Province, Society of Jesus.

In fact, our roots as a diocese extend back to Marquette's first meeting with the Illini Indians.

The Illini—also called the Illiniwek or the Illinois—were a confederacy of Algonquin tribes including the Kaskaskia, Peoria, Cahokia, Tamaroa, and Michigamea. In the pre-contact period they occupied about sixty-five villages in a roughly triangular region comprising most of modern-day Illinois, but also parts of Iowa, Missouri, and northeastern Arkansas. The French called this region the Illinois Country. In the northern reaches of the territory the Illini rubbed shoulders with other tribes. These encounters were not always friendly. From the mid-seventeenth century on, Iroquois raids from the east and Winnebago incursions from the north began to displace the Illini from their traditional lands. The British supplied the Iroquois with firearms, so the Illini cultivated a cordial relationship with Britain's enemy, France.

Indigenous peoples migrated for a variety of reasons, but in the Illinois Country the catalyst was the fur trade. France, Great Britain, and Spain vied with one another

The Illinois Country, c. 1650 to 1763

1

Capitaine de La Nation des Illinois, il est armé de sa pipe, et de son dard. p. 5. f. 9.

An Illini chief with his lance and pipe, c. 1700. C.B. de Granville.
Courtesy of the New York Public Library-Astor, Lenox and Tilden Foundations

to exploit the North American interior. The French were the first to establish a foothold on the mid-continent. They sought out Indian villages so they could trade for beaver and other peltry. In the Illinois Country deerskins comprised the bulk of the trade. These skins were used to make gloves, shoes, and a number of other useful objects.

For their part, Indians desired the European trade goods including metal cooking pots, needles, woven cloth, steel bladed knives, iron ax heads, and ornaments of silver, nickel, and glass. Native women and men used the tools to simplify their labor and the ornaments to enhance their appearance. French traders also distributed firearms, rum, and whiskey to Indians, many of whom became addicted to alcohol.

Trade opportunities drew small groups of the Illini to the French missions on the Great Lakes. In the autumn of 1669, the Jesuit missionary Jacques Marquette met a band of Illini at Holy Spirit Mission at the western end of Lake Superior. The Illini told him that their confederacy numbered about 8,000 people and they invited the Black Robes, the Indian name for the Jesuits, to come and teach the

Catholic faith. In particular, the Kaskaskia, Cahokia, and Tamaroa expressed an interest in Christianity. Perhaps the Illini thought that accepting the Frenchmen's religion would strengthen their alliance, but these three tribes demonstrated a genuine attraction to the faith. The Indians also told Marquette about a powerful river they called the "Missipi" that ran through the Illinois Country. The missionary, his fervor and curiosity aroused, promised the Illini that he would come.

When Marquette set out with Louis Jolliet in 1673 both were seasoned frontiersmen. Marquette was born in France in 1636 and entered the Society of Jesus when he was seventeen. Twelve years later he set sail for New France. While serving at missions on the St. Lawrence and Lake Superior he studied Indian languages and customs. After hearing the Illini talk about the "Missipi" the missionary reported this tantalizing information to colonial officials. Mastery of the waterways was vital to trade. In addition, European explorers hoped to find a water route to the Pacific Ocean because that would facilitate trade with East Asia. Authorities in New France arranged for the Jesuit to team up with the French-Canadian cartographer and explorer, Louis Jolliet. Their task was to map the region and make contact with the Indians.

On May 17, 1673, Marquette, Jolliet, and five other men, who served as canoe paddlers and laborers, set out from Michilimackinac. After a few weeks their canoes floated into the Mississippi which Marquette named the River of the Immaculate Conception. They proceeded as far south as the mouth of the Arkansas. Here, Indians reported that the Mississippi flowed into the Gulf of Mexico. Realizing that they were close to Spanish territory the Frenchmen retreated northward. On the return trip they headed up the Illinois River. Where the Illinois makes a sharp eastward turn the expedition stopped at a large Kaskaskia village on the north shore, near the place later known as Starved Rock. The Kaskaskia

Holy Family Church Cahokia, founded in 1699 as Holy Family Mission, restored to its mid-eighteenth century appearance. Holy Family is the oldest continuously operating Catholic church in the United States.
Courtesy of the Diocese of Belleville.

again expressed interest in Christianity and Marquette pledged to return.

When the Jesuit came back the following spring he founded the Mission of the Immaculate Conception of the Virgin Mary. On Easter, April 14, 1675, he offered the first Mass ever in the Illinois Country. Ill health forced him to stay less than three weeks. He began the return trip to Michilimackinac, but on May 18 he died enroute. Marquette's death, however, was not the end of missionary efforts in the Illinois Country.

About two years later Father Claude Jean Allouez arrived at Immaculate Conception and ministered to the Kaskaskia for the next twenty-four years.

Raids by enemies of the Illini forced the mission to relocate twice. The second time, in 1703, missionaries and Indians settled on a site on the Mississippi near the mouth of the Kaskaskia River. A few years earlier and a few miles to the north, in 1699, the Jesuits founded Holy Family Mission for the Tamaroa and Cahokia. In 1704 the Jesuits turned over Holy Family to the Fathers of the Seminary of the Foreign Missions from Montreal. These two missions were the crown jewels of the church's efforts to evangelize the Illinois Country.

The letters and reports of Jesuit Father James Gravier, stationed at Kaskaskia, provide a glimpse of mission life. Speaking about Father Gabriel Marest, Gravier wrote, "During an entire day he has hardly time to recite his breviary [daily prayers required of all priests], or to eat, or to take a short rest in the middle of the night." Missionaries wrote catechisms in native languages, led prayer services, gave instruction for men and women in separate groups, and generally spent the better part of each day overseeing the spiritual welfare of the newly baptized. They also ministered to the increasing population of French colonists.

French Colonial Society

Canadian-born French traders and hunters were among the earliest colonists to make their homes near the missions. Indian men did the bulk of the hunting and trapping. From Cahokia and Kaskaskia winter hunting parties traveled north up the Mississippi, the Missouri, and the Illinois rivers to hunt deer and other game.

French and Indian together produced a new culture that was a blend of the two. Many traders married Illini women, thus cementing economic ties. Their mixed-blood children exemplify the middle ground or mediating culture. Catholicism was part of that middle ground. Oftentimes Indian women were the first to embrace the faith. Other members of the family would follow the women's example. Gravier reports that at a village of 2,000, all but forty had become converts.

At first missionaries hoped to keep colonists and Indian converts separated, not because they believed the Indians to be inferior, but because the traders and laborers would corrupt the converts with rum, profanity, and illicit sexual activity. A Jesuit father reported to a colleague, "You would be astonished as I myself have been, on arriving at this Mission, to find that a great number of the French are not, by any means, so well instructed in Religion as are these Neophytes. . . ."

No doubt contact was not always of a virtuous kind, but as the native population declined, concern lessened. Precise figures do not exist, but historical demographers estimate that the pre-contact population of the Illini may have reached 30,000. By 1700, one year after the founding of Holy Family Mission, they had declined to 6,000. Disease, more than any other factor, accounted for the decimation of the tribe. Like other indigenous peoples in the Americas the Illini had no immunity to European viruses and bacteria. Upon exposure to small pox, measles, or influenza most Indians died. Intertribal warfare and intermarriage with Frenchmen and other Indians also contributed to the decline.

As the numbers of Illini shrank, the French, mixed-blood, and black slave population increased. After the 1720s the alluvial flood plain on the east bank of the Mississippi became the breadbasket of French Louisiana. The farmers, known in French as *habitants*, grew wheat, oats, rye, corn, and other grains. They raised sufficient surpluses to supply lower French Louisiana and even the West Indies.

The *habitants* settled near the missions at Kaskaskia and Cahokia. They measured off the land in long narrow strips perpendicular to the Mississippi. This way each landowner had access to the waterfront and a parcel of the rich soil. Near the bluff at the rear of the lot they found timber for fuel and other needs. Villagers held pastures and timberland in common.

Two other settlements appeared. St. Philippe, founded in 1720, and Prairie du Rocher founded two years later, were compact villages of the type the French had known in Canada. They preferred this arrangement because it offered mutual defense against hostile Indians and facilitated a lively social life. A town lot consisted of a house, out buildings, and a garden enclosed by a fence about six feet high. In the gardens the *habitants* grew beans, peas, beets, carrots, and pumpkins.

Black slaves made up about one-third to one-half of the work force during the French colonial era. Most were agricultural laborers. Others toiled in the lead mines near Ste. Genevieve and a few were skilled artisans. A 1752 census reported a total population of white, black slaves, and Indian slaves of 1,380. Of these 446 were black slaves, 149 Indian slaves (captives taken in warfare), and 785 whites. In other words, slaves were about 43 percent of the population. Under French law slaves had the right to accuse their masters in court if they felt they had been abused. It appears that in the Illinois Country slaves were treated more liberally than the law required. Slaves were, for example, allowed to carry firearms and gather for entertainment contrary to the law.

People of African ancestry comprised a sizeable portion of the Catholic population. In regard to religion, the law required that slave children be baptized and receive religious instruction. A slave could not be forced to marry against his or her will, but was to seek the owner's permission prior to marrying. Marriages between slaves and between slaves and Indians were celebrated in the Church.

Two of the largest slaveholders were the Jesuit and the Seminary missions. The 1752 census revealed that the Kaskaskia Jesuits owned thirty-four slaves and the Seminary of the Foreign Missions in Cahokia held nineteen. How could the missionaries have justified such a thing?

Reconsructed entrance to Fort de Chartre depicts the fort's mid-eighteenth century appearance.

FESTIVITIES OF THE EARLY FRENCH OF ILLINOIS.

Illustration from Henry Howe's "Historical Collections of Ohio" in <u>This is Illinois</u>.
Courtesy of the Illinois State Historical Library.

Like other Europeans they believed that slavery was part of the natural order of things. After all, the bible contained numerous references to slavery without condemning it and many years would pass before the Church spoke against the enslavement of human beings.

The French built a fort near Kaskaskia to discourage British encroachment and protect the export of grain and other commodities including ham, bacon, venison, buffalo meat, nuts, honey, timber, lead, and copper. Builders completed the first Fort de Chartre, a wooden palisade structure, by 1725. Seasonal flooding soon convinced officials to relocate. The third and final Fort de Chartre, made of stone, was completed by 1753, just before the outbreak of the French and Indian War.

The French houses were not comfortable by today's standards, but the stone and timber-frame buildings provided adequate shelter. By locating on a major waterway the *habitants*, even those of modest means, were able to enjoy imports that later pioneers on the prairies would have envied. The *habitants* seldom lacked for sugar, rice, indigo, and French wine. They also purchased fine fabrics, candlesticks, and glassware.

The parish church, separate from the mission, was the religious and social center of each village. Rich, poor, black, white, red, and mixed-blood gathered in the church to worship. Many of the married couples were French men and Indian women. Baptisms and weddings became occasions for celebration. The space in front of the church was also an important gathering spot. Government notices were posted on the front doors and the priests and civil officials read announcements and proclamations from the steps. Dances, too, enlivened the public square in front of the church.

In the early 1750s French colonial life reached its zenith. Soon after France and England embarked on the French and Indian War (1754-1763). The British in North America vastly outnumbered the French and ultimately prevailed. Great Britain acquired all of Canada and lands east of the Mississippi River. Spain, ally of the British, came into possession of the territory west of the mighty river.

The transfer of Fort de Chartre, in 1776, marks the beginning of British rule. At first little changed for the *habitants*, the slaves, and the remaining Indians. Catholics were permitted to worship as they pleased and to retain ownership of real and personal property, including slaves. Despite minimal day-to-day contact, French settlers became disenchanted and a good number moved into Spanish territory. One of them, Pierre Leclede, founded St. Louis in 1764.

5

The Coming of the Americans

Before the war the *habitants*, traders, and mixed-blood population were French subjects of the King of France. Now they were subjects of the King of England, but the French-born bishop of Quebec still possessed ecclesiastical jurisdiction. With the change of government the bishop was reluctant to act where he had no influence with the civil government.

Unfortunately, the end of the war coincided with the expulsion of the Jesuits. Their withdrawal was a tremendous blow to the frontier church. Prior to the transfer of civil power, French authorities in New Orleans ordered the Jesuits, in 1764, to withdraw from both Indian missions and parishes. This move had nothing to do with the impending governmental changes. The Society had fallen into disfavor and was, in fact, suppressed by the the Pope in 1773.

In the post-war upheaval, hardly any priests remained to serve the people. One exception was Father Louis Meurin, a former Jesuit who returned as a secular priest to the Illinois Country. After a few years in Ste. Genevieve, Missouri, he moved to Kaskaskia. Meurin was a crotchety old man, but his companion and co-laborer; Father Pierre Gibault helped smooth relations with the remaining Catholics as well as with the new British authorities.

A trickle of British fur traders and adventurers made their way to the Illinois Country. Great Britain attempted to control the fur and alcohol trade, but the military presence on the frontier was too small to enforce the regulations. Soon farmers from Kentucky and the Ohio Valley were wandering into the flood plain around the French settlements. The term "American Bottom" was probably coined at this time to describe this slice of land extending southward from present-day Alton to Kaskaskia. Old French colonials and British Americans eyed each other suspiciously, but for a while there seemed to be enough room for everyone.

The situation changed dramatically during the American Revolution (1775-1783).

Father Pierre Gibault. He aided the Americans during the Revolutionary War.
Courtesy of the Diocese of Belleville.

At the beginning of the war the British occupied just a handful of western forts. George Rogers Clark, a Virginian, came to the Illinois Country and with the support of Gibault secured the towns of Kaskaskia and Cahokia for the American cause. Several months later, in 1779, Clark permanently secured Vincennes. Gibault's diplomacy, again, helped pave the way because he persuaded the French to support the Americans.

After the war the United States acquired the territory between the Appalachian Mountains and the Mississippi. They referred to this region as the West—not to be confused with the Far West beyond the Mississippi. (The term Midwest came into usage in the late nineteenth century.) Illinois became a county of Virginia and the state guaranteed Catholics freedom to worship and, with some modifications, allowed the French to maintain their own civil code.

The American population began to increase. Scores of Virginian and British veterans decided to stay on the frontier. Differences in language, law, religion, and customs led to cultural clash. As had happened twenty years before, more *habitants* moved west. Most of the remaining Illini, who had peacefully coexisted with the French, found it impossible to live with the Americans who regarded them with a mixture of contempt and fear. The Illini migrated to the west and in 1800 their number in Illinois had dwindled to eighty.

Illinois Catholics and the Church

The shift from British to American government after the Revolution put Illinois Catholics in a delicate position. The Catholic population remained subject to the Diocese of Quebec even though they had experienced two changes in the civil government.

The Holy See appointed Father John Carroll to address the organizational and pastoral needs of the church in the new nation. He was the ideal candidate. Carroll was born in 1736 into the Maryland aristocracy and received his education from the Jesuits in Flanders. He joined the Society of Jesus, but after its suppression Carroll returned to America. Carroll understood that the Roman Catholic Church would be one of many. As Prefect and as the first Bishop of Baltimore, consecrated in 1790, he labored to promote equal rights for Catholics and to show the compatibility of Catholicism and democracy. American Catholics breathed a sigh of relief when the First Amendment was ratified in 1791.

When Carroll became bishop Catholics comprised a small minority of the population. His flock was scattered, poor, and suffered for want of priests. He dispatched clergy to the West to serve the French-speaking Catholics.

They were a majority in Illinois, but most American Catholics were of English ancestry and lived in Maryland and Pennsylvania.

After the American Revolution some of them homesteaded in Kentucky and a generation or so later many of them took up land in Illinois. Within the present boundaries of our diocese Aloysius and Elizabeth Brown were the first Catholic settlers. In 1817, the year before Illinois became a state, they came from Bardstown, Kentucky and put down roots near the North Arm of Coal Creek in Edgar County. Over the next few years other Catholics, many of them relatives, came to the area. In 1835 they planned to begin construction of a church, St. Aloysius. As far as can

be determined, this was the first church built in what became the Diocese of Springfield in Illinois.

The Catholics on Sugar Creek (near present-day Glenarm) also came from Kentucky. The Burtles, Ogdens, Gattons, and others took advantage of the affordable land available in Illinois. Joseph Logsdon and his wife came to Illinois in 1824 and within a few years more than a dozen relatives by blood and marriage had arrived. Extended kinship groups shared labor, tools, and draft animals.

Protestants oftentimes married within their denomination, but Catholics married other Catholics at even higher rates and continued to do so well into the twentieth century. Sibling exchange, when two or more sisters marry men who are brothers, was common. Mixed marriages did occur despite harsh ecclesiastical criticism. One example is the Catholic Josephus Gatton, a widower from Sugar Creek, who married Eveline Husband. The Jesuit missionary who baptized their first two children recorded that Eveline was not Catholic and, in fact, opposed baptism "in which she does not believe, as having no form of belief."

The Sugar Creek community appealed in 1829 to the bishop of St. Louis for a priest. Shortly thereafter the first Mass in Sangamon County was offered in the home of Joseph Logsdon. Eventually, the families formed a parish, St. Bernard's, founded in 1849 at Glenarm.

Most American pioneers were Protestants and on the frontier many were caught up in the enthusiasm generated by the Great Revival. This movement began in the 1790s in Kentucky and Tennessee. People of every age and class, including slaves, gathered at camp meetings to hear preaching and to engage in robust singing. The highly charged atmosphere produced a startling effect on some believers. Spastic movements of the head and limbs, known as the "jerks," were taken as a sign of spiritual favor.

The Great Revival spawned a generation of circuit riding preachers who catered to the spiritual needs of the pioneers. In Illinois, the Methodist Peter Cartwright was one of the most famous of the itinerant preachers. He was typical in that he had no theological training. "The great Mass of our Western people," he asserted, "wanted a preacher who could mount a stump, a block, or old log, or stand on the bed of a wagon and without note or manuscript, quote, expound, and apply the word of God to the hearts and consciences of the people."

Catholics had different expectations in regard to worship. The Tridentine Mass was somber indeed compared to some of the boisterous Protestant services. Catholic ritual gestures, such as the sign of the cross and genuflecting, were precise and scripted.

Catholic missionary priests rode a circuit like their Protestant counterparts, but were much better educated. In fact, by virtue of their seminary training, priests were among the best-educated men on the frontier. Well into the 1830s and beyond, priests rode from settlement to settlement. One of them was Father Irenaeus St. Cyr who ministered to Catholics at Springfield, Sugar Creek, and Quincy. Writing in 1918, Father Anthony Zurbonsen of the

Diocese of Alton paid tribute to St. Cyr:

> The manifold hardships he underwent in those now distant pioneer days, are almost beyond belief, and yet he but did what almost any one priest had to do in those early years, building rough log churches for the growing flocks, gathering scattered members into congregations, riding for months from one town and village to another, fording streams, driving over impossible roads, often sleeping on saddle-bags or wrapped in a blanket seeking a night's rest under some protecting tree, sharing with the poor settlers their scanty meals which mostly consisted of but rancid bacon and hard corn bread, etc.

St. Cyr and other priests usually devoted Saturdays to baptisms and hearing confessions. They offered Mass the next morning and in the afternoon assisted at marriages and gave religious instruction. On Monday morning they departed for the next station. After decades of service, St. Cyr retired to the motherhouse of the Sisters of St. Joseph of Carondolet, near St. Louis, and served as chaplain until his death at age eighty in 1882.

With the passage of time there were enough clergy to celebrate Masses in each settlement during the Easter season, thus enabling Catholics to fulfill the Easter duty. Most of the time, however, Catholics gathered in a private home or some public place for worship. Even those with a church, such as the settlers at North Arm, participated in services led by a respected layman of the community. Aloysius Brown at the church at North Arm, for example, baptized infants, prepared children for First Communion, officiated at burials, and led devotions.

In temporal matters Catholics and Protestants lived similar lives. Both initially avoided the prairies because immigrants and native-born alike came from woodland cultures. They did not understand the prairie environment. The wide-open spaces, called "the barrens," seemed threatening. Besides, their plows could not cut the dense roots of the prairie grasses. Another impediment was the fact that the prairies were often swampy and poorly drained. As late as the 1850s the Irish

Father Irenaeus Saint Cyr, misionary priest to Springfield, Sugar Creek, and Quincy.
From Zurbonsen's *Clerical Bede Roll of the Diocese of Alton, Illinois*

Catholic settlers near Dalton City were draining swamps. The inhospitable prairies became common pastures.

Unlike the *habitants* of the French era, most frontier farmers eked out a living with little surplus. Farm wives made a vital economic contribution by selling butter and eggs. The family used the cash thus obtained to purchase coffee, salt, gunpowder, and other things that could not be produced at home. Throughout the southern half of Illinois many families even grew and processed their own cotton. It was not until the 1840s and beyond, with improved plows and steam power that Illinoians could engage in commercial agriculture.

Religious communities, too, faced hardship. In 1810, a community of Swiss Trappists settled on 400 acres of land northeast of Cahokia, the gift of a benefactor. The site included the prehistoric Mississippian Indian mounds. The largest of the earthwork structures was called simply "Big Mound," but after the arrival of the Trappists it was renamed "Monks Mound." Like most newcomers to the frontier, the monks became ill with fever, probably malaria. They never recovered from that rocky beginning. A typhoid epidemic further weakened the struggling community and they withdrew in 1813.

Eine Farm Mit Blockhaus
From Briefe Aus Amerika, 1854. Courtesy of the Illinois State Historical Library

Growth of Dioceses in the West

Despite trials and tribulations the Catholic population of the West continued to grow. Upon the recommendation of Carroll, the Vatican erected the Diocese of Bardstown (Kentucky) in 1808. Bishop Benedict Joseph Flaget, consecrated in 1810, presided over the church of the Blue Grass State as well as the territories that became the states of Ohio, Michigan, Indiana, Illinois, and Wisconsin. Flaget had been a pastor at Vincennes so he understood frontier conditions including the tense situation between the Indians, most of them former British allies, and the territorial government. The War of 1812 rocked the northeastern portion of his diocese for two years. In Illinois, peace was not secured until 1832 with the end of the Black Hawk War.

There were never enough priests. After the erection, in 1826, of the Diocese of St. Louis, the bishop of Bardstown arranged with Bishop Joseph Rosati, a Vincentian, to cover the west-

Ecclesiastical Jurisdiction

Diocese	Year Erected
Quebec	1674
Baltimore	1789
Bardstown	1808
Saint Louis	1826
Vincennes	1834
Chicago	1843
Quincy	1853

ern and northern portions of Illinois, including Chicago. Under Rosati's care the first women religious came to Illinois.

The Nuns of the Visitation from Georgetown, arrived, in 1833, with six sisters and one postulant. Their goal was to establish an academy for young women. After disembarking from a steamboat they piled into a wagon for the ride to Kaskaskia. The nuns searched the horizon for sight of the village and were startled when the driver informed them that they had already arrived. They transformed the barroom of the old Kaskaskia Hotel into a combination refectory, play room, and classroom. The curriculum was typical of nineteenth cen-

Ruins of the Visitation Convent at Kaskaskia. A flood in 1844 destroyed the convent and school. This photograph was taken some years later.
Courtesy of the Illinois State Historical Library.

tury academies. In addition to reading, writing, and mathematics, boarders and day students covered sacred and profane history, philosophy, rhetoric, mythology, chemistry, and astronomy. The fine arts included vocal and instrumental music, and needlework. Annual tuition was $100 for a nine-month term.

Floodwaters, in 1844, compelled the sisters and pupils to abandon the academy. They took refuge in the home of Pierre Menard. This was the same year that Pope Gregory XVI erected the Diocese of Chicago. As it happened, Bishop Rosati was escorting Bishop William Quarter, head of the new diocese, to Kaskaskia to meet the sisters. The two men discovered the dire condition of the convent and Quarter arranged for a steamboat to rescue the community's belongings. Sister Josephine later recalled,

> The boat [was] lashed to the house through the doors and windows. The bishops and priests assisted in carrying the furniture on board. Pianos, harps, stoves, desks, and benches, etc. were put in the hold to serve as ballast... By 2 o'clock in the afternoon, they had gotten a sufficiency of freight on board and, bidding goodbye to Kaskaskia and their long-loved convent, they turned their course northward to St. Louis. This was June 26th, 1844.

Unfortunately for Quarter, the Visitation community permanently relocated to St. Louis. The Catholic population of his diocese by the mid-1840s was mushrooming. Immigrants from Germanic Europe flooded the upper Mississippi Valley.

The typical German immigrant entered the United States through the port of New Orleans, but few stayed in the South. Skilled craftsmen, including carpenters, masons, and other builders, moved up the Mississippi to St. Louis. Some turned eastward and settled in Cincinnati. Others made new homes in Milwaukee. Farmers from the old country filled in the "German Triangle" formed by these three cities. The changing political landscape in Europe also compelled Germans to immigrate. The revolutions of 1848, for example, led to a massive exodus. In religion the immigrants were mostly Catholic and Lutheran with each group settling close to their own kind.

Chain migration, that is, family members assisting other relatives to immigrate, accounted for the increased numbers, but some Germans came as members of well-organized colonization companies. Three groups settled within the present-day boundaries of the Diocese of Springfield in Illinois: the Swiss at Highland, the Alsatians at Ste. Marie, and the Germans at Teutopolis. Pooling financial resources allowed them to purchase huge acreage, thus assuring a certain homogeneous quality to their neighborhood. Proximity gave immigrants emotional and material support and helped them preserve their language and customs, in some cases well into the twentieth century. A brief examination the history of the three groups illustrates these points and highlights the role of the church.

At first glance it seemed religion was not very important to the Swiss German- speaking Catholics who colonized Helvetia Township, Madison County, in 1831. About two-thirds of the eighty families who came from Lucerne were Catholic, but they did not attempt to establish church until 1843, and even then it was the missionary priest who took the initiative. They called the town Highland and it grew rapidly, in part, because the organizers offered a free lot to anyone who pledged to build a brick house. Within ten years nearly every family had done so. Highland also boasted a sawmill, woolen mill, gristmill, pottery, brewery, distillery, bakery, two stores, and a tavern.

This degree of success should not mask the sacrifices made by the people. Father August Hohl, Pastor at Highland in the 1920s, reflected,

> The first settlers were all farmers and lived in log huts often rudely constructed. Corn was the principal crop and furnished the greater part of food for man and beast and whatever little cash money the people could lay their hand on to purchase the other necessaries of life, was derived from its sale.

Candlestick at St. Mary Church, Ste. Marie, reportedly brought from Alsace.

10

Highland Catholics laid the cornerstone of their church, St. Paul's, in 1844 and within a few years the congregation had grown to 800 persons.

To the Alsatian Joseph Picquet, the founder of Ste. Marie, religion was so important that he consulted with priests and bishops before selecting land in Jasper County, Illinois. Like other colonizers he did a great deal of research through correspondence and on-site inspections to locate the most propitious site. On the banks the Embarrass River he found rolling land that offered timber, pastures, and good fertile soil.

Picquet returned to Alsace and soon he and an advance party of twenty-eight men and two women went to Jasper County for a final inspection. In October 1837 the Picquet's Company of the Brothers filed for some 10,700 acres of federal land. Afterward, to take possession they held a brief religious service. They offered prayers, sang hymns, and placed the new community under the protection of the Blessed Virgin Mary.

Every Catholic settlement experienced conflict to a greater or lesser degree. In Teupololis the animosity involved the high and low Germans. This town is so closely identified with the Franciscan Friars that we almost forget it was founded over twenty years earlier by *Die Deutsche Landkompagnie oder Ansiedlungsgesellschaft,* the German Land Company or Settlement Society. Initial membership cost ten dollars and monthly dues amounted to another ten dollars. These German immigrants hailed from the principalities of Hanover, Oldenburg, and Westphalia. In fact, most of the Catholics coming to the southern half of Illinois came from these three places. The party found land in Effingham County, Illinois, and in 1839 they filed on 10,000 acres at $1.25 per acre. The land was advantageously located on the National Road.

As part of the overall plan the Land Company envisioned a church. The first priest was Father Francis Joseph Masquelet and with the help of the men he erected a log building. Trouble brewed from the beginning because Masquelet spoke only high German and the many of the people could under-

William de Fluerville, one of the founders of Saint John the Baptist Church, Springfield

stand him only with difficulty. Feelings of bitterness were so intense that Masquelet built, at his own expense, a second church outside the town. He withdrew altogether in 1842. By that time Teutopolis had ninety families, making it a major German enclave.

The examples from Highland, Ste. Marie, and Teutopolis show that the majority of the German Catholic immigrants highly valued the presence of the church and the preservation of the faith. Examination of the records of other German parishes—St. Boniface at Quincy and St. Mary at Alton, for example—reveal the same concern.

Irish Catholics were present from the earliest days of statehood, but did not arrive in large numbers until the late 1830s. Some of those who came before the great famine of 1845-1848 were the descendents of displaced Irish landowners. Within our present boundaries the first Irish parish was St. Alexius in Beardstown. By 1838 about 200 Irish immigrants lived and worked at this Illinois River port. The other early Irish parish was St. John the Baptist in Springfield, established in 1839. Both towns had a sizeable German element and, in time, the Germans established their own parishes. Father George A. Hamilton, one of the itinerant priests, remarked on the poverty of the people and said that it would not be possible for them to build a church. They met in homes and various public halls. Even though Springfield was little more than a village, Hamilton and other clergy thought the city would someday be a suitable location for a diocesan see.

One of those assuming the role of host was William de Fleurville (also spelled Florville or Floriville), a Creole of French and African ancestry born in the West Indies. De Fleurville was a contemporary of Abraham Lincoln and the two first met in 1831 when the Creole passed through New Salem. De Fleurville later became Lincoln's barber, but we remember him as one of the founders of St. John the Baptist, later renamed St. Mary's, in Springfield.

11

The No-Popery Movement and other Challenges

In addition to facing the day-to-day challenges of life, Illinois Catholics of the 1830s and 1840s battled a rising tide of anti-Catholic sentiment. Until about 1830 Protestants had peacefully coexisted with Catholics in the United States because there were relatively few Catholics. Furthermore, Catholics of English ancestry spoke English and shared many cultural traits with other Americans.

Nearly 300,000 German and Irish immigrants flowed into the United States in the 1830s. Many of the Germans were Protestant, but significant numbers of Catholics were in the mix. The Reformation had begun more than 300 years before, but animosity remained like an ember buried in the ashes. With the arrival of the foreign Catholics, the flames leapt to life.

Anti-Catholicism, or No-Popery, as it was called at the time, was strongest in the northeast where the concentration of poor Irish was the greatest, but the West did not escape. Leaders of the No-Popery movement included the highly regarded Congregational minister Lyman Beecher. Catholics attribute the 1834 burning of the Ursuline convent in Charlestown near Boston to his inflammatory sermons. The following year his book, *A Plea for the West*, alleged that the pope had organized a conspiracy to take over the West and thus destabilize the whole country. When the United States was at its weakest, Rome would take over.

The 1836 publication of *The Awful Disclosures of the Hotel Dieu Nunnery of Montreal* by Maria Monk marked the zenith of the anti-Catholic novel. She claimed to have been a postulant and described secret passages between the convent and the priests' residence. Even more scandalous were her assertions that infants born to the nuns were immediately baptized and then strangled. Monk was later thoroughly debunked, but the damage was done. Over 300,000 copies sold between its release and the beginning of the Civil War.

No-Popery, the flood of immigrants, a clergy shortage, and other issues were on the agenda when the American bishops and archbishops met in the spring of 1852 in Baltimore for their First Plenary Council. They addressed organizational, educational, liturgical, and sacramental issues. Council decrees included mandates for the appointment of a chancellor and censor for each diocese, the opening of parochial schools, and procedures for incardinating European-born priests. The council encouraged bishops to appoint priest consultors to act in an advisory capacity and it strongly recommended the erection of a seminary in each diocese in order to develop a native clergy.

Catholic schools were viewed as a safeguard to the faith. Had the common or public schools dropped religion from their curriculum, Catholic bishops might have been more agreeable to placing Catholic children in these schools. The Philadelphia Bible Riot of 1844, when

Awful Disclosures
of the Hotel Dieu Nunnery

by
MARIA MONK

With an introduction by
RAY ALLEN BILLINGTON

Facsimile of 1836 edition

ARCHON BOOKS
HAMDEN, CONNECTICUT
1962

A facsimile of the anti-Catholic book by Maria Monk.
Courtesy of the Illinois State Historical Library.

Protestants rioted after Catholics protested the exclusive use of the King James Version in the schools, convinced the bishops that accommodation was not possible.

Diocese of Quincy

Another matter taken up by the bishops was the advisability of creating more dioceses in the United States. They recommended that Illinois be divided and on July 29, 1853, Pope Pius IX erected the Diocese of Quincy. Its bishop would be suffragen of the archbishop of St. Louis. The northern boundary was the same as today's Diocese of Springfield in Illinois and it extended south to the Ohio River. When the diocese came into existence there were fifty-one churches, thirty-four missions, twenty-three priests, and approximately 42,000 Catholics within its boundaries.

Quincy, in 1853, was a bustling river town, an ideal location for a bishop to take advantage of the steamboat connections. That seemed to be Quincy's only advantage. Illinois was in the early stages of a railroad boom, but overland travel to the interior and eastern edge of the diocese would be arduous. Furthermore, the parishioners of St. Boniface, the pro-cathedral, had a reputation as a fractious lot.

Pius IX appointed Joseph Melcher, the vicar general of St. Louis to be the first bishop of Quincy, but he declined the honor. Melcher's refusal has never been explained. A short time later he served as administrator of the Diocese of Chicago. Perhaps he felt it was a more important duty. He became, in 1868, the first bishop of Green Bay, Wisconsin, and served in that capacity until his death in 1873.

Quincy never functioned as a diocesan see, yet the Diocese of Springfield in Illinois dates its birth from that official beginning. Almost immediately a few Catholics in the new diocese agitated for the transfer of the see to a more central location.

Rt. Rev. Joseph Melcher, D.D., was Bishop-elect of Quincy. This photograph shows him as the Bishop of Green Bay, Wisconsin, c. 1870.
Courtesy of the Diocese of Green Bay, Wisconsin.

Springfield was mentioned, but on January 9, 1857, Pope Pius IX moved the see to Alton. Alton, like Quincy, was on the western edge of the diocese, but it was more central to the Catholic population in the southern half of Illinois. Henry Damian Juncker (pronounced Yunker), a parish priest from Ohio, accepted appointment as Bishop of Alton, and in the spring of that year took possession of his diocese.

Building A Foundation
1857-1886

Unless the Lord build the house, they labor in vain who build.

Psalm 127: 1

1857		1886	
58	churches	210	churches
30	stations	10	stations
28	priests	177	priests
3	women religious	418	women religious
0	colleges	2	colleges
1	girls academy	9	girls academies
?	parochial schools	100	parochial schools
0	hospitals	13	hospitals
0	orphanages	3	orphanages

The Diocese of Alton at the beginning of Bishop Juncker's term and at the death of Bishop Baltes.

CHAPTER TWO

Building Up the Faith

The episcopates of Henry Damian Juncker and Peter Joseph Baltes were a time of building, in both the literal and figurative sense. Anti-Catholic bigotry spurred the expansion of Catholic institutions and our diocese contained its share. When Juncker assumed office the Diocese of Alton was poor and struggling. Many years later, at the death of Baltes, the diocese was still poor, but there had been substantial progress thanks to the efforts of the first two bishops and thousands of laity, priests, and religious.

The No-Popery movement had died down only to be replaced by the Know-Nothing political party. This rabidly anti-Catholic and anti-immigrant organization peaked in influence in the election of 1856. Not every American, however, shared the sentiments of the Know-Nothings. In fact, diocesan parish histories list numerous instances of non-Catholics providing financial support for the building of Catholic churches and schools. Even so, conditions varied throughout the state. Generally, Anglo-Saxon Protestants remained uneasy with the growing Catholic population.

Without their own schools, hospitals, and other institutions Catholic immigrants would be compelled to use facilities where the faith would be ridiculed and held in low esteem. In some locales, Catholics were not even admitted to public facilities. In the face of such bigotry, the American bishops envisioned a parallel universe of Catholic institutions that would address the unique temporal and spiritual needs of their flock. This separation would provide the climate necessary for the preservation of the faith. Bishop Juncker shared these views and when he assumed office he began to plan the building of various institutions, but his top priority was to recruit priests for the sprawling diocese.

Bishop Henry Damian Juncker
April 26, 1857 to October 2, 1868

Napoleon reigned when on August 22, 1809, Henry Damian Juncker was born in Fenetrange, Lorraine. Over the centuries the province of Lorraine changed hands many times between the French and the Germans. Juncker's family belonged to the German element of the population and so his first language was German. A local parish priest taught the boy Latin, but when Juncker enrolled in a nearby seminary, his poor French limited his ability to study. He withdrew after two years and moved to Paris where, presumably, his French improved and he worked as a clerk for a notary public.

Hoping to better his situation, Juncker immigrated to the United States. Like thousands of other Germans he headed for Cincinnati. While working as a clerk, Juncker became a friend of a diocesan priest who rekindled his desire to become a priest. Juncker completed his theological studies and on March 16, 1834, Bishop John B. Purcell ordained him to the priesthood.

Juncker was not a scholarly man, but he did possess certain characteristics that made him a good priest and eventually an admirable bishop: piety, good judgment, and administrative ability. Juncker, furthermore, could communicate in German, English, and French. Another factor was his familiarity with American customs and attitudes. Prior to his appointment at Alton, the Holy See had considered Juncker for the bishoprics of Vincennes, Indiana, and Covington, Kentucky. It was clear that the man had stamina and ability, and in 1856 the Pope Pius IX appointed him to be the first bishop of Alton. Purcell who had ordained Juncker twenty-three years earlier, consecrated him a bishop in Cincinnati on April 26, 1857, and Juncker departed for Alton.

Bishop Henry Damian Juncker, first bishop of Alton.

The new bishop, age forty-eight, took up residence near Ss. Peter and Paul Church, then under construction. It became the cathedral church and during Juncker's tenure the building was completed. Next door the bishop built an enormous mansion designed to serve as bishop's residence, cathedral rectory, and seminary. Alas, the seminary proved impractical, but the 52 room building did for many years house all the diocesan priests for their annual retreat.

Bishop Juncker had an amiable, easy-going personality. The annals of the Springfield Ursulines, for example, record many touching stories of his kindness. He often brought them gifts and on one occasion visited a sick postulant. When in residence at the Cathedral, Juncker himself responded to sick calls at any hour and in all sorts of weather. Under his leadership a firm institutional and spiritual foundation was laid. Catholics of the Diocese of Alton mourned the loss of their first bishop who died on October 2, 1868. His remains lie in repose in the crypt at Ss. Peter and Paul.

Ss. Peter & Paul Cathedral, Alton, as it appeared in 1899.

Bishop's Residence, Alton, erected 1858-1859

Priests for the Diocese

The 50,000 Catholics of the diocese were mostly Germans, Irish, and Americans of English heritage. Enclaves of Czechs, Poles, and French Canadians rounded out the mix. The majority were immigrants or the children of immigrants and lived in the country and small towns. Only those in the larger cities of Alton, Springfield and Quincy were lucky enough to have Mass every Sunday. Although many of the churches in the smaller towns had a resident priest, that man also ministered to the surrounding mission stations. Not only were there not enough priests, there were not enough pastors speaking the languages of the people to hear their confessions or prepare them for reception of the sacraments.

After a six-month tour of the diocese Juncker issued, in the autumn of 1857, his first pastoral letter to express concern about the cradle Catholics who left the Church because there were not enough priests to provide the sacraments. He was aware that many German families joined Lutheran congregations because in the Lutheran church they could worship in their native tongue. In some places, the Germans were simply unwilling to share a church building with the Irish, but in others including Mattoon, Pittsfield, and Raymond where the Germans were a minority, they learned to get along. Still

other Catholics stopped worshiping altogether. "To supply wants so pressing, to obviate evils of such magnitude, " he wrote, we have undertaken at this [hurricane] season, the dangerous voyage across the ocean."

Juncker set sail with two priest companions. Father Augustine Brickwedde, pastor of St. Liborius in Piopolis, was a native of Hanover. He served as liaison in the German principalities. Father James Dempsey of St. Lawrence O'Toole (renamed St. Peter's in 1862), Quincy, covered Ireland. Juncker himself visited both places, as well as Belgium, Italy, Lorraine, and other locations in France. The three men hoped to attract ordained priests and seminarians who desired to minister in America.

Father Michael Clifford.

All Hallows Seminary in Dublin, an institution dedicated to the training of priests for the Irish Diaspora, became a wellspring of vocations to the young diocese. The men hailed from several counties including Armagh, Cork, Derry, Hamilton, Killkenny, Limerick, Longford, Tipperary, Waterford, and Wexford. Michael Clifford was one of the dozen All Hallows graduates to come to America at Juncker's invitation. He arrived in 1863 and Juncker ordained the young man at the cathedral in Alton. For the next forty-five years Clifford served the people as a parish priest at Virden, Bunker Hill, Springfield, and Mt. Sterling.

Among the Germans who answered Juncker's call, Louis Hinssen was typical. Almost 20 percent of the foreign-born clergy in the diocese were—like Hinssen—born in Westphalia. He met Juncker when the bishop spoke at St. Maurice Seminary in Muenster, a school like All Hallows in that it prepared men to serve abroad. In the summer of 1858 Hinssen arrived in the United States and on September 21, Juncker ordained him in Ss. Peter and Paul Cathedral. Hinssen served the churches at Edwardsville, Belleville, and Cairo, but was best known as director of St. John's Hospital, Springfield, a post he held from 1886 until his death in 1905.

The foreign vocations filled out the ranks of the Alton clergy. Some of the Germans spent several weeks at All Hallows to learn English before coming to the United States. Although a few eventually returned to Europe, most of the immigrant priests lived their entire lives here as competent pastors. Juncker also recruited priests from more settled parts of the United States and by the time of his death the number of clergy had swelled to eighty.

Father Augustine Brickwedde.

Teutopolis, a Center of Franciscan Life

In Westphalia, Juncker and Brickwedde called upon the Recollect Franciscans of Paderborn. The bishop very much desired to have a friary in his diocese because the community could provide both pastors and educators. He convinced Father Gregory Janknecht, the Minister Provincial, to send nine friars including two theologians. The nine ranged in age from twenty-five to fifty and collectively had all the skills needed to make a go of it in America. The nine could weave cloth, make and repair shoes, cook, bake, and play the organ. There were also a theologian, carpenter, sacristan, preacher, and bursar.

Father Gregory Janknecht, O.F.M. Courtesy of the Order Friars Minor, Sacred Heart Province, St. Louis.

Teutopolis became a center of Franciscan life. By train, wagon, and horseback, the Franciscans covered forty-eight mission stations in nineteen counties. Stations within the present Diocese of Springfield in Illinois included Paris, Marshall, Mattoon, Casey, Trowbridge, Neoga, Sigel, Lillyville, Green Creek, Bishop Creek, Dieterich, Island Grove, Shumway, Effingham, Altamont, Louden, St. Elmo, Howard's Point, Vandalia, Mason, Edgewood, Greenville, and Pocahontus.

The Franciscan presence became indispensable for the pastoral care of the people. As important as this work was, their contributions in education are equally significant. When Janknecht sent six additional friars in 1859, they opened a college in Quincy. St. Francis Solanus College was a combination high school and junior college for young men. From that small beginning grew today's Quincy University. During the episcopate of Bishop Baltes the friars built a dormitory and began to accept boarding students.

Meanwhile, back in Teutopolis, the friars in 1862, opened St. Joseph's Seminary. Its purpose was twofold: the education of Catholic laymen and the training of future priests. Juncker arranged for the Franciscan institution to serve as the diocesan seminary and discontinued classes at the bishop's residence. In its first two years St. Joseph's was both a minor and major seminary. Due to a lack of friars who could teach philosophy and theology, Juncker and the Franciscans closed the major seminary and henceforward the bishop sent most of the candidates to the Seminary of St. Sulpice in Montreal. St. Joseph's continued as the minor seminary into the 1890s and thus nurtured dozens of diocesan and Franciscan vocations.

St. Joseph Seminary, Teutopolis, Illinois
Circa 1900

St. Joseph's Seminary, Teutopolis.
Courtesy of the Franciscan Monastery Museum, Teutopolis

First home of Quincy University, c. 1860.
Courtesy of Brenner Library, Quincy University.

Women Religious
Building the Foundation of Catholic Institutions

Several communities of women religious came to the diocese during the episcopates of Bishop Juncker. Seven of them specialized in education and three in nursing. Without the sacrifices and hard work of the sisters, the institutional infrastructure of the diocese would not have been built.

The classifications of women religious can be confusing, so a word of explanation is in order. Until the Second Vatican Council popularly, the term "nun" was applied to almost all women religious regardless of status under canon law. The ideal, as embodied in the rules and constitutions of nuns, envisioned an ascetic life of prayer, penance, and isolation from the world. Most apostolic communities in the United States, which ministered to the laity directly, were governed by these rules. The women gallantly tried to be both nuns and apostolic sisters, that is, they taught school or nursed while striv-

ing to maintain the prayers and penitential practices observed by nuns. Although dispensed from some of the traditional practices of nuns in communities of apostolic sisters, many of the tensions between these two ways of life were not resolved until after Vatican II.

The Daughters of Charity of Emmitsburg, Maryland, hold the distinction of being the first women religious to serve in our region. (At the time they were usually referred to as the Sisters of Charity.) In fact, their arrival predates that of Bishop Juncker by about three years. They lived and taught at the Mansion House on State Street in Alton. Today the Mansion House is a charming restored building near the *Alton Belle* casino, but in 1854, it was a damp rat-infested boarding house. The three sisters withdrew in 1858.

Before Juncker traveled to Europe to recruit priests, he began to negotiate with the Ursulines of Brown County, Ohio to open a school in Springfield. These Ursulines were of Irish ancestry and so they spoke English. The bishop, no doubt, hoped they would educate the better-off Irish-American girls of the capital city and attract both Catholic and Protestant boarders.

As was customary in those days, the sisters traveled in secular clothes so as not to be harassed by anti-Papists. They spent their first night in Springfield at the St. Nicholas Hotel. Here they made an unplanned, but favorable, first impression. The following morning the sisters, accompanied by Father Patrick McElherne, gathered in a parlor to wait for a visitor. According to the annals a "very gay coterie

Ursuline Motherhouse and St. Joseph Academy, Springfield. Sangamon County Atlas, 1874.

These school boys are probably better-dressed than their real-life counterparts in the Diocese of Alton. Sadlier's Catholic Directory, 1874.

The Ursulines and School Sisters worked with the African-American children long before the decree of the 1866 Second Plenary Council of Baltimore. Locally, Bishop Baltes issued directives that parochial schools were to admit all children of the parish "irrespective of nationality or color." By that time the Ursulines and School Sisters were already old hands at handling mixed race classrooms. Baltes specified that "white and colored children shall not sit on the same bench" and if there were a sufficient number of black children they should have their own school. While his approach does not conform to our understanding of racial justice, we should give the bishop credit for taking a stand. The diocese covered the southern half of Illinois where many people, including Catholics, opposed integration for any reason.

Other teaching communities included the Sisters of Loretto, the Sisters of St. Joseph, and the Sisters of the Holy Name of Jesus. Juncker also secured the services of the Brothers of the Holy Cross to conduct schools for boys in Alton and Springfield. Of all the teaching religious to enter the diocese during the Juncker era, only the Ursulines have maintained a significant presence to this day. They are also the only group in the diocese with a connection to the Underground Railroad.

of ladies and gentlemen" were already in the room. One of the ladies began to play the piano. When she finished Father McElherne asked Mother Mary Joseph Woulfe "to favor us with a little music, intimating that a little publicity, though disagreeable to their personal feelings, would probably be of advantage to their glorious Institution." Mother Mary Joseph reluctantly played, but with such skill and beauty that people came from other parts of the hotel to hear her. Shortly thereafter the Ursulines opened St. Joseph's Academy and not surprisingly, many young ladies took advantage of the musical offerings.

Two of the earliest teaching communities in the diocese were also the first to provide education for black Catholic children. Both groups arrived in 1859. The St. Louis Ursulines opened an academy in Alton as well as a free school for children whose families could not afford tuition. Some of the latter included black pupils who were taught by Sister Ursula Gruenwald at the Alton academy. The School Sisters of Notre Dame accepted black pupils at their schools in Quincy.

Near the end of the Civil War, nine black children were admitted to St. Boniface School, Quincy, where their presence caused such an uproar that some of the nine transferred to the public Colored School Number One. The others, including the teen-ager Augustine Tolton—the first black Catholic priest in the United States—enrolled at St. Lawrence O'Toole School, where classmates accepted them.

The Civil War

The years leading up to the Civil War were turbulent and filled with sectional strife. Alton and Quincy were important entry points for slaves trying to escape from the South. No hard evidence has come to light to show that Catholics played a role in the Underground Railroad, but the Ursulines possess an oral tradition claiming participation. According to their community stories, the Alton convent was one of the safe houses. Runaways dressed in the Ursuline habit and further altered their appearance by donning the mantle with its large hood. Thus attired, the freedom seekers made their way to the next stop.

In the years leading up to the war German and Irish Catholics usually supported the Democrats which in Illinois meant that they supported Stephen A. Douglas. (Douglas, who was married to a Catholic, became a convert just before his death.) Neither abolition nor states rights seemed to interest Catholics very much. In fact, if one relied only on the documentary evidence it would seem that the Civil War had little effect on Catholics in the diocese. Just one official statement from the bishop survives. In an 1864 pastoral letter, Juncker exhorted Catholics to "Pray to God asking for forgiveness of sins and to grant peace to the nation." Every family, however, was touched by the tragedy of war to a greater or lesser degree. Farmers benefited from rising prices, but had to deal with labor shortages because most of the young men either enlisted or were drafted. Factory workers in Quincy, Alton, Jacksonville, and Decatur enjoyed steady work during the war years and in the economic boom that followed.

Cairo, in the southern part of the diocese, became a major staging area for the Union. Its strategic location at the confluence of the Mississippi and Ohio Rivers assured that Cairo would be a busy port.

Over 5,000 steamers carrying troops and supplies docked at Cairo each year during the War. Well behind the lines, but nonetheless important, were Union camps near Springfield, Riverton, Quincy, and Carrollton.

The first nursing sisters came to the diocese of Alton in 1861. The Sisters of the Holy Cross of Notre Dame, Indiana, at the request of General U. S. Grant, tended the wounded as they arrived at Cairo. They also took charge of the U.S. General Hospital at Mound City, about ten miles upriver on the Ohio. The Holy Cross Sisters were educators, but responded generously to the demands of the times. Mother Augusta Anderson recalled,

> Many wounded men
> whose limbs had been
> amputated were there
> with little or no care.
> We pinned up our habits,
> got brooms and buckets
> of water, and washed the
> blood-stained walls. We
> were not prepared as
> nurses, but our hearts

A Holy Cross Sister on the Red Rover, a hospital ship that often docked at Cairo.
Courtesy of the Illinois State Historical Library.

made our hands willing,
and with God's help, we
did much toward alleviat-
ing the suffering.

In 1864, the United States government asked Juncker to supply nursing
sisters for the federal prison at Alton.
Formerly the Illinois State Penitentiary,
the building was so wretched that the
State had stopped using it, but it now
housed some 3,000 Confederates prisoners and 1,000 Union deserters.
Juncker contacted the Daughters of
Charity at St. Louis and their annals
describe the first visit: "The poor sick
were so delighted to see us that we
heard, 'Sisters!' re-echoed in every direction . . ." They nursed prisoners suffering from typhoid, fever, diarrhea, and
small pox, as well as battle wounds.
Men with small pox were isolated on an
island in the Mississippi and to this day
it is called "Pox Island."

About two weeks later "the doctors
acknowledged that a change for the better was already visible; there were fewer
deaths, said they, and despondency had
nearly disappeared." The sisters also
responded to the spiritual needs of the
patients and reported that several prisoners requested baptism. "Thus did our
merciful Lord make us, in those fright-
ful dungeons of horror and despair, the
means of saving many souls who otherwise, would have died in enmity with
God, whom they knew not, and whom
they now thanked for His many and single favors for them."

When the sisters were no longer
needed at the prison, the people of
Alton prevailed upon them to open a
hospital for civilians. Thus St. Joseph's
Hospital came into existence and contin-
ued to function until 1989 when the
Sisters St. Francis of the Martyr St.
George assumed charge and renamed it
St. Clare's Hospital.

Tragic as it was, the war benefited
Catholics in a number of ways.
Catholic immigrants had proved their
loyalty to the Union and bigotry
declined during the war. On the
home front farmers enjoyed high com-
modity prices and factory workers
gained from steady employment. But
perhaps the most dramatic change was

*Window in the Cathedral of the Immaculate Conception, Springfield,
depicting Abraham Lincoln commissioning Archbishop John Joseph
Hughes of New York to represent the United States in France.*

in the attitude of Protestants towards women religious. The Holy
Cross and the Charity sisters, by virtue of their contact with non-
Catholics, did much to overcome the Maria Monk stereotype. In Illinois
and across the country, Americans had witnessed first-hand the self-sacri-
ficing work of the sisters and treated them with a new respect. During
the war over 600 women religious served as nurses on the battlefield and
in military and prison hospitals.

Several years later, in 1874, when the statue of Lincoln was to be
unveiled at his tomb in Springfield, President U.S. Grant asked that
two sisters be given the honor as a sign of gratitude for the services of
religious during the War. Sister Josephine Meagher and Sister Rachel
Conway, Dominican Sisters of Jacksonville, graciously accepted the
invitation. The choice of Catholic sisters symbolized the decline of
anti-Catholic bigotry and the growing acceptance that Catholics could
be loyal Americans and faithful to their church at the same time.

Bishop Peter J. Baltes

January 23, 1870 to February 15, 1886

*Bishop Peter J. Baltes,
second bishop of Alton.*

Bishop Peter Joseph Baltes was, like his predecessor, an immigrant. The family lived in Ensheim, Bavaria, where on April 7, 1824, the future bishop was born. When he was six he came with his parents to the United States and settled in Oswego, New York. Here Baltes learned the cabinetmaking trade from his father, but about the same time began to study Latin and at the age of sixteen enrolled at Holy Cross College in Worcester, Massachusetts. He continued studies at St. Mary of the Lake, Chicago, and completed the theological course at the Grand Seminary in Montreal. Baltes was ordained a priest for the Diocese of Chicago on May 21, 1853. Soon, he took up duties as pastor at Waterloo about fifteen miles south of Cahokia. In 1855, Baltes took charge of a new church in Belleville where he acquired a reputation as a builder. Under his direction St. Peter's Church was erected and a fine church it was. Today it is the cathedral church of Belleville. Baltes honed his skills in administration and fund raising—two essential qualities in a bishop-to-be.

Juncker and Baltes had a cordial relationship. The younger priest served as Juncker's theologian at the Second Plenary Council of Baltimore. That same year, 1866, Junker made his protégé the vicar general. When Juncker died about a year later Baltes became administrator of the Diocese of Alton. At that time he took steps to legally incorporate the diocese and Articles of Incorporation were filed with the Illinois Secretary of State in 1869. This action helped protect church property from independent-minded church trustees.

Baltes performed well and on September 24, 1869, Pope Pius IX named him bishop of Alton. Bishop John Henry Luers of Ft. Wayne consecrated Baltes at St. Peter's Church, Belleville, on January 23, 1870. The consecration occurred during the First Vatican Council. Because there was no bishop until the council was underway, the diocese was not represented at Vatican I which, among other things, declared the pope infallible in proclaiming dogmas of the church.

Baltes was a churchman in tune with his time. His first official acts were to bring diocesan practices into conformity with the decrees of the Second Plenary Council of Baltimore and the First Vatican Council, especially in regard to parochial schools. Every parish with a sufficient number of children was to have its own parochial school. Parishioners who refused to support a school were not to receive the sacraments. He effectively regulated building projects so that parishes would avoid overwhelming debt and he insisted that all new construction be of brick so as to prevent destruction by fire.

Although his predecessor had not been lax in enforcing church discipline, Baltes strove with particular zeal to bring uniformity of practice to the diocese. "From the time we were placed at the head of the diocese," he wrote, "up to the present moment, our unremitting endeavors have always been directed toward the bringing about as complete a uniformity as possible in matters pertaining to the government of the parishes as well as in the observance of the rites and ceremonies of the church at divine service and the administration of the sacraments."

His diary of confirmations and dedications contains biting references to irregularities and violations. At Assumption, for example, he recorded "foot of chalice and ciborium not clean." He often complained about the use of styrene candles rather than the more costly ones of beeswax. At Pittsfield, the bishop was miffed when he entered the town that the boys failed to doff their hats or salute him in any way.

A highlight of the Baltes episcopacy was the ordination to the priesthood of the first vocation to come from the diocese. Father John Molitor was born in Germantown (in the present Diocese of Belleville) in 1845. He was ordained in 1875 and served for many years as pastor at St. Thomas in Newton.

One might say that whereas Juncker had presided, Baltes ruled. Nonetheless, under his guidance the diocese of Alton continued to grow and in some respects even to prosper. Baltes died February 15, 1886 and was buried next to his predecessor in the crypt beneath the Cathedral.

Three Motherhouses Established in the Diocese of Alton

As administrator and bishop, Peter J. Baltes actively recruited women religious for the diocese of Alton. Three of the communities—the Springfield Dominicans, the Hospital Sisters of St. Francis, and the Sisters Adorers of the Precious Blood—founded motherhouses. A motherhouse was the administrative center of a religious community and in those days housed the novitiate. The motherhouse was also the place to which infirm sisters came home to recover or to die.

In the early 1870s Father Peter Mackin hoped to find sisters to teach at St. Patrick's School in Jacksonville. He specifically desired to obtain the services of religious who would teach boys as well as girls. Baltes made arrangements with the Dominicans of St. Catherine, Kentucky, and late in the summer of 1873 six sisters arrived in Jacksonville. Our Saviour's Church provided a tiny cottage and the first night, as they mounted the steps to the half-story "dormitory," they beheld what appeared to be six white coffins. Startled, but curious, they investigated and found that the mattresses had been overstuffed. The annalist recorded that:

> Word had circulated that the Sisters had to sleep on straw ticks. Farmers had gone beyond the call of duty to contribute to the cause from their stacks. The woman who filled the ticks, equally big-hearted, had stuffed in the straw to the very last wisp. Consequently, the pioneers spent their first night in a precarious commingling of hilarity and caution as they tried vainly to keep atop their impressive mounds.

Jacksonville sprang up around Illinois College, a school founded by New England Presbyterians in 1829. There was always a certain unease between the New England element and the Irish who began to arrive in the 1840s. Many of these immigrants were "famine" Irish. They were extremely poor and most were illiterate and uneducated. The Irish clustered in an area northeast of the church called "The Patch." Here they lived in boarding houses and two-story tenement buildings. Irish men comprised the bulk of the labor force at the railroad shops, farm implement factories, and lumber mills. Young Irish women worked as domestic servants in the better part of town. Older women, usually widowed, sometimes ran boarding houses. School attendance was sporadic because even the children worked in the mills and other factories. Jacksonville thrived in large part because of the affordable labor provided by the Catholics.

After a few lean years in the 1870s new sisters joined the Dominicans and they accepted teaching assignments in Carrollton, Jerseyville, Mt. Sterling, Beardstown, and Prairie du Rocher. Almost all of the sisters were born in the United States and in those early years, most were of Irish ancestry. In 1893 they moved their motherhouse to Springfield where they later opened Sacred Heart Academy.

The Hospital Sisters of the Third Order of St. Francis from

Arrival of the Hospital Sisters of the Third Order of St. Francis as depicted in stained glass at the Franciscan Motherhouse, Springfield.
Courtesy of the Hospital Sisters of the Third Order of St. Francis.

First Convent of the Dominican Sisters, Jacksonville.
Courtesy of the Dominican Sisters of Springfield in Illinois.

1875

Woodcut of the first St. John's Hospital, Springfield

the Franciscans for some time and began to teach them English. The capital city was now home to flour mills, railroad shops, and other industries so the Hospital Sisters tended the victims of industrial accidents as well as disease. Within a short time the sisters spread out to provide nursing services in Belleville, Effingham, East St. Louis, and Litchfield.

An old college in Ruma became, in 1876, the first motherhouse of the Sisters Adorers of the Most Precious Blood. Some years earlier nine sisters came from Baden, Germany to teach the pupils at Belle Prairie (Piopolis). Baltes wanted them to establish a motherhouse in Springfield, but the American superior informed him that she must first obtain the permission of the superior-general in Germany. He replied that they would found a motherhouse or leave the diocese. Years of strained negotiations with Baltes and the expulsion of all religious from Baden contributed to a split within the Precious Blood community. A group of ten sisters moved into the old Sacred Heart College which had been operated by St. Patrick's Church. The early years at Ruma were very harsh. The sisters subsisted on meals of thin soup and black bread. For coffee they concocted a mixture of roast acorns and wheat. Although cheap manufactured cloth was available, the sisters economized by spinning and weaving their own wool, flax, and hemp.

The Precious Blood sisters assumed responsibility for a number of parochial schools in the southern portion of the diocese, the part that in 1887 became the Diocese of Belleville. Within the present-day boundaries of the Diocese of Springfield in Illinois, these sisters ministered at Marine, Black Jack, Carlinville, Mt. Sterling, and Taylorville.

A spirit of self-sacrifice characterized all the religious communities. The Hospital Sisters, for example, actually begged for food for themselves and their patients. Nurses and teachers alike were happy to accept payment in kind. Another group of nursing religious were the Franciscan Sisters of the Poor (then called the Poor Sisters of St. Francis). They originated in Germany and in 1858, established a foundation in Cincinnati. Responding to a call from the Germans of Quincy, the sisters opened St. Mary's Hospital in a small cottage in 1866.

Muenster, Westphalia, arrived in 1875. Bishop Baltes invited them to open hospitals where they could serve both the German- and English-speaking Catholics. In the autumn of 1875, twenty-one sisters stepped off the train in Springfield. The city had grown significantly since the arrival of the Ursulines, who hosted

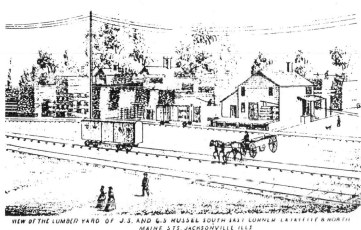

VIEW OF THE LUMBER YARD OF J.S. AND G.S HUSSEL SOUTH EAST CORNER LAFAYETTE & NORTH MAINE STS. JACKSONVILLE ILLS

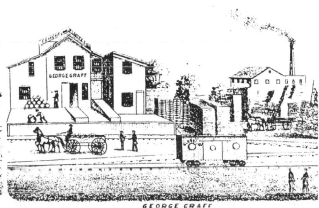

GEORGE GRAFF
DEALER IN LUMBER, LATH, SHINGLES, DOORS, SASH, BLINDS, CEMENT, LIME, PLASTER PARIS, &C. OPPOSITE OF T.W.&W. RAILWAY JACKSONVILLE ILLS.

Two views of Jacksonville.
Atlas Map of Morgan County, 1872.

Other Needs Addressed by Women Religious

Although life expectancy gradually increased by the end of the nineteenth century, disease and accidental death claimed a number of adult lives. So it was not uncommon for children to be orphaned. The death of one or both parents put children in a precarious position. Abandonment was another hazard to children of the era. Some parents, feeling overwhelmed by the responsibilities of child rearing, left their children in the care of relatives or insti-

First Catholic Orphanage, Alton.

tutions. For many there was no recourse except to the orphanage.

The Catholic Orphanage, today the Catholic Children's Home in Alton, traces its origin to 1883 when it opened in a house near the cathedral. It replaced the two smaller orphanages at Piopolis and Belleville. The Precious Blood Sisters assumed charge and continued to minister at this institution for nearly 100 years.

As the nineteenth century neared its end yet another social need emerged. Following the Civil War, thanks to improved sanitation, and other factors life expectancy for adults increased and more and more elderly and infirm needed institutional care. In Quincy they found a haven at the St. Vincent's Home. Here the Poor Handmaids of Jesus Christ, Ft. Wayne, Indiana, cared for Catholics and non-Catholics alike.

The existence of the Orphanage and the St. Vincent's Home exemplify the nineteenth century Catholic approach to the care of the poor and helpless. The low wages paid to the sisters, little more than room and board, made it possible for Catholics of the diocese to support such institutions through an annual appeal. At this time most Catholics were relatively poor. The presence of the sisters also assured that a Catholic atmosphere would prevail in which the residents could continue to practice their faith and receive the ministrations of the Church.

By the time of Bishop Baltes' death there were over 400 women religious in the diocese. It is impossible to calculate the value of their ministries. Without them the mandate of the Second Plenary Council of Baltimore for parochial schools and Catholic institutions would have been unfulfilled.

St. Vincent Home, Quincy.

First church building of St. Mary, Pittsfield, erected 1850-51.

Building Up the Spirit

The role of religious communities was essential for institutional growth, but equally important was the support of the laity. This support took two forms: infusions of cash from abroad as well as cash and in-kind contributions of local Catholics. The early parishes could not have attained stability during the pioneer era without the financial support of immigrant aid groups such as the St. Raphael's Society for the assistance of German immigrants. Informal networks of support were also important. Many a diocesan priest solicited funds from relatives and friends back in the old country. Some even went on begging tours.

Within the diocese pew rents were the major source of revenue. Payment of pew rent on a quarterly basis gave the pew-holder and dependents the right to sit in a particular pew. It was a sign of responsible membership in the local parish. Those too poor to pay pew rent were also entitled to a seat and access to the sacraments. Bazaars and other activities also added to church revenues, but at some point, every parish incurred debt,

especially when building a new church or school. A talented pastor was one who could inspire liberal giving and rapidly pay down debt.

The church building was, and continues to be, an important symbol of Catholic identity. In the Diocese of Alton, most of the churches employed the basilica plan, that is, they were long and narrow. The larger structures had a transept and aspe. Usually, in our diocese the most common plan was a Gothic Revival style church with a center bell tower over the main entrance. The cathedral in Alton was one of the few to have double towers.

Oftentimes Catholics first met in existing buildings. This was the case, for example, in Effingham where the people of St. Anthony's met in a log cabin. After two years the pastor, Father Thomas Frauenhofer, and the people made plans for a proper church and rectory of brick. Forty families each donated $100, but in-kind contributions were equally important. "Accordingly, in 1856, the farmers set to work cutting the cord wood which would be needed the following year in the making of brick," recorded a parish history. A generation later, in the mid-1870s, the congregation had outgrown the building and at a cost of $40,000 erected the present structure.

Some priests also made in-kind contributions through their manual labor. Father J. A. Marks, of St. Mary's in Marshall, for example, was a master carpenter. With a young assistant he did all the carpentry work on the still intact brick church completed in 1872. They also helped build the school and rectory.

As important as the buildings were, parish life was more than bricks and mortar. The church was the setting for the celebration of the sacraments and various devotions. Infants were baptized, couples were married, and the dead were buried with the rites of the Church.

27

Many Catholics were not well catechized, so Juncker and Baltes promoted the spiritual welfare of the people by addressing a number of issues including illegal marriages, mixed marriages, intemperance, and secret societies.

In regard to marriage, Juncker exhorted pastors to publish the banns three times as required by canon law unless the proper dispensation was obtained. The banns helped to prevent fraud by unscrupulous parties and bring to light impediments to contracting a valid marriage. Juncker also condemned evening weddings held either in the church or in private homes. "It is at the foot of the altar, ' he wrote, "that the sacred obligations should be assumed, and the blessing should ever, according to the ritual, be bestowed amid the solemnities of the sacrifice of the Mass, or at least immediately after it."

Mixed marriages received harsh condemnations. Baltes wrote that such marriages "were always looked upon as productive of much evil." Yet, mixed marriages were tolerated as evidenced by the fees collected for dispensations. In rural areas of the diocese where Catholics were a small minority, officials viewed mixed marriage as a necessary evil because there were not enough unrelated Catholics to supply spouses.

The bishops, like almost everyone else, believed that intemperance or drunkenness was a sin. Drunken revelry at wakes, weddings, and church events was condemned in the harshest terms. Juncker referred to "scandalous and diabolical wakes" in which the drinking became more important than praying for the dead. Baltes, too, exhibited concern for good order when he prohibited suppers, picnics, fairs, and balls—occasions when drinking occurred—to be held on church property. He also prohibited dancing and kissing games.

The Caholic Church had long condemned secret societies, but Baltes singled out the Masons and the Fenians in particular. The Masons were associated with the Protestant power structure and the Fenians he denounced not only because they were a secret society, but they advocated violent means to achieve Irish independence.

Baltes also criticized the Ancient Order of Hibernians, an Irish-American organization. His objections rested on his belief that most Hibernians were Catholics in name only and that some Hibernians used the organization as a cover for radical advocacy of the independence cause. Perhaps the bishop let his Teutonic heritage cloud his judgment. Irish in the diocese enthusiastically supported the organization and established, in 1852, a chapter in Springfield. The Hibernian goals were to promote charity among its members, loyalty to the United States, and by all legitimate means to advance the cause of Irish independence. Eventually, there were chapters in Greenview, Riverton, Cantrall, Gillespie, Staunton, Auburn, Pawnee, New Berlin, and Witt. The Hibernians and the ladies of the Auxiliary also provided social support to other Irish-Americans through payments during sickness and a death benefit sufficient to cover the cost of a funeral. The ultimate irony, in view of Baltes' distaste for the Hibernians, is the fact that one of his successors, Bishop James A. Griffin was the organization's state chaplain.

Devotional and service societies, in contrast to non-religious organizations, received official endorsement. Catholic popular literature and family stories suggests that devotions were an integral part of lay spirituality. The Tridentine Mass was in Latin and throughout most of the service each person was free to engage in silent prayers of one's own choosing. Reciting the rosary was common, but meditations on the Passion were considered praiseworthy, too. Full, active, and conscious participation in the Eucharistic liturgy is a consequence of Vatican II.

Commercially produced booklets and pamphlets, such as *The Garden of the Soul* and *The Imitation of Christ*, distributed through parish missions, promoted devotional practices. Papal approbation and the granting of indulgences for certain forms of devotions increased their popularity. Juncker, for example, promoted the Archconfraternity of the Most Holy and Immaculate Heart of Mary. By 1860 this society was functioning at the cathedral and the bishop hoped to extend it to every church in the diocese.

Numerous parishes in the diocese had a Confraternity of the Holy Rosary. Marian devotions, in general were very popular especially after Pope Pius IX proclaimed the dogma of the Immaculate Conception in 1858. The Sodality of the Immaculate Conception, for example, was a group for young unmarried women. Nellie Eck, a member of the Sodality, organized, in 1866, the first May devotions at her church, Ss. Peter and Paul, Collinsville. The church was so poor that a woven straw beehive served as the tabernacle. "It can be imagined that that particular altar did not make a very imposing appearance," observed a parish historian. Even so, the young women placed the statue of Mary at the altar and decorated it with flowers. Juncker was so touched by the fervor of the young women that he made a special effort to find a resident priest for Collinsville.

Service societies provided another avenue for Catholics to express their faith. An altar society was usually the first to be organized in a new church. Ladies of the parish worked to keep the linens, vestments, sacred vessels, and accoutrements in good order. Of the charitable groups, the St. Vincent DePaul Society was the most widespread. The earliest reference in the diocese dates from 1866, when a chapter was founded at Ss. Peter and Paul, Springfield. In time, almost every parish had a St. Vincent DePaul Society. The concept of advocacy for systemic change would have been foreign to nineteenth century Catholics. They perceived charity as a personal responsibility and the St. Vincent DePaul Society gave the laity a way to pool their resources for the benefit of others.

Moving Towards a New Century

At the death of Baltes in 1886 the Catholics of the Diocese of Alton could look back with pride on all that had been accomplished since the founding of the diocese thirty-three years earlier. The institutional infrastructure of schools, hospitals, and orphanages was secure and poised for continued growth. During the interim between Baltes' death and the appointment of the next bishop, Father John Janssen, the vicar general, served as administrator. He was a good choice. Janssen had served both bishops and was familiar with the inner workings of the diocese. He maintained a cordial relationship with both the German and Irish elements.

In 1887 the Holy See established the Diocese of Belleville from the southern portion as the Diocese of Alton. Janssen became its first bishop and served with distinction until his death in 1913. The new Bishop of Alton was James A. Ryan of the Diocese of Peoria. He was the first Irish bishop of the diocese, although he had come to America as a child. Little could he have known that he would usher the diocese through some of its most turbulent years.

John Janssen

First Bishop of Belleville

When the Vatican created the Diocese of Belleville in 1887, the logical choice for bishop was John Janssen. Years before, he had been one of the first seminarians Bishop Juncker persuaded to come to Illinois. After Janssen's ordination in 1858 he served in Springfield, New Berlin, Quincy, and Alton. Both Juncker and Bishop Baltes had complete faith in Janssen and allowed him to gain administrative experience as chancellor and vicar general. After Baltes' death Janssen became the administrator of both the Diocese of Alton and the new Diocese of Belleville. Janssen was consecrated a bishop at St. Peter's Cathedral, Belleville, on April 25, 1887. After an episcopacy of twenty-six years Janssen died at the age of seventy-eight.

Bishop John Janssen,
first bishop of Belleville.

Bridge to the 20th Century

1886-1923

Jesus said, "Let the children come to me, and do not prevent them; for the kingdom of heaven belongs to such as these."
Matthew 19: 14

Father Augustine Tolton.
Courtesy of Brenner Library, Quincy University.

CHAPTER THREE

A Time of Transitions

Bishop James Ryan was a member of the generation that experienced the change from horse and buggy to automobile. He witnessed the Civil War, the industrial revolution, the rise of organized labor, the birth of the progressive reform movement, and the enfranchisement of women. He appears to have been more a spectator than participant, but even so, his presence was like a bridge from one century to the next. He was no risk taker, no innovator, but he tended his flock with competence and coordinated the expansion of Catholic institutions.

Like every bishop, Ryan faced the task of tidying up the unfinished business of his predecessor. In the closing days of the Baltes episcopacy, a young African-American man from Quincy began to study for ordination. Baltes had been largely indifferent toward this man, but Ryan—for better or worse—helped to shape his destiny. That man was Augustine Tolton, recognized as the first African-American priest in the United States.*

Father Augustine Tolton

Today, Catholics of the diocese take pride in the knowledge that Father Augustine Tolton is from our diocese. Yet, the Tolton story is simultaneously a source of shame. The racism and indifference of two bishops and the hostility of some diocesan Catholics remain a cause of sadness and regret. The 1850s were one of the most tumultuous periods in American history. The debate over slavery was as hot then as today's discourse over abortion. By 1860 a minority—about one in twenty northerners—advocated the emancipation of approximately four million blacks in the South. Generally, abolitionists believed that persons of African descent should be accorded citizenship and full civil rights, but their hopes were dashed in1857 when the Supreme Court of the United States ruled in the Dred Scott case that blacks were not and could never become citizens.

Tolton was born in 1854, the same year that trouble flared in the Nebraska territory over the expansion of slavery into the West. His parents were Martha Chisley Tolton and Peter Paul Tolton, Catholic slaves on a farm in Ralls County, Missouri. When the Civil War began the Toltons continued working as before, but at some point the father ran away to St. Louis in hope of aiding the Union. He died a short time after arriving in the city. Compounding the tragedy, Mrs. Tolton did not learn the fate of her husband; it seemed that in the confusion of the war he had simply disappeared.

Hearing that slave traders were coming to Ralls County, Mrs. Tolton made a bold move. She ran away and took her three children with her: Augustine, age seven, an older brother, Charles, age eight, and Anne, age twenty months. After a harrowing escape across the Mississippi, the family made its way to Quincy. Mrs. Tolton obtained work at a cigar factory, one of Quincy's major industries. About two years later the older boy, always sickly, died.

---

* The Healy Brothers—James Augustine, Patrick Francis, and Alexander Sherwood—of North Carolina were the first American priests of African descent. Their father was white and their mother black. In their own lifetimes, however, they "passed" as white and the public was not aware of their African ancestry.

Father Peter McGirr.

The Toltons, like most of the other black Catholics in Quincy, attended St. Boniface. Augustine, called Gus, gradually learned German by listening to the sermons and scripture readings. Eventually, he became quite proficient. With the encouragement of Father Herman J. Schaefermeyer, the pastor, Mrs. Tolton and other black parents enrolled their children in St. Boniface School. The German children harassed and intimidated the dark-skinned pupils. Like Tolton, who began to work in the cigar factory when he was nine, many of the African-American pupils worked most of the year. Schooling was sporadic. Sister Chrysologus, a School Sister of Notre Dame, provided additional instruction before and after school so these children could begin to catch-up. Hostility persisted and parishioners threatened to have Schaefermeyer removed from the pastorate unless he expelled the black students. With great reluctance, Schaefermeyer did so.

For a while, Tolton attended the Illinois School for Colored Children, a state institution in Quincy, but even here, the very dark-skinned adolescent endured rejection by African-American children with lighter complexions. About 1869 he began to attend St. Peter's, a predominatly Irish school. He later recalled, "As long as I was in that school, I was safe. Everyone was kind to me. I learned the alphabet, reading, and arithmetic." Sister Herlinde, a School Sister, tutored Tolton and the other black children before and after school. It was about this time that Tolton became an altar boy and talked with the pastor, Father Peter McGirr, about a priestly vocation. Bishop Baltes confirmed Tolton in 1872 and, as was customary in those days, he probably made his first Communion.

McGirr nurtured the young man's vocation and worked tirelessly to find a minor seminary that would accept Tolton. St. Joseph's, the diocesan seminary, turned him down, but McGirr—encouraged by the bishop's promise to pay tuition and expenses at any seminary that would accept him—kept trying. Given the widespread prejudice and institutionalized racism of the time, it is not surprising to learn that every seminary in the United States refused to admit Tolton.

Tolton, however, was a man of remarkable perseverance. While searching for a seminary and pondering his future, he began to study Latin and philosophy with various priests in Quincy, including two Franciscan Fathers at St. Francis Solanus College. Tolton became the first African-American admitted to the college. During these trying years, he taught at the Quincy Colored Sunday School and when St. Joseph's School for Colored Children opened in 1878, he taught religion to the children. This school was the result of a joint effort of St. Boniface parish and the School Sisters of Notre Dame. Tolton's old teacher, Sister Herlinde, was in charge. All the while, Tolton continued to work in various Quincy factories.

Finally, in 1880, through the intervention of his Franciscan friends, the Urban College of the Propaganda Fide in Rome accepted Tolton. This institution trained priests for the mission fields. Most likely, Tolton could expect to be missioned to a country in Africa. After six years of study, on Holy Saturday, 1886, Cardinal Giovanni Parocchi ordained Tolton to the priesthood. The new priest was astonished to learn that instead of being sent to Africa he would be missioned to his home diocese.

Meanwhile, back in Quincy, McGirr prepared a reception worthy of the nation's first black man to be ordained a Catholic priest. Quincians met Tolton when he arrived in Springfield and escorted him the rest of the way. A band struck up the hymn "Holy God, We Praise Thy Name" as the train pulled into the station and a four-horse hitch drew Tolton's carriage to St. Peter's. There, parishioners, including his mother, and other well wishers, lined up to receive the new priest's blessing. After celebrating his first high Mass in Quincy at St. Boniface—the only Catholic church able to accommodate the crowd of 1,500—Tolton assumed his duties as pastor of the recently organized mission church, St. Joseph's.

St. Joseph Church, Quincy.
Courtesy of Brenner Library, Quincy University.

Bishop James Ryan
May 1, 1888 to July 2, 1923

*Bishop James Ryan,
third bishop of Alton.*

Our third bishop, James Ryan, sprang from humble origins. He was born in County Tipperary, Ireland on June 17, 1848, and came at the age of seven to America with his parents and a sister. They took up residence in Louisville, Kentucky. The father died a short time later, but the intelligent boy caught the attention of the bishop of Louisville, Martin J. Spalding. The Spaldings were one of the most prominent Catholic families in the United States and their patronage proved beneficial to Ryan's career. The bishop more or less adopted young Ryan and made him part of the episcopal household.

Ryan attended the minor and major seminaries in Bardstown, Kentucky, and completed his theological education at Preston Park Seminary, Louisville. The day before Christmas in 1871, Bishop William G. McCloskey ordained Ryan to the priesthood. John Lancaster Spalding, nephew of the former bishop (by now Archbishop of Baltimore), preached the sermon. For a few years Ryan served in country parishes and for a time taught at St. Joseph's College, Bardstown. In 1877 John Lancaster Spalding became bishop of Peoria, and Ryan transferred to his diocese. At Wataga, Danville, and Ottawa the young priest supervised the construction of new churches and raised money to cover the debts.

Meanwhile, in the Diocese of Alton, Bishop Baltes had died. The impending change of leadership made it a propitious time to divide Alton into two dioceses and in 1887 Pope Leo XIII established the Diocese of Belleville for the southernmost portion of Illinois. The Holy See appointed Father John Janssen, the administrator of Alton, to be Belleville's first bishop. The Pope selected Ryan, whom John Lancaster Spalding nominated, for Alton. It must have been a happy day for the bishop of Peoria when, on May 1, 1888, at the Alton cathedral Spalding consecrated his protégé a bishop.

Little could Ryan have imagined that he would have the longest tenure of any bishop of our diocese: a little over thirty-five years. Yet, surprisingly, fewer documents survive from his episcopate than from any other. The lack of documentation tends to give the impression that Ryan was a caretaker bishop who took little initiative, but the record of institutional and parish growth suggests otherwise. The estimated number of Catholics rose from 70,000 at the beginning of his tenure to 87,000 at the time of his death. Forty new churches were opened and six hospitals were founded in the diocese. But Ryan is especially remembered for his active role in expanding the Alton orphanage. Having been deprived of a father in his youth, he seems to have had a soft spot for the children.

*Chess, apparently, was an acceptable pastime for priests.
From left: Fathers Joseph Meckal, Anton Jaschke,
and Ferdinand Stick at St. Mary's, Alton, c. 1910.*

Another significant accomplishment of the Ryan episcopacy was the Diocesan Synod of 1889. The bishop convened this assembly of diocesan and religious clergy to adopt rules and regulations that would bring the diocese into compliance with the decrees of the three Plenary Councils of Baltimore. Among other things, the synod addressed issues of church and school building projects, finances, and the behavior of priests. Priests were the most visible members of the Catholic community and their public appearance could create an impression for good or ill. Priests, for example, were never to attend the theatre or dances. Many Protestants of the day found these activities morally objectionable; Catholic

Monsignor Edward L. Spalding.

leaders thought them frivolous.

Ryan was the first Irish bishop of the diocese. Throughout the nation, Irish and Irish-American priests dominated the hierarchy. Ryan's appointment reflects the declining influence of the German Catholics in the diocese. Fortunately, there were still enough German-speaking priests to mollify the Teutonic element and Ryan was astute enough to include German priests among his consultors. Although huge numbers of Germans continued to immigrate into the United States, within the diocese the influx of Italians, Poles, Lithuanians, Slovaks, Croatians, Slovenians, and other eastern Europeans—called the New Immigrants—outnumbered the German Catholic arrivals.

Ryan took a dim view of immigrant Catholics who shunned assimilation. He was even harsher in his attitude towards those who challenged ecclesiastical authority. The New Immigrant Catholics, as the Germans before them, demanded priests who spoke their languages. Ryan found "the multiplicity of tongues the curse of Babel" reported his vicar general, Edward L. Spalding (yet another member of the Kentucky clan). In some cases Ryan attempted to supply such priests, but "after the good bishop had tried every foreign speaking priest available in a belligerent parish," Spalding stated, "he could succeed in bringing about good working conditions by sending a big, vigorous Irish priest into the Parish. This type of Pastor usually brought order out of chaos and confusion." The vicar general's comment in itself testifies to the power enjoyed by the Irish clergy.

Spalding recalled that Ryan was a reclusive man who lived in almost monk-like austerity. Ryan abstained from all intoxicating beverages, although he enjoyed smoking a pipe. He was a voracious reader and stayed abreast of current affairs by reading the weekly and daily newspapers. His hobby was baseball, the national pastime, and it is said that Ryan knew all the statistics for every player in the National League.

Bishop Ryan apparently grew even more reclusive in his later years. Diocesan clergy have handed down a story about a clever scheme whereby the bishop could avoid receiving visitors. One room of the bishop's residence was named the Quincy Room and another Springfield. When someone came to see the bishop he would duck into one of these rooms. The maid could then, truthfully, tell the visitor that the bishop was not available because he was in Quincy or Springfield.

Ryan died on July 2, 1923. *The Western Catholic* reported, "though we knew he had been ailing we had hoped he had rallied." Ryan had enjoyed decades of good health and his death, after a short illness, came as a surprise. Following the funeral at the Cathedral, Ryan was laid to rest at St. Patrick's Cemetery, Alton.

Children from the Alton Catholic Orphanage brought flowers to the grave of Bishop James Ryan.

From left: Fathers Clement Sommer, Francis Recouvreur, Bishop Ryan, Peter Peters, P. J. O'Halloran, Anthony Zurbonsen. At St. Michael's, Staunton, September 29, 1895.

Tolton Leaves the Diocese and His Final Return

Father Thomas Bruener of St. Boniface had organized St. Joseph's in 1882. This was an attempt to meet the pastoral needs of Quincy's black Catholics and to evangelize unaffiliated African-Americans. Bruener had obtained a second-hand church building and for two years he served without salary as the pastor. By that time about twelve families attended. School enrollment fluctuated between thirty and forty pupils. When Tolton assumed charge, the enrollment increased to fifty-five and a second School Sister joined Sister Herlinde. Over the next two years parish annual receipts increased steadily from $248.05 in 1886 to almost $700 in 1888, but a debt of $3,000 to St. Boniface remained. This loan had covered the initial purchase of the second-hand building. In the 1887 annual report, Tolton stated that about thirty African-Americans attended, but the church was "filled up with others." The pastor had acquired a reputation as a good preacher and understanding confessor

Tolton became, against his will, something of a celebrity. Other Quincy parishes, without his permission, sold his photograph. He received numerous invitations to give lectures and missions. He accepted a few, but mostly Tolton devoted attention to his own flock. Things seem to have been going well. The number of African-Americans attending seldom exceeded thirty, but a number of white Catholics came to St. Joseph's and some of them contributed generously when the plate was passed. But a cloud loomed on the horizon.

Father Michael Weiss, late in 1887, became the new pastor of St. Boniface and dean of the Quincy Deanery. When the new bishop was installed in 1888, he and Weiss had already been friends for some time. Ryan, no doubt, hoped that Weiss would be able to pay down the parish debt, an amount exceeding $8,000. Weiss did not want to continue subsidizing St. Joseph's and he openly criticized St. Boniface parishioners who donated money to the African-American parish. Furthermore, personal and racial animosity seems to have motivated the Bavarian-born Weiss. Using his authority as dean, Weiss informed Tolton that St. Joseph was to minister only to African-Americans. The bishop backed up Weiss who demanded that Tolton instruct the whites attending St. Joseph to stay away. To compensate for the lost revenues Tolton began to accept more speaking engagements outside of the diocese.

Weiss began to pressure Tolton to seek a transfer to another diocese. So did the bishop. When Tolton asisted at the wedding of a couple against the wishes of the woman's mother—a wealthy Catholic matron—Weiss insisted that Tolton pack his bags. A few bishops, desiring an African-American priest to serve their black Catholics, discussed possibilities with Tolton. In 1889, less than four years after his installation as pastor in Quincy, Tolton transferred to the Archdiocese of Chicago.

In the Windy City Tolton enjoyed the support of the bishop and many of his fellow priests. Nineteen of the black converts who came into the church under Tolton moved to Chicago with him as did his mother and sister. Even so, his assignment, to develop a parish for African-Americans, was a daunting task. Tolton expended himself trying to build St. Monica's, but gradually his health declined.

In July of 1897, Tolton returned to Chicago from the National Congress of Colored Congress (later renamed the National Black Catholic Congress). It was a very hot day and Tolton suffered a heat stroke. He died on July 9. The parishioners were shocked by the sudden loss and a very large crowd, including more than 100 priests, attended the funeral Mass. A few days later on July 13, back in Quincy, his friends waked the body. In compliance with Tolton's request, they buried America's first black priest at St. Peter's Cemetery.

Franciscan Architect Brother Adrian Wewer

Brother Adrian Wewer, a professional architect, designed and supervised the construction of dozens of buildings erected by the Sacred Heart Province of Franciscans. He was born in 1836 in Westphalia and entered the Order of Friars Minor in 1858. Wewer began to train as an architect before he came to the U.S. in 1862 and in this country he designed numerous churches, schools, and other religious institutions. Many, including four in our diocese, are still standing.

- St. Rose of Lima, Montrose (1879, razed 1956)
- St. Michael, Sigel (1880-81)
- St. Francis Solanus, Quincy (1884-86)
- St. Mary's, Alton (1892-93)
- St. Aloysius, Bishop Creek (1893-94)

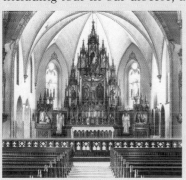

Interior, St. Francis Solonus Church, Quincy.

Brother Adrian Wewer, O.F.M.,
Franciscan friar.

Courtesy of the Order of Friars Minor, Sacred Heart Province, St. Louis.

Changing Face of the Diocese

Between 1880 and 1920 thousands of newcomers made homes within the boundaries of the diocese. Many of these immigrants were Roman Catholic although Eastern Orthodox and Eastern-rite Catholics accounted for sizeable minorities.

Ryan thus contended with more than a dozen ethnic groups and rivalry among them was one of the major challenges of his episcopate. Ryan deplored resistance to assimilation, in part, because it gave credence to the stereotype of the unpatriotic Catholic. Citizens of British ancestry tended to think it was impossible for Catholics to be loyal to both the church and to the nation, but Ryan saw no contradiction. Nonetheless, Ryan did recognize the desirability of offering preaching and confession in the native tongue of the faithful and tried to supply priests who spoke the various languages. He was, in fact, the first bishop of the diocese to monitor systematically the languages within his jurisdiction by including a language category in the annual parish reports.

Coal Miners from Macoupin County.
Courtesy of Pat Obertino, Staunton.

Foreign born in Illinois by Nationality

Nation	1880	1890	1900	1910
Ireland	117,343	124,498	114,563	93,451
Germany	235,786	338,382	332,169	319,182
Italy	1,764	8,035	23,523	72,160
Austria Bohemia Hungary	16,707	37840	63,516	163,020

*Based on "The Movement of the Population of Illinois, 1870-1910,"
Ernest L. Bogart. Transactions of the Illinois State Historical Society, 1917. p. 5.*

Most of these immigrants came to work in mines and factories. Deposits of bituminous coal underlay about 75 percent of Illinois' land surface. Demand for coal increased after the Civil War as railroads expanded and the number of factories mushroomed. In 1880, Illinois mines produced over six tons of coal. Production peaked at ninety million tons in 1918.

Mining is inherently dangerous, but even more so in the days before unions and government regulations. For most of the nineteenth century miners worked a ten-hour day beginning at 7 o'clock in the morning. The United Mine Workers of America organized in 1890 to secure fair pay and safer working conditions. Sometimes violence erupted when miners agitated for reforms.

The Brumleve homestead on the National Road near Effingham. Courtesy of Rosalee Hinkle, Tuetopolis.

Henry & Mary Hank Homestead, near Teutopolis, c. 1910. Courtesy of Margie Clayton, Effingham

In the 19th century farming remained a mainstay in many areas of the diocese.

The Virden Riot was one of the bloodiest incidents and it touched the lives of many Catholics. On October 12, 1898, striking miners from Mt. Olive and other nearby mining towns converged on Virden. That day the mine owners attempted to bring in 180 African-American miners, non union men from Alabama, to take the place of striking workers. As the train bearing the strikebreakers approached, union members—including many Catholics—tried to block its progress, but the train made it into a stockade. Then the shooting began as mine guards and strikers fired at one another. The battle lasted about ten minutes. None of the Alabamians were shot, but seven miners, four of them from Mt. Olive, and five guards were killed. Eventually, the United Mine Workers of America and the operators reached a settlement. The Virden Riot is remembered as a turning point in the strike of 1897 1898 that marks the rising power of the union.

New Parishes for the Coal Towns

By 1920 about 25 percent of the parishes in the diocese depended on the coal industry. In some places existing parishes absorbed the increasing numbers of Catholics. St. Louis, Nokomis, for example, founded two years before the Civil War, grew so much that the parish built a parochial school in 1912. Ss. Simon and Jude in Gillespie was another parish that learned to accommodate the newcomers. German and Irish farmers founded the church in 1879, but between 1899 and 1905, Italians and eastern Europeans moved in. They built a new church with double the seating capacity and, in 1913, opened a school.

Even with the adjustments, several new churches were necessary. At Witt, people of several nationalities joined forces to erect a church. Slovaks, Hungarians, Lithuanians, Poles, Irish, Italians, and Germans contributed to the cause, but were not able to raise enough money for a building. The longer established Catholic farmers of the area refused to contribute to the project because they were content to continue worshiping at Nokomis, but Father Clemens Johannes had an idea. The old St. Louis Church building was just four miles away and could be moved to Witt. In 1904, parishioners dismantled and reassembled the structure at the new site. They named the church St. Barbara in honor of the patroness of miners.

Many people are surprised to learn that mining was once a thriving concern in Springfield and Riverton. In the capital two new parishes served the mining families: St. Vincent DePaul for the Lithuanians in 1906 and St. Barbara for the Slovenians in 1909. St. Vincent's was the only national parish for Lithuanians in the diocese although several of the coal towns had a sizable Lithuanian minority. In Springfield, they began to arrive in the 1890s and attended St. Mary's where Monsignor Timothy Hickey helped them secure the services of a Lithuanian priest. The people wanted a parish of their own, but settling on a location was difficult because the Lithuanians were scattered throughout the city. After some wrangling they decided to build a little northeast of downtown.

The influx of Italians into Riverton expanded the parish roll at St. James. Catholics of German, Irish, and English ancestry founded

Ss. Simon & Jude Church,
Gillespie, c. 1900.

St. Barbara Church, Witt, c. 1910.
Courtesy of Jean Sarsany, Witt.

the parish a few years after the Civil War. Even with the newcomers, St. James was able to make do with the existing building, perhaps

Holy Trinity School and Convent, Mt. Olive, 1925.

because Italians tended not to attend as regularly as other groups.

One might think that ethnic Catholics would have united in the face of prejudice and bigotry, but most immigrants preferred to socialize with members of their own group. Unless absolutely necessary, they much preferred their own parish rather than mingle with other ethnic Catholics. The Slovaks in Virden founded Sacred Heart Church in 1912, and in Mt. Olive they built Holy Trinity Church in 1915. The Croatians at Mt. Olive, apparently less numerous, continued to worship at the Church of the Ascension with the English speakers. The isolation, however, did not extend to the union hall. There, men of the various nationalities managed to unite to advance their common interests.

Growth of the Tri-Cities

Coal fueled the industrial revolution that resulted in the growth of cities. The towns of Madison, Venice, and Granite City boomed in the late 1890s and their factories attracted immigrants like a magnet. St. Mark's, Venice, founded in 1871, was the earliest Catholic Church in the area. It is ironic that what is today one of the smallest and poorest parishes in the diocese was then a model parish of the early industrial era. At first, most of the families either farmed or worked for the Wabash or the Chicago and Alton railroads. Father Peter Kaenders arrived in 1880 and labored for forty-one years. His efforts to accommodate the New Immigrants were so successful that St. Mark's membership declined. He helped both the Poles and the Ukrainian Byzantine-rite Catholics to build their own parishes. The school opened in 1883, but St. Mark's found it impossible to retain

Father Peter Kaenders, St. Mark's, Venice. Kaenders also founded St. Elizabeth Hospital, Granite City.

teaching sisters for very long. Malaria and typhoid were constant companions in low-lying Venice. Eventually, the Sisters of Divine Providence arrived in 1921 and remained into the 1970s. St. Mark's, for a time, sponsored a high school, the only one in Venice. Kaenders himself taught the commercial classes including stenography, typewriting, bookkeeping, and commercial law. But the parish declined as more people moved to Madison and Granite City.

In Madison the "Car Shops" (Madison Car and Foundry) opened in 1891 and soon other factories, including the Standard Oil barrel works, Helmbacher Forge, and

Laclede Steel, provided jobs. The Catholics initially attended St. Mark's in Venice, but by 1912, there were enough Poles in Madison to establish their own church, Our Lady of Czestochowa, usually called St. Mary's. The bishop even

KOŚCIÓŁ M. B. CZĘSTOCHOWSKIEJ W MADISON, ILL.

OUR LADY OF CZESTOCHOWA POLISH R. C. CHURCH, MADISON, ILL.

Our Lady of Czestochowa Church (St. Mary's), Madison, 1912.

managed to provide a Polish priest. The future looked promising. The new building seated 200 and had two classrooms where Polish Franciscan sisters taught school. During World War I, however, prospects dimmed. As a parish history reports, "dissentions arose within the congregation owing to Polish national and radical leaders." Soon a schismatic group, the Polish National Catholic Church, built a church in Madison, and St. Mary's languished until the mid-1920s.

The presence of so many foreigners disturbed some native-born Americans. Anti-Catholic bigotry declined after the Civil War, but as the immigrant tide continued to rise in the closing years of the century, bigoted nativists took action. The American Protective Association (APA) became, in the late nineteenth century, the most virulent of these groups. Within twelve years of its 1887 founding, the APA claimed a membership of 2.5 million members, mostly in the Midwest. The APA was not very active in the diocese. In fact, several parishes of "old immigrants" (English, German, and Irish) report generous assistance on the part of non-Catholics.

The Knights of Columbus

The late nineteenth century witnessed the emergence of dozens of fraternal and benevolent societies. Americans had a long history of forming voluntary associations to promote various causes and Catholics proved to be no exception. Working people and immigrants with meager resources formed mutual aid societies to assist members in times of crisis. In the era before Social Security or government programs, the death benefit met a genuine need. When a member died, surviving members contributed a sum of money to cover the burial expenses for the deceased and provide some ready cash for the deceased's family. Oftentimes these societies also furnished an outlet for socializing.

Program for the institution of the Knights of Columbus council #1143, Edwardsville.
Courtesy of Genevieve C. Morrissey, Alton..

One of the best-known Catholic lay organizations dates from this period. The Knights of Columbus came into existence in 1882 in New Haven, Connecticut. Father Michael J. McGivney and some men of his parish created a society to render mutual aid, promote fellowship, encourage good citizenship, and battle against anti-Catholic bigotry. They chose Christopher Columbus as their patron. Today, some would say they romanticized the navigator's role as a defender of Christianity, but Catholics of the late nineteenth century saw Columbus as an apt symbol of Christian manhood. The Knights of Columbus, in fact, were part of a larger Columbian movement that, in the United States, climaxed in 1893 with the World's Columbian Exposition in Chicago.

In 1899 some Catholic men in Springfield were the first in our diocese to organize a council of the Knights of Columbus. By the end of 1921 an additional twenty-four councils were scattered across the diocese. Each council engaged in a variety of activities. The Tri-Cities Council at Granite City, for example, donated the Knights of Columbus edition of the *Catholic Encyclopedia* to both the Catholic school and the public libraries. At Staunton, in 1921, the council gave a Christmas package to each child at St. Michael's School. The Beardstown Council distributed copies of *Our Sunday Visitor* to parishioners. Local councils also helped support seminarians and The Catholic University of America. To address the social needs of members, the Knights held picnics, barbecues, and balls and organized baseball teams. In most places the Knights erected their own clubhouse or hall. In sum, the Knights gave Catholic men a structure to contribute to the well being of the church and society and meet their social needs at the same time. Other men's societies, some of them national, addressed similar concerns, but the Knights of Columbus was by far the most popular.

THE CATHOLIC
ENCYCLOPEDIA

AN INTERNATIONAL WORK OF REFERENCE
ON THE CONSTITUTION, DOCTRINE,
DISCIPLINE, AND HISTORY OF THE
CATHOLIC CHURCH

EDITED BY
CHARLES G. HERBERMANN, Ph.D., LL.D.
EDWARD A. PACE, Ph.D., D.D.   CONDÉ B. PALLEN, Ph.D., LL.D.
THOMAS J. SHAHAN, D.D.   JOHN J. WYNNE, S.J.
ASSISTED BY NUMEROUS COLLABORATORS

FIFTEEN VOLUMES AND INDEX
VOLUME VIII

SPECIAL EDITION
UNDER THE AUSPICES OF
THE KNIGHTS OF COLUMBUS CATHOLIC TRUTH COMMITTEE

New York
THE ENCYCLOPEDIA PRESS, INC.

Cover page of The Catholic Encyclopedia, special edition sponsored by the Knights of Columbus, 1913.

Catholic Women and the Domestic Church

Catholic Order of Foresters, women's division, c. 1900.
Courtesy of the Sangamon Valley Collection, Lincoln Library, Springfield.

Catholic women also participated in a variety of organizations to promote faith, family, and responsible citizenship. The Catholic Daughters of America began in 1903 under the patronage of the Knights of Columbus, but attained independent status in 1925. Ethnic Catholic women had their own societies, including the First Catholic Ladies Slovak Union, the American Lithuanian Roman Catholic Federation, and the American Catholic Hungarian League. Other groups were auxiliaries of men's organizations. The Ancient Order of Hibernians, for example, established an auxiliary in 1896 and the German Central Verein, formed a women's group in 1916. They wisely renamed themselves the National Catholic Women's Union in response to the anti-German sentiment of World War I. The Catholic Order of Foresters also had an auxiliary.

Over a dozen of the women's groups established a federation, the National Council of Catholic Women, in 1920. The federation gained the approval of the recently organized National Catholic Welfare Conference of American bishops. Under the auspices of these two groups, Diocesan Councils of Catholic Women came into existence, but in our diocese such developments did not occur until the time of Bishop James A. Griffin.

Catholic women discovered strength in numbers, but usually refrained from political advocacy. They did not, generally, support the female suffrage movement that climaxed in 1919 with the passage of the Nineteenth Amendment enfranchising women. Several factors account for the absence of Catholic women from this movement. First, they were not interested in systemic reform. The women focused on home and parish. Second, the American clergy and the hierarchy opposed suffrage. They believed that giving women the vote would undermine good order within the family and the family was the backbone of the faith. In this period laity tended to respect the opinions of church authorities, so women leaders followed the guidance offered. Furthermore, most Catholic women saw the suffrage movement as the pursuit of middle-class Protestant ladies. Immigrant Catholic women, especially, were too busy trying to

Catholics have always viewed marriage as a sacramental bond. Marriage cements not only the couple, but the wider community of relatives and friends. Note the make-shift dance floor laid out beside the barn.

Wedding celebration of Christie Bueker and Ben Meyer, near Teutopolis, May 23, 1899.
Courtesy of Betty Koeberlein, Teutopolis.

An Irish-American family from St. Mary, Pittsfield. Mr. & Mrs. Pat McCary and children (from left) Blanche, Myles, Carroll, Urban, c. 1905.

make ends meet by taking in boarders or laundry and working in factories.

The lack of support for suffrage, however, did not mean that Catholic women were unaware of events in the civil sphere, but they tended to embody their contribution to the common good by providing stable homes and raising children to be honest, generous, and obedient to authority. Many parishes, St. Michael's in Sigel, for example, had a Society of Christian Mothers. Through such groups, older and more experienced mothers provided practical and moral support for younger mothers.

Mothers were expected to establish a

First Communion certificate.
Courtesy of the Franciscan Monastery Museum, Teutopolis.

Holy card, c. 1880.
Courtesy of the Franciscan Monastery Museum, Teutopolis.

First Communion photograph of Annie Wegman (Hatke), Teutopolis, c. 1875. Courtesy of Betty Koeberlein, Teutopolis.

The German-American family of Mr. & Mrs. Henry Wilde, Sr., from St. Boniface, Quincy. Top from left: Katherine, Helen, Anna, John, Itha, Godfrey. Middle from left: Otto, Theresia, Anna (Mrs. Henry), Henry, Harry. Bottom from left: Marion, Genevieve, Cornelius, Carl, Herbert.
Courtesy of Mrs. Frances Schulte, Quincy.

extended family. In the minds of many Italian-American mothers, praying before the statues and protecting the family from the "evil eye" was more important than attending Mass. Italian men thought religious observance best left to the women, except for the festivals and processions. Pastors, usually Irish-American, in the mining communities throughout the diocese complained that the Italians seldom attended religious services and failed to give financial support to the parish. But when it was time for a baptism, wedding, or funeral, the pastors lamented, the Italians expected the church to provide. The piety of Polish and Irish women, in contrast, centered on the parish. Both groups held novenas and other devotions in the church as well as in the home.

Regardless of ethnicity, the Catholic mother was the first teacher of religion to her children. She taught them how to pray, make the sign of the cross, genuflect, and if she was literate, she quizzed them on the catechism. She schooled the children in the rituals and customs that would help them to make their way in the church and the world. Mothers looked to the Blessed Virgin Mary as their model, and bishops and priests encouraged such imitation through their preaching as well as in Catholic literature.

distinctive Catholic atmosphere within the home. They accomplished this by erecting home shrines and displaying religious pictures, statues, and sacramentals. Inexpensive pictures of Mary and the Sacred Heart of Jesus were especially popular. Each ethnic group had its own customs and preferences.

For Italians religion was home-centered rather than parish-based. Statues or pictures of the Holy Family, including St. Anne, adorned their homes. Jesus, Mary, Joseph, and the saints were part of the

Procession, St. Maurice, Morrisonville, c. 1900. Note the two facers at the far right window.

Catholic Education Enters the 20th Century

St. Teresa Academy, sponsored by the Ursulines, Decatur, c. 1920.

Sacred Heart Convent, Chapel, and Academy, Springfield, 1914.
Courtesy of the Dominican Sisters of Springfield in Illinois.

During the Ryan episcopate Catholic school enrollment increased from 7,000 to 12,911, although the number of parochial schools increased by just eleven. In the mid-nineteenth century the academies had been little more than finishing schools and the men's colleges offered a classical curriculum based Latin, Greek, ancient history, and mathematics. As the twentieth century approached the academies began to offer classes in the new science of home economics. Sewing, cooking, home decoration, and other practical subjects were designed to inspire Catholic women to make comfortable and attractive homes for their families-to-be. Business courses entered the course of study. Stenography, typewriting, and business mathematics enabled young women to obtain positions as secretaries and clerks. The traditional subjects of literature, history, geography, music, and art continued.

The institution that experienced the most growth was the school operated by the Dominican Sisters. After several years of teaching at the parochial school in Jacksonville, the sisters opened an academy or girls' high school in that city in 1886. It soon became apparent that a larger facility would be needed to accommodate the number of young women seeking admission to both the academy and religious life. After careful study, the Dominicans moved the Motherhouse to Springfield in 1893.

Two years later, their new school, Sacred Heart Academy, began to accept pupils. Eventually a complex, completed in 1910, included a Motherhouse, chapel, school, and dormitory.

Jacksonville may have lost the Dominican Motherhouse, but it gained a coeducational high school, the first in the diocese. Initially called the Public High School for Catholics, later renamed Routt, this institution opened its doors in 1902. The first class consisted of five men and six women. A new building was erected and at the 1905 dedication it was announced that William R. Routt donated $50,000 as an endowment for the school. Over time other members of the Routt family made additional donations even more generous than the

Girls exercise class at Notre Dame Academy, Quincy, 1915.
Courtesy of the School Sisters of Notre Dame, St. Louis Province.

43

first. For many years the school charged no tuition. Over the years the curriculum expanded to include not only the high school offerings, but also a full four-year college education. During these years the institution was called Routt College.

The two Franciscan colleges underwent dramatic changes during the Ryan episcopate. St. Joseph's at Teutopolis became a Seraphic College, meaning that, beginning in 1898, St. Joseph's accepted only aspirants to the Franciscan order. At the same time, St. Francis Solanus College, Quincy, enrolled priestly candidates for the diocese, men who previously would have gone to Teutopolis. St. Francis had for some years offered a business course of study for lay men and this program was strengthened during the 1890s. The Franciscans endeav- ored to equip young men with the skills needed to succeed in the business world.

Commercial Department, St. Francis Solanus College (Quincy University), Quincy.
Courtesy of the Brenner Library, Quincy University.

Varsity baseball team, St. Francis Solanus College (Quincy University), 1898-99. Intercollegiate baseball became popular in the late 19th century.
Courtesy of the Brenner Library, Quincy University.

Routt College, Jacksonville, erected 1905.

St. Francis Solanus College (Quincy University), c. 1890.
Courtesy of the Brenner Library, Quincy University.

Window in the Cathedral of the Immaculate Conception, Springfield, honoring Catholics who served in World War I.

A New Home for Catholic Orphans

Catholic Orphanage, Alton, 1923.

Classroom at the Orphanage.
The teacher is a member of the Sisters
Adorers of the Most Precious Blood,
Ruma, c. 1925.

Since 1883 Catholic orphans had found a refuge in the Alton Catholic Orphanage near Ss. Peter and Paul Cathedral. All too soon, this facility became crowded and when Bishop Ryan came into office he immediately contemplated an expansion. In the early 1890s the diocese received a bequest from the estate of the Jacksonville philanthropist Charles Routt. Ryan decided to use the $10,000, along with other funds he set aside, to construct an addition to the existing home. Architect J. L. D. McCarthy of St. Louis developed a master plan calling for additions and eventual replacement of the original structure. When completed in 1908, the remodeled orphanage could accommodate 200 children plus the Precious Blood sisters who cared for them. Within a short time the orphanage was again bursting at the seams.

Living in such close quarters, the orphans were among the hardest hit when the Spanish influenza epidemic spread to the United States in the winter of 1918-1919. Apparently, two recently admitted children were the source of contagion. Within three days eighty children were stricken. A few days later, the number topped one hundred. The sisters attempted to isolate the sick children and when the infirmary could hold no more, they began to use hallways. Miraculously, only two children died. That so many survived is a tribute to the care exercised by the sisters, the lay nurses who were brought in to assist, and to Father Michael A. Tarrant, the chaplain. All provided excellent care under the most trying circumstances.

In the wake of the epidemic even more orphaned children flooded into the home. Building a new facility became imperative and the bishop made it the special project of his final years. The diocese purchased a thirteen-acre site on State Street, about five blocks from the cathedral. The enormous five-story building was designed to accommodate 500 children. Ryan began raising funds in the spring of 1919 and continued until his death. "A gift to the orphan is a pure gift to God," he wrote in one of the solicitation letters. Catholics responded generously and raised over $300,000

towards the total that exceeded half a million dollars. Alas, the bishop did not live long enough to see the opening of the new orphanage. He died three months before its completion.

By the time the new home opened, professional social workers were advocating the deinstitutionalization of orphans. Foster care was, they believed, a better and more humane way to provide for needy children. Ryan and Tarrant may not have been aware of trends in modern social work, but considering conditions within the diocese, the decision to build a large orphanage made sense. Protestant children were accepted at the home, but its principal goal was to provide a Catholic upbringing for Catholic children. Many Catholics were so poor that they had no alternative but to send young relatives to orphanages. Placement in a Protestant or non-religious foster home was an unattractive alternative. The Catholic Orphanage continued to function for several decades. As the twentieth century advanced the number of orphans declined. The institution shifted its focus to children with special needs and today, as the Alton Catholic Children's Home, continues to assist children and youth through a variety of services.

Hospitals & Homes Founded during Bishop Ryan's Tenure

1896   Our Saviour's Hospital, Jacksonville, Sisters of the Holy Cross, Notre Dame, Indiana

1903   St. Joseph Home for the Aged, Springfield, Franciscan Sisters of Peoria

1905   St. Vincent's Hospital, Taylorville, Sisters Adorers of the Most Precious Blood, Ruma

1906   St. Joseph Home for the Aged, Alton, Sisters Adorers of the Most Precious Blood, Bosnia

1910   St. Elizabeth's Hospital, Granite City, Sisters of Divine Providence, St. Louis

1913   Huber Memorial Hospital, Pana, Sisters of Misericorde, Montreal

1919   St. John's Sanitarium, Springfield, Hospital Sisters of the Third Order of St. Francis, Springfield

1920   St. Joseph's Hospital for Aged and Chronically Ill Female Patients, Quincy Franciscan Sisters of the Poor

St. Joseph Home, Springfield, erected 1925.

Getting to Church

Parishioners from St. Mary's Marshall, posed for a photograph at Sharkey Cross Road on a Sunday morning in the 1920s. Although millions of Model T automobiles were on the road by this time, horse-power continued to be used in rural areas of the diocese as late as the 1930s.

From left: (standing) unknown, Barney Curran, Jimmie Curran, Mike McManus, Pat Sharkey. (seated) Jack Curran, unknown, Ossie McManus, Sr., Benny Gallagher, Jimmy Sharkey, Tom Curran, Pat Curran. Taken at Sharkey Crossroad on the way home from St. Mary's, Marshall, 1920s. Courtesy of Donald Guinnip, Marshall.

The End of an Era

The closing years of Ryan's episcopate were trying ones for the diocese and the nation. Our popular conception is that the 1920s was a prosperous era of flappers and Model T automobiles. And for many Americans, it was just that. We tend to forget, however, that the mining and agricultural sectors were in depression long before the stock market crash of 1929.

Prejudice and racism, too, disfigured the American landscape. The 1908 race riot in Springfield shocked the nation and led to the founding of the National Association for the Advancement of Colored People (NAACP). Ironically, at St. John's Hospital where many of the wounded were treated, no one complained when patients of different colors were placed side by side in the emergency room and the hallway.

German-Americans faced suspicion during World War I even though discerning eyes can find dozens of German names in the roster of Catholics who served during the conflict. The Knights of the Ku Klux Klan were anti-Catholic, anti-immigrant, and anti-black. This sometimes violent white supremacist group was active throughout the diocese—notably in Sangamon, Macoupin, and Cass counties. *The Western Catholic* newspaper, published by two diocesan priests and a layman in Quincy, often reported on anti-Catholic activity.

The bishop was seventy-five years old when he died on July 2, 1923. He had steered the diocese through a period of tumultuous growth. We best remember him for his work on behalf of the orphans, but it would be the next bishop, James A. Griffin, who awoke the social conscience of the diocese and ushered it into the twentieth century.

Fide et fortitudine

The Diocese Comes of Age

1924-1948

A city set on a mountain cannot be hidden. Let your light shine before others, that they may see your good deeds and glorify your heavenly Father.
Matthew 5: 14b, 16.

CHAPTER FOUR

"We must let our light shine before all men, before our nation and the nations of the world, so that they may see our good works and glorify our Eternal Father. How can the world see our good works unless we have wide publicity? We have kept silent too long." Although Bishop James A. Griffin spoke these words in 1938, they capture the essence of his approach to running a diocese—let the world know what the Catholic Church is doing and what it has to offer. In the nineteenth century most Catholics refrained from participation in civil affairs lest they stir up animosity, but in the 1920s and beyond, they exercised greater economic and political clout. Bishops wielded influence far beyond Catholic institutions.

Geographic considerations played a role in the transfer of the see to Springfield, but the fact that Springfield was the seat of state government was duly noted by the new bishop. It was only fitting that the seat of diocesan government—literally the *cathedra* or bishop's seat—should be in the same city. Griffin developed a network of friends in government and business. He exercised direct power, too. In 1927 he was appointed to the State Welfare Board. Most of the time, however, Griffin filled the role of watchdog on behalf of all the Illinois bishops.

The Cathedral of the Immaculate Conception
"It is God's Work. God wills it."

Nothing better symbolized the ascendancy of the Roman Catholic Church in central Illinois than the building of the Cathedral of the Immaculate Conception. The new cathedral, dedicated in 1928, was everything a cathedral should be. It was big. It was constructed of the finest materials. It cost a lot of money. Construction and furnishings totaled more than $1 million, a staggering sum when one remembers that many area Catholics were

Main aisle of the cathedral, 1928.
Photograph by Chicago Architectural Photographing Company.

Architect Joseph W. McCarthy's rendering of the proposed Cathedral of the Immaculate Conception. From left: school, church, bishop's residence.

Main altar of the cathedral as depicted in an advertisement of the Deprato Statuary Company, Chicago. Official Catholic Directory, 1929.

poor. Griffin was never one to cut corners when it came to setting the right tone, and in this respect he was simply executing lessons learned from Cardinal George Mundelein of Chicago. At one level the cathedral and the adjacent school, convent, and chancery were a monument to Griffin. It is easy to spot his winged mascot, the griffin, inside and out. On another level, however, the imposing nature of the structure displayed the power and prestige of the Catholic Church.

The Cathedral Campaign fund-raising effort began two years earlier and was so timed that the new building would be dedicated during the Diamond Jubilee of the diocese. Griffin also commissioned a book to mark the seventy-fifth anniversary. In its own way, it was as huge an undertaking as the cathedral. Griffin engaged the services of a Catholic historian and writer, Thomas J. Thompson, who did a masterful job of assembling the 882-page work. It included individual parish histories as well as the story of each diocesan institution. *The Diamond Jubilee History of the Diocese of Springfield in Illinois* remains an indispensable reference, but the dedication of the cathedral was the centerpiece of the anniversary celebration.

The campaign slogan was "It is God's work. God wills it." Such a catch phrase would raise an eyebrow today, but whatever doubts individuals may have harbored, it did not prevent them from digging deep into their pockets. Within the first month the campaign reached its goal of $750,000 and topped the million-dollar mark. Springfield's non-Catholic businessmen held the bishop in such high esteem that they asked to be solicited. In other parts of Sangamon County the Ku Klux Klan still flourished, but as Griffin observed, the new cathedral was "not only a house of prayer but also a symbol of lovely friendship and an incentive to greater civic service."

The bishop turned to his childhood friend, Joseph W. McCarthy, of Chicago to design the new complex. McCarthy is best remembered as architect of the chapel at St. Mary of the Lake University in Mundelein. The similarity of the two structures is apparent. Both employed classical elements–the chapel in the Georgian mode and the cathedral in the Neo-Classical style. McCarthy turned to early nineteenth century Greek Revival buildings for inspiration. This style of architecture has been long associated, in the American mind, with ideals of democracy, stability, and dignity.

The architect employed the basilica plan in which the nave is longer than it is wide. The exterior is Mankato stone, a golden colored marble. The interior is graced by marble in various colors and custom-designed art glass windows. A mosaic of the Immaculate Conception of Mary, just above the high altar, is based on a painting by Bartolomé Esteban Murillo, a seventeenth-century Spanish baroque artist.

The two-story school, at peak enrollment, accommodated nearly 300 children. The convent, located between the school and the church, contained sixteen bedrooms. The Dominican teachers occupied the second floor and the Franciscan housekeepers for the bishop and cathedral clergy lived on the first.

The bishop's residence, compared to the homes of most Catholics, was palatial. Spanish Baroque Revival furnishings graced the interior. Three guest bedrooms, each with connecting bath, awaited visiting prelates and clergy friends. Griffin's own bedroom held a twin bedstead with his coat of arms carved into the headboard. The dining room could easily accommodate a dozen, but Griffin hosted smaller and larger groups as well. In sum, the residence was a sort of stage for entertaining, a stage set where Griffin could perform his role as prelate and power broker.

It is tempting to view the cathedral and bishop's house as nothing more than Griffin's monument to himself, but that would miss the greater significance of the cathedral group as a symbol of the church's institutional maturity in American life. The buildings are also a tribute to the generosity of the donors and an expression of their hopes for the future.

Bishop James A. Griffin
February 5, 1924 to August 5, 1948

Providence smiled on James Aloysius Griffin, born February 27, 1883, to Thomas J. and Catherine Woulfe Griffin. He was one of ten children and the Griffin household on Chicago's South Side was a happy one. His Irish-born father, educated at Trinity College, Dublin, instilled in the boy a love of learning. Young Griffin also came to respect those who earned a living by the sweat of their brow. The nearby Armour meatpacking plant, where Griffin's father worked, employed many of their neighbors, too.

The family's church, St. Gabriel's, was one of Chicago's now-legendary parishes that reached its zenith during Griffin's childhood and youth. The parish was founded just a few years before his birth and when Griffin was five years old, St. Gabriel's dedicated its new church building. The Irish parishioners and the whole neighborhood took pride in the edifice designed by John Wellborn Root. Griffin, thus, experienced the Catholic Church as a confident and powerful institution. In Chicago, after all, Catholics were an unapologetic majority. Years later, as bishop, Griffin's self-assurance and commanding presence rested on this foundation of strength.

There were three vocations to the church in Griffin's family. Two of his sisters became Sisters of Mercy and while in high school he chose the diocesan priesthood. He studied at Kenrick Seminary, St. Louis, and in 1909 completed his theological education at the North American College in Rome. By this time it was common for American prelates to send their brightest and best to study abroad. A few years in the Eternal City strengthened loyalty to the Holy Father and fostered a deeper connection to the universal church, traits essential to develop in men who showed an aptitude for leadership. Griffin also picked up several academic and ecclesiastical degrees including a Ph.D. and the S.T.D. (Doctorate in Sacred Theology), degrees qualifying him to teach in a seminary or pontifical institute.

Bishop James A. Griffin, fourth bishop of the diocese.

After ordination on July 4, 1909, Griffin returned to Chicago. For the next seven years he cut his teeth as an assistant pastor in urban parishes. In 1917 he moved to Coal City to become pastor of Assumption of Mary Church. Griffin's fluency in Italian helped smooth the way with the numerous Italian immigrants, but he also managed to work successfully with the eighteen other ethnic groups to begin a parochial school. On occasion he served as a mediator between coal miners and operators, experiences that proved invaluable when Griffin dealt with the mining crisis of the 1930s.

St. Mary's Church, Springfield, the pro-cathedral from 1924 to 1928.

Drawing Room of the bishop's house, Springfield, 1928.
Photograph by Chicago Architectural Photographing Company.

Pope Pius XI appointed Griffin as bishop on November 10, 1923, just a few days after announcing, on October 26, the transfer of the see from Alton to Springfield. Following his consecration at Holy Name Cathedral, Chicago, on February 25, 1924, Griffin traveled to Springfield where an enthusiastic crowd of Catholics and non-Catholics greeted him for a day of celebrating. His installation was carried on a local radio station. Later in the day Griffin attended a reception at the Illinois State Armory where the Mayor of Springfield and other dignitaries welcomed him.

The bishop's first task was to establish a new cathedral and move the chancery. St. Mary's in downtown Springfield became the pro-cathedral, but from the beginning Griffin envisioned a structure in keeping with the dignity of a cathedral church. Griffin toured his new territory and by 1928, the Diamond Jubilee of the diocese, he had instituted a number of programs including the Holy Name Society and Catholic Social Services, the predecessor of Catholic Charities.

Dining Room of the bishop's house, Springfield, 1928.
Photograph by Chicago Architectural Photographing Company.

In many respects the new bishop patterned himself on Mundelein. In that era the American hierarchy were like aristocracy. It was neither unusual, nor scandalous, for prelates to live lavishly and rub shoulders with high-ranking civil and business leaders. The bishop's residence, part of the new cathedral group on Sixth Street, was designed for entertaining. Furnishings included monogrammed sterling silver flatware and porcelain dinnerware embossed with Griffin's episcopal coat of arms. His vestments for church ceremonies were embroidered in gold and silver. Precious stones adorned his mitre. Today, all of this seems an ostentatious display, but in the inter-war period it symbolized the increasing influence and status of the Catholic Church in America.

Catholic Charities, Springfield, c. 1930.
Photograph by the Illinois State Register.

Griffin, an outgoing man by nature, reveled in the role of prelate and in Springfield became something of a celebrity. He numbered J. Emil Smith, editor of the *Illinois State Journal*, among his new friends, and he soon made the acquaintance of several politicians. He mingled with mayors and governors. Governor Henry Horner (1933-1940), became Griffin's best friend. Some thought it an odd friendship because Horner was a Jew. Whatever one's religion, high office can be a lonely experience, but the two unmarried men were able to communicate as equals. It was not unusual for the bishop to stroll over to the Governor's Mansion in the evening where they would review the trials and triumphs of the day. Horner died while in

From left: William H. Hellhake, Bishop James A. Griffin, Archbishop Samuel A. Stritch of Chicago, an unidentified man, Bishop Aloysius J. Muench of Fargo, South Dakota. National Convention of the Catholic Central Verein of America and the National Catholic Women's Union, Springfield, 1943. The prominent display of American flags and George Washington symbolized the wartime loyalty of the predominately German-American membership.

In 1939 Griffin and other American bishops traveled to Mexico to investigate the state of the church. Because of Mexico's anti-clerical laws, they wore secular attire. Here, Griffin (middle) is seen at the Shrine of our Lady of Gualdalupe, Tepeyac.

office and to Griffin it was a great personal loss.

An invitation to dine with the bishop was a coveted prize. The *Illinois State Journal* reported "As a host none is more congenial than Bishop James A. Griffin. His home, known as the Bishop's House, is a house of friendship. Within its portals all are made to feel at home." Women, however, were never on the guest list, so how can this statement be true? Griffin, in keeping with the clerical conventions of his day, did not sit at table with women, even female relatives. Protestants, however, were not aware of this practice and no less a personage than Governor Dwight Green (1941-1949) was caught by surprise. Upon receiving an invitation, the Governor assumed it included his wife and replied that they would be happy to attend. In response, the bishop immediately telephoned to inform Green that the dinner was strictly a men's party.

On a day-to-day basis, Griffin administered the diocese much as a businessman would run a company. Monsignor Michael A. Tarrant, former secretary to Bishop James Ryan, provided continuity in the transition to Springfield. They centralized the administration of the diocese by creating a number of new offices. A director of parochial schools, for example, coordinated textbook selection and organized teachers' institutes. A comptroller assumed responsibility for fiscal affairs.

Creation of Catholic Social Services in 1925 exemplified the new management style. Today, it is known as Catholic Charities and no other apostolate of the diocese has had more impact on non-Catholics. The priest director, trained in social work, coordinated the efforts of Catholic institutions and lay organizations. He also hired Elizabeth Kuhlman, another social worker, to work with women's organizations. As far as can be determined, she was the first professional woman hired by the diocese. During the Depression, Catholic Social Services, in cooperation with St. John's Hospital, began a program to feed the hungry. St. John's Breadline for some time operated directly from the kitchen of the hospital, but eventually became a freestanding operation. The office also helped families and individuals to apply for relief and take advantage of many New Deal programs.

Griffin appointed priest moderators to oversee a number of new lay organizations including the Catholic Youth Organization (CYO), the Holy Name Society, Laymen's Retreat League, the Diocesan Council of Catholic Women, the Confraternity of Christian Doctrine, the Legion of Mary, and the Legion of Decency. The centralizing trend was consistent with the progressive philosophy that well managed programs could improve social conditions.

Compared to his predecessor, Griffin was more accessible. Not only did he fulfill his sacramental responsibilities to confirm and ordain, he spoke to countless church and civic groups on topics ranging from Scripture, the New Deal, foreign affairs, and changes in family life. Griffin was also active in the National Catholic Welfare Conference, precursor to the United States Conference of Catholic Bishops. In 1939, he was part of a delegation of bishops to Mexico where anticlerical laws made it difficult for priests to function.

He shepherded us through some of our most trying days. When Griffin arrived both the farming and mining economies were in shambles. The Great Depression of the 1930s and the coal miners' war (1932-1937) intensified the suffering. By the time the mining crisis was resolved, Americans were watching with apprehension the rise of Hitler in Germany. Catholics shouldered their share of sacrifices during World War II and after the war Griffin launched a $500,000 capital campaign to build and remodel churches in the postwar period.

Throughout his tenure, Griffin held fast to the teachings of the church. He encouraged the people through personal example, preaching, public speaking, and advocating for Catholic concerns at the Statehouse. When he died after a lengthy illness on August 5, 1948, the loss was keenly felt. A longtime friend, J. Emil Smith, wrote in the *Illinois State Register* that Griffin personified the Golden Rule. The same paper editorialized: "Priest, builder, genius of organization, and a friend of all mankind, Bishop Griffin has in a quarter of a century swiftly expanded the dominion of the Catholic Church in the Diocese of Springfield in Illinois despite a great economic depression and the vicissitudes of a World War."

Catholic Action:
Cornerstone of the Griffin Era

Catholic Action was Griffin's top priority. Strictly speaking, Catholic Action consisted of structured lay apostolates sanctioned by the bishop, such as the Catholic Youth Organization (CYO). Griffin also encouraged the less structured form of Catholic Action in which lay persons, inspired by their faith, perform acts of charity and justice. Throughout his tenure Griffin relied on the work of lay societies, the Catholic and secular press, and Sunday preaching to promote Catholic Action.

"The cry today," Griffin wrote in 1929, "is Catholic Lay Action—but we can have no Lay Action till our Catholic men and women have a working knowledge of the Doctrines of their Church." To this end, three years earlier, Griffin required pastors to preach on designated topics over the course of each liturgical year. Annual topics included the Apostles Creed, Grace and the Sacraments, Liturgy, Divine Revelation, the Ten Commandments, and Catholic Action.

During the Great Depression, beginning with Advent in 1936, the Sunday Gospel was to be the basis of the sermon. That became the standard practice after Vatican II, but in those days it was fresh and innovative. In any given year, however, a number of Sundays were reserved for other topics such as the Legion of Decency (and subsequent pledge), Lenten regulations, the evils of mixed marriages, and other teaching considered vital to leading a life of faith.

Griffin recommended the "catechetical discourse," a style of preaching popular at the time. The preacher employed scripture, familiar sayings, and illustrations from life to explain Church teachings. Otherwise, the Mass remained unchanged. Most Catholics continued to offer private prayers while the priest faced the high altar. The liturgical reform movement was in its infancy, but Griffin was aware of the trends in this area. He understood the link between liturgy and social justice, and hence, the mandate to cultivate Catholic Action through preaching.

Lack of space prohibits a comprehensive survey of the many forms of Catholic Action in our diocese, but we will examine a few representative endeavors. Although each organization had a priest moderator, the emphasis was on lay action.

The Legion of Mary

In the middle decades of the twentieth century the Legion of Mary was one of the most popular expressions of Catholic Action. It is a tightly structured organization, founded in Dublin, Ireland, in 1921, with local, regional, national, and international levels. Father James Haggerty introduced the Legion to our diocese in 1936 by starting a *praesidium*, or local unit, at the cathedral. Soon there were additional *praesidia* throughout Springfield and in the 1940s the Legion spread to Alton and Quincy.

The allusion to the Roman Legion is deliberate. To the Irish founders this military entity represented the values of courage, discipline, honor, endurance, success, and loyalty. Members of the Legion of Mary think of themselves as an army under the banner of the Blessed Mother. This lay organization of men and women promotes both good works and spiritual enrichment. Active members commit to attend a weekly meeting to pray and encourage one another. They also pledge to perform at least two hours of apostolic work each week. Within our diocese these good works have included visiting the sick both at home and in hospitals, visiting the imprisoned, and doing parish census work.

Emblem of the Legion of Mary.
Courtesy of Marie Therese Henebry, Springfield.

The Holy Name Society

The Holy Name Society traces its origins to the sixteenth century, but in the United States it grew dramatically after 1900. Griffin considered it suitable for every Catholic man, and in 1925 mandated that a branch be established in each parish of the diocese. The organization combined piety and practical action. First and foremost, members promoted reverence for the Holy Name of Jesus and to the person of Jesus. Members were to receive Holy Communion in a body every three months, in part because this example would inspire others to good works and deeper faith. Members also organized baseball leagues and participated in other activities to build up a sense of community.

As for Catholic Action, the Society advanced the cause of justice by fighting against anti-Catholic bigotry. "Prejudice is a cataract in the eyes of the soul," wrote the priest moderator, Father Thomas Fennessy, "and this must be removed before the light of truth can be seen." Society members also spoke out against indecent motion pictures and literature. In short, they endeavored to be good Catholics and good citizens. For many years the Holy Name Society remained

Championship baseball team from the Holy Name Society, St. James, Riverton, 1927.

the principal parish-based outlet for men to express their religious sentiments and channel their good works.

The Catholic Youth Organization—the CYO

Many Catholics recall the happy times spent participating in the Catholic Youth Organization, better known as the CYO. Dominican Sister Philip Neri Crawford, for example, recollected that it was at the Springfield CYO in the Knights of Columbus building that she learned to swim, attended dances, and generally had a good time with her friends. To the bishop and the adult organizers, the CYO was more than a recreational venture. It was a comprehensive program designed to strengthen the faith and encourage Catholic Action.

Griffin organized the CYO, a national movement within the Church in America, shortly after coming to the diocese. The CYO program employed a variety of social, religious, cultural, and athletic programs to enhance the development of Catholic youth. The bishop also believed that the CYO would bear the fruit of Catholic Action. Shortly after World War II the diocese issued a revised CYO manual for the adult leaders. "This book," the bishop wrote in the introduction, "strives to correlate Catholic activity and Catholic action, with the overwhelming emphasis, of course, on the latter." Griffin continued,

> With the whole-hearted cooperation of all our parish priests, this program should readily succeed in forming the minds and hearts of our young people according to the pattern of Him Who has, for twenty centuries, fired the aspiration of millions of youth to go forth and do battle in His Name. This is precisely the task that faces our Catholic youth in the post-war world.

The CYO Camp was yet another way—one of the most enjoyable, no doubt—to inspire Catholic youth. The Diocesan Camp at Pere Marquette State Park began in 1939. According to the 1946 brochure, a stay at the camp worked toward "the socialization of boys and girls, under the influence of religion and by using the advantages afforded by the Camp and its

facilities" so that each youngster would become a useful citizen. The camp operated for about two months each summer, but one week was reserved exclusively for the children of the Catholic Orphanage in Alton. In 1946 parents paid $10 per week per child. Activities included swimming, life-saving instruction, hiking, crafts, singing, and morning and evening prayers. A classes in nature lore "opens a new world to the younger camper, especially the city-bred boy or girl," stated the brochure. And parents could be assured that respect for the nation was cultivated by the daily raising and lowering of the American flag.

First all-city C.Y.O. night at the Knights of Columbus Hall, Springfield, 1945. It was not unusual for girls to dance together if the boys were too shy to ask.
Courtesy of the Clerics of St. Viator, Chicago Province.

Holy Childhood Association

Younger children, too, were encouraged to serve humanity and grow in faith. The Holy Childhood Association, a branch of the Society for the Propagation of the Faith, began in our diocese in 1925. Older readers will associate the Holy Childhood with an unusual fund raising method. To fund the missions and foster a sense of connection with those served, the Association encouraged children to assist a pagan baby. For $5 an individual boy or girl, or a whole class, could assure that an abandoned baby in a non-Christian culture would be raised in the Catholic faith. An added incentive was that the sponsor could name the baby. The children understood that they were helping the salvation of the baby's soul. The youngsters of our diocese responded generoulsy. After Vatican II the Association of the Holy Childhood dropped the pagan baby idea, but to this day our diocese consistently ranks in the top ten in contributions to the Holy Childhood Association.

Kindergarten graduation class from Cathedral School, Springfield, 1936. The baby dolls (at either end of the first row) represent the pagan babies sponsored by the class.
Courtesy of Sister Mary Alice Mannix, O.P., Springfield.

African-Americans and the Bishop

Some forty years had passed since the closing of the diocese's only parish for African-American Catholics when in the late 1930s Bishop Griffin decided to erect a mission in Quincy for black Catholics. It was called St. Benedict the African. By 1939, St. Benedict's membership had risen to a mere ten or so families. The following year, the Franciscan Friars assumed control of the mission. Despite donations from the Society for the Propagation of the Faith, St. Benedict's foundered and in 1949 the mission closed.

Elsewhere in the diocese, Griffin reported that there were about twenty black Catholic families in Springfield and about forty in Alton. The trend in those days was to establish separate parishes if there were enough African-American Catholics to make a go of it, but as the bishop noted, "We have made three attempts to establish a colored Catholic Church here in Springfield, but never had any great success." In Springfield many blacks attended Cathedral and in Alton many went to Ss. Peter & Paul.

Although diocesan attempts to evangelize African-American Catholics failed, the bishop personally received high praise from Springfield's black community. In a radio tribute after Griffin's death, the Reverend Andrew Richard Parks of the St. John's African Methodist Episcopal (A.M.E.) Church, stated, "Negroes of Springfield who have lived here for many years, tell of the sterling character of Bishop Griffin that was marked by a spirit of tolerance. They regarded him as a leader in bringing about interracial amity." Among other things, the bishop supported equal treatment of African-Americans in regard to New Deal programs. Griffin appears to have had good intentions, but it would be another two decades before substantial improvement began in race relations within the church in our diocese.

Sisters of St. Francis of the Martyr St. George Arrive in Alton

The first Sisters of St. Francis of the Martyr St. George to arrive in Alton, 1925.
Courtesy of the Sisters of St. Francis of the Martyr St. George.

In 2000 the Sisters of St. Francis of the Martyr St. George celebrated seventy-five years of service to the Church in the United States. They trace their origins to Thuine, Germany. There, in 1869, Sister Mary Anselma Bopp gathered a small group of women to serve the poor and sick. Most women's communities founded in the nineteenth century dedicated themselves to either teaching or hospital work, but from the onset, the foundress of this community organized it in such a way that it could assume any apostolate.

After World War I the Thuine sisters decided to send missionaries to the United States and, in 1923, five sisters arrived in St. Louis to work in Father Peter J. Dunne's Home for Newsboys. Conflict with Dunne led the sisters to seek another apostolate and they began to ask for the intercession of St. Therese of Lisieux. Soon, they received word that the Precious Blood sisters from Croatia, who operated the Nazareth Home for the aged and infirm in Alton, were looking for a religious community to take over the institution. As arrangements were made for the transfer, the Franciscan superior, Sister Mary Columbe, discussed a plan to transform the home into a hospital for those with contagious or chronic illness. The new institution would also continue to serve the aged and infirm and the new facility would be known as St. Anthony's Infirmary. St. Joseph's Hospital, sponsored by the Daughters of Charity and the oldest hospital in town, would provide acute, surgical, and obstetrical care.

It was an expensive proposition, but trusting to Providence and the Little Flower, the sisters borrowed $60,000 to remodel and expand the old Nazareth Home. Time and again in the late 1920s and throughout the Great Depression, the sisters would be on the verge of bankruptcy when a benefactor would appear or a poor person found the means to pay a bill.

The immigrant sisters realized that they must become fluent in English in order to serve the patients and to continue to study advances in nursing. So they learned English from the School Sisters of Notre Dame at St. Mary's parish. The Franciscans also prepared to assume American citizenship and in 1926, seventeen of them did so. As the years passed St. Anthony's grew and so did the Franciscan community. Today they sponsor not only Saint Anthony's Health Center, but also a number of other health care facilities, most of them outside of Illinois. They also engage in teaching, diocesan administration, and serve as domestic staff in the archbishop's residence at St. Louis and at the Apostolic Nuncio's residence in Washington, D.C.

Rural Revitalization

Edith Feldhake,
Co-op Parish Activities Services.

Out in the countryside, Father Charles Nell, working in the Effingham deanery, began an innovative and successful program to reinvigorate the diocese's rural parishes. With the help of Miss Edith Feldhake, a parishioner at St. Anthony's, he set up the Co-op Parish Activities Services. This non-profit organization served rural churches and schools throughout Illinois. Participating parishes paid a subscription fee that entitled them to information, catechetical aids, film strips, charts and other supplies for parish and school. Feldhake served as secretary, general manager, and advisor. She was also active in the National Rural Life Conference. In fact, Feldhake helped organize Rural Youth rallies all over the country.

Nell, Feldhake, and the Parish Co-op Services were part of a larger movement, the National Catholic Rural Life Conference, established in 1923. Rural Life founders hoped to improve the condition of rural Catholics. A major concern was the decline of the rural population. In our diocese Nell, although born and raised in Chicago, embodied the spirit of the Rural Life Conference. To this day rural Catholics still reap the benefit of his initiatives.

In 1922 the bishop transferred Nell to St. Joseph's, Island Grove. "I was pretty dumb about farming," he said in a *Prairie Farmer* interview, "but the people gave me an education." When Nell came to Island Grove, farm families were in the midst of the post-war agricultural slump. Part of the problem was over-cropping. The fertility of the soil was exhausted. Twenty farms in the vicinity had been abandoned. Nell approached the Farm Bureau and invited them to organize in Jasper County.

The priest also addressed the social needs of the community. Living on a farm sounds idyllic to many of us, but without electricity, telephones, and radio farm life was all too often months and months of unrelieved labor. Many still farmed with horses. To foster social life, the young priest organized picnics, baseball games, and other activities. He cultivated improved relations between Catholics and non-Catholics. "We just agreed to disagree on religious matters to start with," he told the *Prairie Farmer,* "and have since kept religion and community activities apart, believing that both have their own place."

Nell consulted the Effingham County farm agent to work out a plan for crop rotation. He also organized study clubs so farmers could learn more about the benefits of modern farming techniques. In some locales, dairy farming was a better alternative and the county agent helped many Catholics make the transition from grain to milk production.

Despite Nell's work on behalf of local farmers, the Co-op Services was not neglected. Almost as soon as he moved to Island Grove, Nell asked Feldhake to become parish secretary. She also assumed the role of sacristan and number of other functions. Illness forced Nell to discontinue the Co-op Parish Activities Services in 1956. It continued, however, in Detroit under the auspices of the Third Order of St. Francis. Feldhake, along with two associates, helped to set up the new office. Co-op Parish Activities Services is truly one of our diocese's contributions to the American church.

Father Charles Nell, founder Co-op Parish Activities Services.
Courtesy of Bernice Probst, Island Grove.

Ursuline Institutions Go Co-ed

For hundreds of years the sisters of the Order of St. Ursula educated young women and young women only. The Ursulines maintained this tradition in our diocese. High school age men could attend the secondary program at Ss. Peter and Paul in Alton or Routt in Jacksonville, but boys in the other cities had no alternative but boarding school. The bishop approached the Ursulines, first in Alton and then in Decatur, requesting that they transform their academies into coed high schools. In this regard he was innovative and forward looking, but at first the proposal took the Ursulines by surprise.

Marquette Catholic High School, Alton and St. Teresa High School, Decatur

"At first, we were actually struck dumb," wrote the Ursuline annalist in Alton, "but after a realization of what the request would mean to the community, every argument that could be brought against such an upheaval of our life's work was offered, but in vain." When Griffin visited Holy Family Convent in July 1924, just months after becoming bishop, the sisters planned to make a pitch for building a new convent. The Danforth Street facility was crowded and run down. Some of the sisters even slept in the windowless attic. After a top-to-bottom tour by the bishop approval of a new convent seemed imminent, so the sisters were stunned when Griffin proposed not only a new convent, but a coeducational high school as well. Thus, Marquette Catholice High School came into existence.

While construction at Marquette was underway the bishop and the Ursulines at Decatur began to contemplate a new building for St. Teresa Academy. Sister Eugenia, the community's historian, described how plans suddenly changed in 1929:

His [the bishop's] final conclusion was that what Decatur needed was a Catholic coeducational high school, and he was asking that we, the Ursuline nuns, undertake its erection and control, either on

Marquette Caholic High School, Alton.

the academy grounds or on some suitable site. He assured us also that boarding schools would soon be outmoded, and that both boys and girls needed a high school where religion was taught.

Sister Eugenia added, "...the old nuns wept when they heard the proposal," but they decided to comply with wishes of the bishop who promised to assist with fundraising.

Difficult as it was initially to accept, Griffin was right about the future of boarding schools. St. Teresa could probably have continued to function for another twenty-five or thirty years. Although the Ursulines lamented the emphasis on sports in the co-ed school, they were consoled in the knowledge that the new St. Teresa High School was accredited by the North Central Association of Schools and Colleges.

Architect's rendering of the proposed enlargement of St. Teresa Academy, Decatur, c. 1928.

Springfield College in Illinois

Dawson Hall, Springfield Junior College, Springfield

For a third time the bishop persuaded the Ursulines to include young men in their plans. In 1929 the sisters in Springfield announced their intention to open a women's junior college. The new institution would benefit area women as well as Ursuline novices beginning college work. The school offered two courses of study, secretarial or liberal arts. A total of 135 women enrolled for the first semester.

Bishop Griffin encouraged the Ursulines to make Springfield Junior College, today known as Springfield College in Illinois (SCI), a coeducational institution. In its second year the school added courses in business administration and pre-law. During World War II aviation studies rounded out the curriculum. Over the years, thousands of graduates went on to complete bachelor and

Manual Training Department, Notre Dame High School, Quincy, 1940.
Courtesy of the School Sisters of Notre Dame, St. Louis Province.

advanced degrees in education and numerous other fields. Many of today's diocesan priests took their junior college seminary studies at the college.

It may come of something of a surprise that the Springfield Junior College was the first institution of higher education to open in the state capital. (Sangamon State University, now the University of Illinois-Springfield, and Lincoln Land Community College were founded in the 1960s.) From the beginning the new college accepted Catholics and non-Catholics alike. Part of the appeal was that a high school graduate could begin college without leaving the stabilizing influence of home. Pat (Mrs. Jack) Nattermann was one of the hundreds of local girls to do just that. After graduation from Ursuline Academy in 1939 she enrolled at the college. "In those days," she recalled, "you lived at home until you got married."

Students from the aviation program of Springfield College during World War II.
Courtesy of the Springfield College in Illinois, Springfield.

St. James Trade School & Cathedral Boys High School

St. James Trade School, Riverton, sponsored by the Franciscan Brothers of the Holy Cross, 1946.

As Griffin became familiar with the diocese he decided to build two educational facilities for boys in the see city. Cathedral Boys High School would be a prep school, and St. James Trade School would provide training in the manual arts.

The Catholic Charity Bulletin in the fall of 1930 reported that St. James Trade School had just opened near Riverton. The trade school accepted both day and boarding students and was sponsored and staffed by the Franciscan Brothers of the Holy Cross. Brother James Wirth in Niederbreitbach, Germany founded their community in 1862. This trade school was their first mission abroad, but was in keeping with their charism to care for orphans, the sick, and poor.

The curriculum included farming, dairy work, poultry raising and processing, butchering, baking, shoemaking and repairing, carpentry, tailoring, mechanics, and electrical work. The school occupied a 254 acre site so there was plenty of room for the cattle and poultry as well as the various departments. At first, the brothers assigned boys to a department without regard for the interest or ability of the student. The drop-out rate was high. Results improved somewhat when the boy's wishes were taken into account. The baking, butchering, and mechanics programs were the most successful. Many of the graduates in these areas found a trade for a lifetime.

In 1948 St. James Trade School added an academic element to the curriculum. Boys in this program spent one-half of each day studying traditional subjects such as English, mathematics, and history. All students had the opportunity to participate in extra-curricular activities.

The boarding school operation could accommodate thirty. "[It] is intended for boys coming from needy families," stated the Charity Bulletin, "whose parents cannot afford to give them more than an eighth-grade education and who would like to learn a trade in order to be able in later life to earn a suitable livelihood." St. James continued to take boarders until 1964 and the trade school

continued until 1972. At that time the Franciscan Brothers of the Holy Cross began their ministry to developmentally disabled men. The facility was renamed Brother James Court and the buildings modified to meet the needs of the new endeavor.

Even as the Franciscan Brothers were busy preparing to open St. James Trade School, Griffin was developing plans for Cathedral Boys High School. This institution was the apple of his eye. The bishop wanted the descendants of immigrant Catholics to take their rightful place in American society so a prep school was necessary. Cathedral Boys would turn out Catholic gentlemen for the world of business and the professions. Griffin, no doubt, also hoped that some of the students would discover a vocation to the priesthood.

Cathedral Boys High School opened in the fall of 1930 and initially operated from the Cathedral Grade School. The Clerics of St. Viator served as faculty. The following year Cathedral Boys moved to old St. Mary's where both school and church were transformed into classrooms. Students jokingly called it "the cardboard college" because of the makeshift facilities, but enrollment climbed anyway. In 1939 the school moved to its second home, a former public school building on Springfield's north side. It continued in this location until 1959 when the new Griffin High School opened on Springfield's west side.

Cathedral Boys High School (formerly Old St. Mary's School), Springfield, 1931-39.
Courtesy of the Chicago Province, Clerics of St. Viator.

Catholics and the Coal Miners' War

Hardship abounded during the Great Depression, but within our diocese no group suffered more than the miners and their families. In the winter of 1932-1933 violence ripped across the state's mining towns including Taylorville, Kincaid, Tovy, and Pawnee. Drive-by shootings, bombings of public buildings, and acts of sabotage rocked District Twelve of the United Mine Workers of America (UMWA), an area contiguous with the state boundaries. A split within the union precipitated the chaos. In the summer of 1932 miners of bituminous coal rejected a new contract with the Illinois Coal Operators Association (ICOA) and that autumn the Progressive Miners of America (PMA) came into existence. By the time the miners' war died down in 1937, hundreds of men and women had been harassed and intimidated, dozens injured, and at least twenty-one had died.

Father Francis Dominic Lydon lived and ministered in Christian County where some of the worst violence occurred. In the parish annual report for 1933 he shared his thoughts:

> Spiritual side of the parish:-The people come to church and frequent the Sacraments fairly well when one considers their present lamentable condition and ancestral background and training. Material aspect of the parish:-The parish (and the same is true of the whole immediate locality since both are economically dependent on the mining industry) is suffering intensely by reason of the present strike among the miners. (Punctuation as in original.)

More than a year earlier Griffin expressed his apprehension to a friend at the Peabody Coal Company in Chicago. "At the present time," wrote the bishop, "I am much concerned about the mining situation in this part of the State. We have thirty parishes in mining towns that are absolutely dependent upon the mining industry." Griffin suggested using his connections to persuade miners and operators to reach an agreement. He proposed that Governor Louis L. Emerson, a personal friend, invite representatives from both sides to a conference "in order to talk things over and see if a decision could not

Front page of *The Beneld Enterprise*, August 26, 1932.
Courtesy of Pat Obertino, Staunton.

be reached. Possibly a neutral party might get some machinery working in order to secure a satisfactory solution." For better or for worse, nothing came of Griffin's proposal.

One might have expected Griffin to side with the Progressives because their goal of a just wage was consistent with Catholic social teaching, but Griffin believed that the UMWA would be more effective. Futhermore, he thought that the PMA harbored radicals. To the dismay of the Progressives, Griffin endorsed their rival. Regarding the rebel union members Griffin penned these words to the state UMWA President:

> How one could read [your statement in the *Illinois State Register*] and follow the leadership of the irresponsible element now calling themselves progressives is beyond comprehension. The insurgents are making a mess of it.

The UMWA published Griffin's letter in their state bulletin thus making it public. Soon, the PMA's weekly newspaper, *The Progressive Miner*, reprinted the letter along with a response from three Catholic miners. Each pointed to the corruption of the UMWA. One pointedly reminded the bishop that it was the workhorses (that is, the miners and other laborers) that made it possible for the stable horses (men like Griffin) to eat their oats in the comfort of the barn.

A few days after the publication of these letters a bomb exploded on the front porch of the rectory of St. Joseph's, Benld. Father John J. Goff described the scene in the 1933 annual report: "Feb. 15. Bomb exploded presumably by radicals on front porch of rectory. Considerable damage to front of house. After this deed radical element lost much of their following. Conditions much better last half of year."

Escalating violence and the threat of violence harmed the mining parishes. Several of the annual parish reports for 1932 and 1933 indicate that 50 to 75 percent of parishioners, many of them unemployed Progressives, received state aid. Miners who remained loyal to the UMWA were sometimes too intimidated to report for work. Some Catholic families split up over the dispute, but whatever side one chose, the war compromised the ability of miners to support their families and their parishes.

Griffin made no public statement about the bombing and he seems to have broken off correspondence with friends at Peabody Coal. Extremists on both sides offended his sense of fair play. The Progressives managed to establish a stronghold in parts of Macoupin and Madison counties. By 1937 the UMWA had secured contracts at all the large mines and the coal miners war came to an end.

World War II

Catholics, like the vast majority of their fellow citizens, supported the entry of the United States into World War II. Millions of men enlisted in the armed forces, and civilians cooperated in the war effort by working in defense industries and volunteering in the Red Cross as well as other service organizations. They also complied with government restrictions on the consumption of certain foods (meat and sugar, for example), gasoline, rubber, and other materials needed for the war effort.

Catholics could turn to *The Western Catholic* for coverage from a faith perspective. From its pages we learn that Catholic support for the war differed little from that of other Americans. Students at

World War II mileage ration coupon issued to Bishop Griffin.

Which Will You Get?

Cartoon promoting a scrap metal collection, Marquette [High School] Review, January 25, 1943. Courtesy of Marquette Catholic High School, Alton.

every level held scrap metal drives. High schools put on victory dances. In the weekly feature, "Homemakers in Defense," housewives learned to economize and conserve essential materials. "Beans as a Victory Food" exemplifies the recipes offered to compensate for meat rationing. Catholics of all ages raised money to purchase war bonds.

From our diocese 10,286 persons served in the armed forces. Of those, 314 died. Eight diocesan priests served as chaplains. One of them, Lt. Chaplain Thomas Terence Brady, was killed in action in 1943 in the Solomon Islands. He had been assistant pastor at St. Francis Xavier in Jerseyville. Captain Chaplain Casimir Andruskevitch was more fortunate. The former assistant pastor at Our Saviour's, Jacksonville, received the Legion of Merit for the "meritorious performance of duty" in the Pacific.

On the home front parishes displayed the service flag, a special flag bearing a star for each member of the parish serving in the armed forces. Gold Star mothers, whose sons were killed in action, received a letter from the bishop. Children supported the war effort in a number of ways. The Knights of Columbus, for example, sponsored an essay contest on "God and Country." In a particularly poignant story, readers of *The Western Catholic* learned about a first grader from St. Aloysius, Springfield, who was dying of leukemia. Instead of asking for pennies to buy a toy, Dickie Laswell was saving pennies for another reason: "Maybe I'll have enough to buy a bond before long," he told the reporter.

Catholics had their own spiritual approach to dealing with the trials of war. Griffin, in a special pastoral letter in January 1943, called for the enthronement of the Sacred Heart of Jesus in every home "as a practical way to defend the home front." The bishop exhorted Catholics to "keep on praying." And echoing President Roosevelt's "Four Freedoms" speech, Griffin discussed freedom from materialism, from god-

United States Marine Corps photograph of a Mass held on the island of Iwo Jima.

Elise Beger (Hines), indicated by arrow, a U.S. Army nurse, Japan, sang in the choir for Mass while stationed on Tinian Island, Japan. 1945. Courtesy of Elise Hines, Springfield.

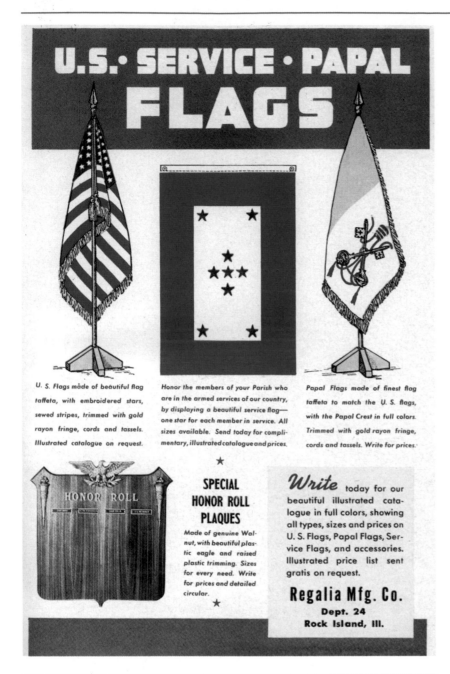

In addition to the U.S. and papal flags many parishes displayed a service flag during the war. Each star represented a member of the parish serving in the armed forces. Advertisement from the Official Catholic Directory, 1943.

lessness, from indifference, and from sin.

Because the Catholic Church is an international body, it was in a unique position to minister to those whose loved ones were prisoners of war, missing in action, or victims of other circumstances. Through the diocesan chancery a spouse or relative could inquire about the status of a loved one. Using Vatican channels, the diocese sought information. Eventually, whatever news could be obtained was sent back to Springfield. Dozens of people were consoled in this manner.

One of the most touching letters sent to Griffin came from the mother of Charles Smith of Lake City, Illinois. Charles had been killed in action, but no details were forwarded to the family. Mrs. John T. Smith, the man's mother, wrote to the bishop pleading for help. "Charles was 20 years of age, a fine model of a young child and a good Catholic child. One you confirmed just 10 years ago." She

hoped to learn more about her son's death. The vice-chancellor, Father Michael O. Driscoll, replied and enclosed a copy of the letter he had sent the Apostolic Delegate. He also informed her of the date when the bishop would offer the Mass she requested for her son. Alas, we do not know the outcome of this particular inquiry.

After the war Catholic servicemen returned to civilian life. In our diocese many attended college on the GI Bill. Others resumed work in coal mines, factories, farms, and their trades. Most shared in the post-war prosperity of the 1950s. Their children crowded into the parochial schools, and in some locales whole new parishes were established to accommodate the growing numbers.

The 1945 graduation class of St. Louis School, Nokomis. Top from left: Bernice Murphy, Eugene Poliak, Father John J. Hogan, Bernadette Poliak, Dolores Caualetto. Bottom from left: Delores Pieper, Gloria Kausic, Veronica Pehapich, Dolores Macalisaky, Mary Kelly. On the homefront Catholic schools continued to operate. The wartime graduates became parents of the baby boomers.
Courtesy of Bernice Murphy Maretti, Nokomis.

The Quonset Hut Churches

Fifteen new parishes were erected during Griffin's episcopate, one-third of them after World War II. As GIs returned from the war many established new households. Couples separated by the war, and those who married afterward, began having children. Lots of children. Families of four to six were common and even larger families were not unusual. These children are the Baby Boomers, the demographic bulge that peaked about 1955 and tapered off in the early 1960s. The building of the five post-war parishes are related to this trend.

Right after the war building materials were at a premium because demand increased throughout the nation. The post war years were a period of "catching up" on the construction of private homes, churches, commercial, and industrial structures. To secure worship and educational space, some churches turned to government surplus. Quonset huts were temporary buildings used during the war to house troops and supplies. After the war the government sold the structures to civilians. In our diocese the new parishes of St. Matthew (Alton, 1946), Little Flower (Springfield, 1948), and St. Frances Cabrini (Springfield, 1949) turned to the Quonset hut to meet their needs. The buyers understood that the buildings had a life expectancy of ten to fifteen years. That would allow enough time to build a school and church. As things turned out, the Quonset huts were more durable than expected. At Little Flower—more than fifty years later—the hut is still used for parish activities including the Sunday morning coffee and donut get-together. Other Baby Boom parishes included St. Ambrose (Godfrey, 1947) and Christ the King (State Park, 1948).

Pre-war parishes kept pace by expanding their schools and remodeling their churches. Fortunately vocations to the teaching orders throughout the 1930s and 1940s enabled schools to secure additional sisters. The Dominicans, School Sisters of Notre Dame, Ursulines, and others in our diocese coped with classrooms of thirty, forty, even fifty and more children at the height of the baby boom.

The death of Bishop James A. Griffin marked a turning point in our diocese. He ushered us into the modern era. After the war he warned of the dangers of communism and exhorted the people to remain firm in the faith. Little could he have imagined that his successor, Bishop William A. O'Connor, would participate in the sweeping changes brought about by the Second Vatican Council.

St. Matthew Church, Alton, late 1940s. With the addition of a special entrance and landscaping the Quonset hut looks more like a church and less like the government surplus it had been.

Reading The Signs of The Times

1949-1975

CHAPTER FIVE

Training a New Generation of Priests
Hilltop and the Diocesan Seminary of the Immaculate Conception

*I*n the early 1950s a new brochure was making the rounds of the diocese. It read, in part:

> Would it be possible to take a good Catholic boy who had finished high school with little or no knowledge of Latin but with a strong desire to be a priest, and in one year's intensive training prepare him sufficiently—intellectually and spiritually—to fit into a seminary program?

Pre-seminarians with Fr. Lawrence H. Wiskirchen (center) at Hilltop, early 1950s.
Mercury Photographers, Springfield.

69

Father Casimir Toliusis (left) and an unidentified student at Hilltop, early 1950s.

Bishop O'Connor answered with an emphatic "Yes." In fact, the brochure was printed at his direction in order to promote the new Latin School located at a farm called Hilltop close to New Berlin. Never had our diocese produced enough homegrown vocations to meet the pastoral needs of the people. O'Connor thought the problem was the lack of fluency in Latin. In those days not only did the priest need sufficient command of the language to offer a valid Mass, but to comprehend theological instruction in Latin. Diocesan boys were at a disadvantage because few of them had the chance to study Latin in high school. So the answer to the lack of priestly vocations was intensive study in the ancient language of the church. The bishop was so confident that he and the people could cultivate more vocations that he resolved to accept only native vocations.

Hilltop opened in September, 1949 and attracted a cross-section of young men from the diocese. Students included public and Catholic high school graduates and World War II veterans as well as men with some work experience. They came from farms, small towns, and big cities. At any given time about eight to ten men resided at Hilltop. Under the instruction of Father Lawrence H. Wischkirchen, rector, and Father Casimir Toliusis, instructor, the students—to borrow a phrase from the booklet—lived in "close companionship as in a family of brothers."

Weekly, students persevered through twelve hours of instruction in Latin. This was the heart of the curriculum. And all conversation at Hilltop was to be in Latin, too. The men also studied biblical Greek, English, and religion. "It was total immersion," remembered Father Frank Westhoff, a Hilltop alumnus. "We had Latin in Latin. We had Greek in Latin. We even had English in Latin," he chuckled. "We spoke Latin at the dinner table and by the end of the year we were sneaking off so we could talk to each other in English."

In O'Connor's plan, Hilltop would function until a suitable facility could be built. In 1956 that dream was realized. The Latin School, built in the Neo-classical style, opened on the shores of Lake Springfield. Latin continued to be part of the curriculum until the seminary closed in 1986. In addition to academic subjects, the seminarians polished their manners. Dining, for example, in the 1950s and 1960s was more formal than today. As a public figure in training, it was important that the future priests know the difference between the salad fork and dinner fork, the soup spoon and the coffee spoon. Not everyone had learned the finer points of etiquette at home. The goal was to help the seminarian to be comfortable in any social setting.

When the seminary first opened most of the candidates had not completed a college education. When deemed sufficiently ready to begin studies, seminarians were sent by O'Connor to a college seminary. By the late 1950s the diocese had worked out an arrangement with Springfield Junior College for the men to obtain an associate's degree. In 1961 the school was renamed the Diocesan Seminary of the Immaculate Conception to reflect the change in status to a minor seminary. As time passed, more and more of the seminarians began their formation with a bachelor's degree in hand, but often needed to take courses in philosophy, theology, and Latin before they entered post-graduate studies in a major seminary. Eventually, all paths led to the major seminary. During O'Connor's tenure many of the candidates for priesthood attended St. John's Seminary, Little Rock, Arkansas. But from the 1950s through today, most of our priests have completed their studies at St. Mary of the Lake, Mundelein, or Kenrick Seminary, St. Louis. A smaller number have been educated at the Pontifical North American College in Rome.

The Diocesan Seminary was the apple of O'Connor's eye, yet his hopes were not completely fulfilled. As early as 1955, the bishop expressed concern over the small number of men who persevered to ordination. The largest class consisted of eleven men in 1964. O'Connor later admitted that he was wrong about limiting candidates to those native to the diocese. After the bishop's retirement the Seminary continued to operate for another eleven years. Declining numbers and changed attitudes towards priestly formation led, in 1986, to the closure of the Diocesan Seminary of the Immaculate Conception. Yet, for most of the men who attended, the seminary served an important function. One alumnus commented that "The people were great. The best thing about the seminary was the camaraderie and the lifetime friendships."

The Latin School, later renamed the Seminary of the Immaculate Conception, Springfield, 1956.

Bishop William A. O'Connor
March 17, 1949 to September 2, 1975

Williiam A. O'Connor has the distinction of being our Vatican II bishop. The beginning of the council, in 1962, neatly divides his episcopate in two halves. The first he devoted to improving Catholic education, the second to implementing the mandates of the Council. Although O'Connor moved too cautiously to suit some, this unflappable man provided a measure of continuity between the two eras. He was a gifted administrator and under his leadership various advisory bodies and new curial offices came into existence.

The fifth bishop was born in Chicago on December 27, 1903. He was one of nine children in the family of John J. and Mary Murphy O'Connor. He attended the school at Our Lady Help of Christians in the Austin neighborhood and upon graduation he enrolled at Quigley Preparatory Seminary. From there he proceeded to the seminary at St. Mary of the Lake. Cardinal George Mundelein ordained O'Connor to the priesthood on September 24, 1927 and then sent the twenty-three year old for additional studies at the College of the Propaganda Fide in Rome.

Upon returning to Chicago in 1930, O'Connor taught Latin at Quigley for five years. Perhaps he showed an interest in charity work, but more likely his superiors sensed his gift for administration because in 1935 the cardinal sent him to study at the New York School of Social Work. About a year later Mundelein appointed O'Connor

Bishop William A. O'Connor seated on the cathedra, the bishop's seat, 1949.
Photograph by Illinois State Journal-Register.

superintendent of the St. Mary's Training School in Des Plaines. Here the reserved Irish-American applied his newly acquired expertise by making the residential facilities more homelike for the 800 girls and boys at the school.

His term at St. Mary's was short. Just two years later O'Connor became the director of the Archdiocesan Catholic Charities. He shepherded this huge department through the closing years of the Depression. By the end of World War II Catholic Charities administered forty-nine agencies with an operating budget exceeding $2 million. O'Connor then turned his attention to new problems emerging in the wake of the war including rising illegitimacy rates, juvenile delinquency, and the needs of the aged. A massive building program began, but O'Connor was not present to witness the fruits of his labors. On December 28, 1948, Pope Pius XII appointed him to be the next bishop of Springfield in Illinois.

Cardinal Samuel Stritch consecrated O'Connor along with two others at Holy Name Cathedral on March 7, 1949. Nine days later our new bishop arrived in Springfield. The installation ceremony took place at the Cathedral of the Immaculate Conception the following day. O'Connor's sermon accented home and parish life. "It is of the family life of the homes of the faithful," he said, "and of the active, vigorous Catholic life of our parishes that we shall preach and for which we shall labor incessantly." A vigorous family and parish life, in turn, would support Catholic institutions including schools, hospitals, homes for the aged, and missionary activity. Later in the day nearly 8,000 people, including Illinois Governor Adlai Stevenson, greeted the bishop at a reception. The ceremonies over, O'Connor dived into the business of leading a diocese.

Comparisons with his predecessor were inevitable. Bishop James A. Griffin had been an outgoing man who loved to mingle with the public. O'Connor, in contrast, was an introvert, and while he handled public duties with competence, he lacked Griffin's enthusiasm. Another difference was that O'Connor never devel-

Bishop O'Connor boarding the train in Springfield for the first leg of the journey to Vatican II, 1962.

oped close friendships with the Illinois political and business leaders. A handful of priest friends traveled from Chicago once a month to play bridge with O'Connor. These men seem to have been his closest friends and confidants.

The new bishop's arrival coincided with the twenty-fifth anniversary of the transfer of the see to Springfield. To celebrate the occasion and to introduce O'Connor to the faithful, the diocese published an untitled commemorative booklet. Because of its metallic green cover it became known simply as *The Green Book*. Through a rectangular cutout one glimpsed O'Connor in violet episcopal attire and a white ermine cape. Each parish and mission were pictured along with its pastor. Photographs of the hospitals and other institutions were included. Thousands of copies were distributed and the booklet did much to raise awareness about life beyond parish boundaries.

O'Connor made Catholic education a priority. He was particularly interested in preparing the next generation of priests. To this end in 1949 he opened the Latin School on land near New Berlin donated for that purpose. The location, however, was temporay until a proper school could be built. In 1956 he dedicated the Latin School located on Lake Springfield.

At the parish level the religious education of children not attending the parochial school was an on-going challenge. In 1950 O'Connor established the Confraternity of Christine Doctrine (CCD) in our diocese, but still the children in rural areas were underserved. To meet their needs the four Rural Confraternity Centers came into existence during O'Connor's tenure.

O'Connor attended all four sessions of the Second Vatican Council. He arrived on October 3, 1962 and soon wrote in his diary, "Rome feels like home again." O'Connor served as one of the five co-presidents of the "American Bishops Council." In this capacity he helped to coordinate and promote the study of subjects pertinent to the council. His brother bishops held O'Connor in esteem and respected his mastery of Latin and administrative skill. O'Connor kept a Vatican II diary. He called it "A Private and A Personal View of a Council Father" although he rarely mentioned his personal opinions or feelings. The diary was instead a meticulous summation of each day's proceedings.

After Vatican II O'Connor began to execute the mandates of the council. The bishop expected compliance with duly authorized changes even though he personally lacked enthusiasm for some of them. He established the diocesan Office for Worship and the Office for Catholic Education in 1969. They were the first of many curial agencies that opened to assist parishes and other Catholic institutions to implement the changes resulting from the council.

O'Connor also authorized the organization of three diocesan advisory bodies—the Priests' Senate, the Diocesan Pastoral Council, and the Sisters' Senate. According to Dominican Sister Mary Harris, who was active in the Sisters' Senate, O'Connor used these bodies to listen to the concerns of the people. In the early years, the Priests' Senate was structured in a way that

Pope John XXIII and Bishop O'Connor at the Vatican, 1962.

tended to favor the concerns of older priests. In fact, tensions between older and younger priests in our diocese ran high after Vatican II.

In the late 1960s O'Connor assumed a more public role representing the Catholic Church to non-Catholics. Some years earlier, for example, the bishop had declined an invitation to diocesan clergy to participate in an Institute on Judaism held at Temple B'rith Sholom in Springfield. "The Bishop feels," explained the reply, "that the attendance of our Clergy at the Institute in your Temple would arouse widespread comment and perhaps lead to considerable misunderstanding." After Vatican II, O'Connor was more willing to be part of interdenominational and inter-religious events.

In 1975, at the age of seventy-one, O'Connor retired. "The diocese should not have to slow down because of my advancing age," he told *The Western Catholic*. O'Connor moved to a house near the cathedral and became more reclusive than ever, in part, because of declining health. Bouts of shingles and a heart condition made an active retirement impossible. Official duties concluded, O'Connor stopped keeping a daybook. The last entry, dated September 2, 1975, reads," Decided not to continue recording daily events. Nothing of special interest or importance is expected to happen worth recording."

Ironically, the retired bishop outlived his successor, Bishop Joseph A. McNicholas, who died unexpectedly on April 17, 1983. At the wake a forlorn O'Connor kept vigil at the casket in the cathedral.

MOTTO: GOD IS OUR SUPPORT

Bishop O'Connor's coat-of arms. The star above the mountains represents his patron, St. William. The oak tree was taken from the O'Connor family coat-of-arms.

Perhaps he was wondering why his successor had been cut down in the prime of life. O'Connor died just seven months later, on November 14, 1983, a few days after a severe heart attack. He was the third bishop to be interred in the Cathedral. *The State Journal-Register* eulogized him:

"Some will remember his warm smile, others his stately manner, and still others his diligent efforts on behalf of his flock, but in whatever way Roman Catholics of the Diocese of Springfield in Illinois recall Bishop William A. O'Connor, one thing is certain: it will be with a sense of loss at the passing of a saintly and dedicated man."

Quincy College first admitted women in 1949. From left: Richard Webb, Myron Pilatz, Gene Cramer (partially hidden) Stevene O'Connell, Don Stockman. Gryfalcon (yearbook), 1949-50. Courtesy of Brenner Library, Quincy University, Quincy.

St. Anthony's Hospital, Effingham, Destroyed by Fire

One of the most tragic events in the history of the diocese occurred on April 4, 1949. A devastating fire at St. Anthony's Hospital claimed seventy-five lives. Just two weeks earlier the institution had passed an insurance review and was found to be in compliance with all safety codes. Fire is always an unexpected threat, so when Sister Edmunda Hiersig, a Hospital Sister of St. Francis, smelled smoke about 11:30 p.m. she immediately reported a fire. The state Fire Marshall later determined that the conflagration began in some insulation and that fresh paint and varnish had contributed to the blaze.

Although the Effingham Volunteer Fire Department arrived quickly, the fire had already spread. Franciscan and the lay nurses rushed to the aid of terrified patients. The women were able to evacuate some, but other patients had no recourse but to call for help from the windows of their rooms. People living near the hospital helped nurses drag mattresses to the ground beneath the windows, but a number of patients, overcome by panic, jumped to their deaths before help arrived.

Civilians handled the fire hoses so the firefighters could concentrate on rescue operations and thus bring a few more individuals to safety. Two lay nurses, Mrs. Hilary Clements and Miss Fern Riley, managed to rescue a number of people before they were trapped in the inferno. Finally, about 5:00 a.m. firefighters extinguished the last flame.

In the days that followed the sounds of requiem Masses and memorial services echoed throughout Effingham and the surrounding towns. Among the dead were two Franciscan sisters, Bertina Himricher and Eustachia Glatki. The bodies were charred beyond recognition. "It is beautifully significant," the Hospital Sisters' historian poignantly recorded, "that when the Sisters' bodies were found, they could be identified in a special way. Sister Eustachia's rosary beads remained partly intact, as did a small portion of Sister Bertina's scapular. The blessed Mother of God had seemingly showed her favor to the two Sisters."

Because the fire destroyed patient records, the Hospital Sisters cancelled all outstanding debts. At least one individual, however, passed up the opportunity to save some money. His wife had died in the disaster, but he desired to help. "I want to pay my bill," he stated. "I know how much it is. The sisters need the money. It would be too bad if I couldn't do this little bit for them." Thanks to that kind of generosity of spirit the Franciscans were able to move forward in erecting a new hospital. Door-to-door canvassing yielded over $100,000 in Effingham alone. From far and wide donations flowed in and the new hospital opened in 1954.

A National Guard soldier stood watch over the ruins of St. Anthony's Hospital, Effingham.
Courtesy of the Hospital Sisters of the Third Order of St. Francis, Springfield

Two Hospital Sisters examine the rubble.
Courtesy of the Hospital Sisters of the Third Order of St. Francis, Springfield.

John B. Franz,

Bishop of Dodge City, 1951-59
Bishop of Peoria, 1959-71

John B. Franz was the first diocesan priest since John Janssen to become a bishop. Franz was born in Springfield in 1896 to Louisa Reisch Franz and Fridolin Franz. He studied for the priesthood and in 1920, Cardinal John Glennon ordained him. For several years Franz was a member of the Springfield Mission Band, a group of priests who traveled throughout the diocese preaching missions. He also acquired pastoral experience including a term as rector of the cathedral. Following the death of Bishop James A. Griffin in 1948, Franz served as the administrator of the diocese for several months. In 1951 the Pope Pius XII appointed Franz as the first bishop of Dodge City, Kansas. The episcopal consecration took place in Springfield on August 29 of that year. Eight years later, Franz was transferred to the Diocese of Peoria where he was installed on August 8, 1959. Franz guided the diocese through Vatican II and retired in 1971. He died at the age of ninety-five in 1992

Bishop John B. Franz of Dodge City (1951-59) and of Peoria (1959-1971).
Courtesy of the Diocese of Dodge City.

The Confraternity of Christian Doctrine

Since the Second Plenary Council of Baltimore in 1866, American bishops endorsed the parochial school as the place for the religious instruction of children. Yet, throughout the history of the church in America only about one-third of Catholic children have attended a Catholic elementary school. Many parishes, especially in rural areas, could not afford to operate a school. Pastors and lay catechists assumed responsibility for the religious instruction of children. The quality of instruction varied and generally did not measure up to the standards set by the teaching sisters. Many adults, too, needed ongoing instruction.

In our diocese, to address the needs of youth and adults, Bishop O'Connor in 1950 introduced the Confraternity of Christian Doctrine, better known as the CCD. That first year some 13,319 Catholics enrolled. Before Vatican II instruction emphasized doctrine, ritual, and traditional devotion. First graders in the late 1950s, for example, learned to make the sign of the cross, say the *Lord's Prayer, Hail Mary,* and other common prayers. Older children memorized more difficult prayers. The *Memorare, Prayer to the Holy Ghost,* and others were tasks for the eighth graders.

Religious education for rural children got a boost in 1953 when the first Rural Confraternity Center opened in

Decree establishing the Confraternity of Christian Doctrine at St. Mark, Venice, 1950.

LIFE AFTER DEATH

15¢

Matthew J. O'Connell, S.J.

DOCTRINAL PAMPHLET SERIES

DISCUSSION QUESTIONS

for Adult Confraternity Groups on Human Life in Our Day

Diocese of
Springfield in Illinois
1969—70

Adult Discussion Club booklets

Arcola with two sisters. Eventually three other centers opened: Carlinville (1955), Hillsboro (1957), and Beardstown (1959, transferred to Springfield in 1969). Students did not come to the centers. The catechists—all of them Springfield Dominicans—traveled to the pupils. From Arcola, for example, two sisters traveled by car each week to five other parishes. Hundreds of children thus received instruction that otherwise would have been difficult to obtain.

Funding for the sisters' residences came, in part, from the 1952 Diocesan Development Fund campaign. The largest center housed five sisters. The diocese also provided the automobile and its upkeep. Each parish paid a per-capita fee for participating children. This covered the sisters' salary and instructional materials. "The people were good to us and we were good to the people," said one of the Dominicans involved in CCD work. "At the beginning of the year most of the parishes held a food

shower for us. The people gave us canned goods and other non-perishable foods. That really helped cut down the grocery bills." After Vatican II the number of sisters available for rural CCD work gradually declined. By the mid-1970s the emphasis shifted to adult catechesis so that a number of lay adults at each parish would be qualified to teach religion to the children.

Dominican Sisters Yvonne McNamara (left) and Mary Edna Walsh, Rural Catechetical Center, Carlinville, 1956.

77

Vatican II

Pope John XXIII took the world by surprise when in 1959 he announced that he would convene an ecumenical council. Soon the word "aggiornamento" entered our vocabulary. The Italian word means "updating." It was time, said the Holy Father, to reassess the relationship of the church to the modern world. Since the last council, held in 1870, numerous social and economic changes had occurred. Not only did the church have some catching up to do, but the pope realized that a better understanding of the present would strengthen efforts to evangelize.

It is important to remember that the council and its immediate aftermath coincided with momentous changes in American life. For one thing, Catholics had attained social equality with Protestants. Nothing better symbolized the acceptance into the mainstream than the 1960 election of John F. Kennedy to the U. S. presidency. Catholics and non-Catholics alike shared the optimism of Kennedy's "New Frontier," but the assassination of the president three years later disillusioned many. About the same time the Civil Rights movement divided the nation. By 1967 a growing body of young and liberal activists began to question the United States' role in Vietnam. And the sexual revolution

Catholics shared the grief of the nation.
Courtesy of Winifred White Howard, Alton.

Participants of Vatican II gather in St. Peter's, 1962.

was underway as well. The convergence of secular and religious change raised anxieties as well as hopes.

The council, of course, functioned independently of any nation or state. The participants of Vatican II understood that their decisions would affect the universal church. By the end of the council they had promulgated sixteen documents touching every aspect of Catholic life. The constitutions and decrees provided a blueprint for renewal and they continue to inspire and guide us. One of these statements, the Dogmatic Constitution on the Church, resulted in a profound shift of the understanding of personal sanctity.

The Dogmatic Constitution proclaimed a universal call to holiness. Every member of the Body of Christ—male or female, lay or ordained—by virtue of baptism is called to holiness of life. Previously, Catholics tended to think of degrees of holiness determined by one's state of life. The most holy were the ordained. Next in rank came the cloistered monks and nuns. Members of the apostolic institutes fell a bit lower. The laity occupied the lowest rung because it was believed that family life and work impeded spiritual development. The idea of a universal call to holiness gave a new vision and enthusiasm to the spiritual life.

Interaction with non-Catholics was another area of dramatic change started by Vatican II. The Decree on Ecumenism held out the hope of unity among all Christians. The church spoke respectfully about other religions, including Judaism. While reaffirming that through the Catholic Church alone the fullness of the means of salvation is present, the church acknowledged the goodness of other traditions.

Vatican II also challenged Catholics to internalize the faith more deeply. Customs and regulations that made sense in their own historical context—the first Fridays, for example—no longer held meaning for many twentieth century Catholics. Praying the rosary, litanies, and novenas were a source of edification to many, but not to everyone. After Vatican II, Catholics were free to explore different ways of prayer and devotion. Some turned to the Catholic Charismatic Renewal, Cursillo, and other movements to meet their spiritual needs.

Large numbers of lay Catholics discovered the beauty of Holy scripture for the first time. One of the myths about Catholics was that we were not allowed to read the bible. This was never true, but with Vatican II the church encouraged the faithful to delve into scripture. The release of the *New American Bible*, a modern English translation, made scripture more accessible. Parish bulletins began to include a list of the daily readings. Individual and group study helped Catholics move toward the interior renewal endorsed by the council.

The most dramatic change for many Catholics was the introduction of the vernacular into the liturgy of the Mass and the other rites. In the United States on the first Sunday of Advent 1964, English replaced Latin for the parts spoken or chanted by the people. Just as startling to many, the priest now faced the people from a freestanding altar. With the introduction of the New Order for Mass (*Novus Ordo*) in 1969 the entire Mass was in English.

St. Teresa High School, Decatur, mid-1960s.
Mass in the round became popular after Vatican II.
Courtesy of the Ursuline Sisters, Central Province, U.S.A.

Liturgical Reforms

Liturgical renewal became the subject of contentious debate even before the release of the Constitution on the Sacred Liturgy. The Catholic press covered the upcoming changes. Still, even for those who welcomed the vernacular, it was a shock to the system when Catholics in America for the first time heard the Mass in English. Use of the vernacular did much to foster the "full, active, and conscious participation" extolled in the council documents, but in retrospect, leaders in our diocese—and throughout the nation—regret that we did not accompany the reforms with more appropriate catechetical instruction. Even the clergy were ill prepared. A significant minority of priests and laity lamented the replacement of Latin, the priest facing the people, and other changes. Some thought the new liturgy was "too Protestant" and that the changes diminished the sense of reverence. No doubt a few also resented the exhortation to active participation because they were expected to give up personal rituals.

In 1969 the Diocesan Commission on the Liturgy conducted a survey on liturgical practices in the Springfield Deanery. This deanery includes city and county parishes and a variety of ethnic Catholics, so the results were probably typical of what was happening throughout the diocese. The goal of the survey was to determine the extent of compliance with the mandates as well as the use of practices currently unauthorized, but expected to be approved in the near future. All but four of the thirty-six parishes, convents, and high schools responded.

Several questions concerned congregational singing. Almost 75 percent included hymn singing for Sunday and weekday liturgies. Far fewer, however, regularly sang the Mass parts even on Sunday. Folk music enjoyed popularity in some parts of the nation, but not in the Springfield Deanery. As one priest put it, "NO! We have no 'folks.'" The proper location of music leaders and instrumentalists was another

Lectors from Ss. Simon & Jude, Gillespie, 1979. The appearance of lay liturgical ministers became more and more common by 1980. At first only men were allowed to fill these roles. Gradually the numbers of women increased.

unsettled matter, especially if the musicians were female.

Women, in fact, were at the time officially banned from the sanctuary. About three-quarters of the parishes responded that laity of either sex were not permitted to enter the sanctuary. A few allowed male musicians to lead singing from that location. Only one parish allowed women to do so and the pastor pledged that "the practice will be discontinued." A couple of Viatorian Fathers expressed the opinion that women should be allowed in the sanctuary. Stated one, "I would not hesitate to have girls or women singers or instrumentalists in the sanctuary. In fact, I would see no reason why we couldn't use girl Mass servers. Why must it be an all male sanctuary?"

Only three locations had women lectors and all three were convents or girls academies. At that time the American bishops were studying the implications of having women proclaim the readings. Eventually church authorities decided that women could fulfill this liturgical ministry. The whole notion of lay lectors upset some. The pastor at St. Patrick's, Springfield, gave this testy response: "I think people come to church to hear the priest speak and not to hear a layman. Reading is not one of the best things the average layman can do."

Reception of Holy Communion was another area of varied practice. In twelve churches the people stood to receive. They knelt in fifteen others

Silver Jubilee Mass of Father James Hughes, 1970. By this time the communion rail had disappeared and the people receive Holy Communion while processing. Older women still cover their heads, but the girls are bare headed and wear pants.

and in the remaining five, the people had their choice of standing or kneeling. Only one priest offered communion under both species on a regular basis. When two or more priests concelebrated it was more likely that both species were offered to the laity. The stumbling block to reception under both species seemed to be the use of lay persons as extraordinary ministers of Holy Communion. Liturgical experts and bishops debated the distinctive roles of priests, laywomen, and laymen and eventually decided that laity of either sex could serve as Eucharistic ministers if a sufficient number of priests are not available.

The response of Catholics to changes in the liturgy mirrored the reactions of Catholics across the nation. By and large, they enthusiastically welcomed the use of the vernacular, were open to the greater use of lay ministers, gave up many traditional devotions, and made confession less often. There were exceptions, of course. With the passage of time and more catechesis, most resisters came to accept the reforms, but a significant minority continued to feel a sense of loss and that their concerns have not been heard. Some speculate that the decline in Mass attendance after Vatican II was related to changes in the liturgy, but that would be a simplistic explanation. A combination of social changes in American society—including those in family life—as well as changes in the church, led to different behaviors than in the past.

Catholic Family Life

Many think of the 1950s and early 1960s as a golden era for American families, but the haze of nostalgia can be deceiving. Memories of *Leave it to Beaver* and *Father Knows Best* obscure Cold War anxieties. On the domestic scene the Supreme Court's 1954 ruling to desegregate schools and the Montgomery, Alabama, bus boycott in 1955 set in motion the modern Civil Rights movement. Even though these tensions ran beneath the surface of America life, most went about their day-to-day activities with a certain optimism.

Catholic baby-boomers were usually two or three generations removed from their immigrant roots. This fact, combined with the prosperity of the era, meant that Catholics finally joined the American mainstream. After World War II Catholics rapidly closed the gap in

The family of Mr. and Mrs. Harry Murphy, Nokomis, 1960s. Despite social change, family remained at the heart of Catholic life. Courtesy of Julio Maretti, Nokomis,
Photograph by C. F. Marley, Nokomis.

81

income and education between themselves and Protestant Americans.

The marriage rate increased and couples tended to marry at a younger age. Until the mid-1960s the average age of first marriage for men was twenty-two. For women it was twenty. A diocesan priest who served in Decatur remembered that many of the brides were only seventeen to nineteen years old. In fact, half of all American brides were still in their teens. Earlier marriage resulted in larger families. Nationally, three or four children became the norm. Catholic families tended to be somewhat larger. After twenty to twenty-five years of marriage it was not unusual for a Catholic woman to have borne five or six children, although a mere 5 percent of all American mothers bore ten or more. How Catholic family life differed from that of Protestants is the subject of study, but this much seems clear: before Vatican II many couples did observe Church teaching about birth control.

By 1968, when Pope Paul VI issued the encyclical *Humanae Vitae*, much had changed. Research by the Gallop Poll and the University of Chicago indicated that increasing numbers of Catholics were using artificial contraceptive methods including the Pill. Many theologians and lay persons consulted by the pope, advised the approval of "the Pill" and certain other forms of contraception. Anticipating a change in church teaching, some priests began to advise married and engaged couples that the Pill was acceptable. So, it was something of a surprise to many Catholics in the United States when the pope upheld the artificial birth control ban. Some church leaders believe that *Humanae Vitae* undermined the moral authority of the pope because many Catholic couples felt that church teaching did not relate to the challenges of married life. However, the influence of secular society in general should not be overlooked as a contributing factor to dissension in the church. The sexual revolution, the women's movement, the Watergate crisis, and other events influenced American Catholic attitudes towards authority. During the 1970s the controversy over *Humanae Vitae* contributed to the divide between so-called conservative and liberal Catholics, a gap that continues into the present.

Wedding of an unidentified couple, St. Charles, Charleston, early 1970s.

Polio patient in an iron lung, Saint Anthony's Hospital, Alton, 1950s. The iron lung was a kind of respirator for victims of poliomyelitis who were not able to breath unaided. Thanks to an effective vaccine introduced in 1954 the number of cases dropped dramatically. Courtesy of the Sisters of St. Francis of the Martyr St. George, Alton.

Ministry with the Deaf Community

The subject of ministry with the deaf community is worthy of a study unto itself. Because the Illinois School for the Deaf, which opened in 1846, is located in Jacksonville, Our Saviour's Church has developed a strong ministry with deaf Catholics. Historically, the hearing have viewed the deaf as passive child-like objects who merited pity and charity. Gradually, attitudes changed among both the deaf and the hearing. We now speak of ministry with, rather than to, the deaf. Locally, the ground work for this change was laid by deaf Catholics and the hearing parishioners of Our Saviour's, who over the decades learned sign language and served as catechists, drivers, babysitters, and chaperones for various activities.

During the latter half of Bishop O'Connor's episcopate a number of initiatives began to improve ministry with the deaf. In 1964, O'Connor appointed Father Terence Tracey to coordinate the pastoral care of this community, a position he occupied until 1978. Tracey, who had served at Our Saviour's in the 1950s, had learned sign language and acquainted himself with the deaf culture. He was, by the way, just one of several priests whose time in Jacksonville called forth a gift for working with the deaf.

Tracy, along with Dominican Sisters Patricia (John) Francis and Alverna Hollis, and Redemptorist Father David Walsh, organized in 1974 the first Community Week with the Deaf Community. This was a family experience held at Camp Star of the Sea adjacent to the Diocesan Seminary on Lake Springfield. With the support of the Knights of Columbus and private donations, the organizers were able to offer religious education and recreational activities in a retreat setting for families with deaf members.

Ministry with the deaf continues to be an important part of parish life at Our Saviour's, but other locations in the diocese also serve the deaf community. By 2000, signed Masses were regularly offered in Effingham, Springfield, Quincy, Decatur, and Granite City.

Renewal of Religious Life in the Diocese

A look at the O'Connor years would not be complete without a few words on developments in religious life. The path of renewal varied for each institute, but all of them turned to the Vatican II "Decree on the Appropriate Renewal of Religious Life" which stated that revitalization "comprises both a constant return to the sources to the whole of the Christian life and to the primitive inspiration of the institutes, and their adaptation to the changed conditions of our time."

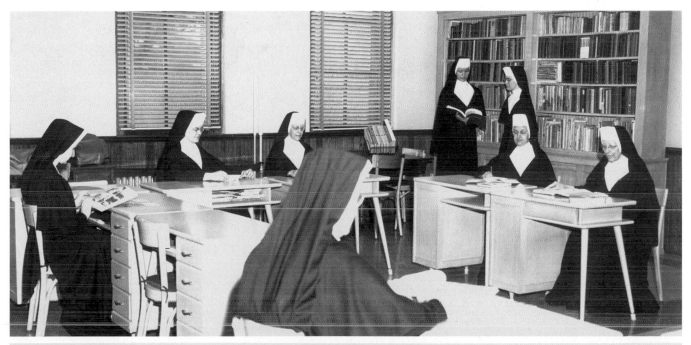

School Sisters of Notre Dame grading papers, c. 1960. Before Vatican II convent life was highly structured. Sisters gathered in common for prayers, Mass, meals, work, and recreation. Courtesy of the School Sisters of Notre Dame, St. Louis Province.

In response to this statement and the other directives in the conciliar decree, men and women religious engaged in more theological and scripture study in order to understand better the implications of Vatican II. They prayerfully scrutinized every aspect of their communal life. In their general chapters, the governing body for most communities, members set the direction for renewal and made decisions about their lives together. Prayer in common, for example, was now in English, a change that almost everyone welcomed. External changes, of course, were the most visible to the laity and diocesan priests, but exterior changes—such as habits—tell only part of the story.

Another aspect of renewal was the study of the "primitive inspiration of the institutes." Franciscan women and men, for example, re-examined the life of St. Francis. Ursulines turned their attention to St. Angela Merici, the Dominicans to St. Dominic, and so forth. The purpose was to grasp anew the charism of the founder or founderess and consider how the gifts the Holy Spirit lavished on their order could be applied in the present time. The handing on of the charism is one of the most important challenges facing religious communities today. The Ursulines, for instance, treasure their motto, *Serviam* (Latin for Service) which springs from the earliest days of the order. Since their origins in the diocese more than 150 years ago, these sisters cultivated in their pupils a spirit of service to church and society.

An Ursuline Sister at the ceremony transferring the sponsorship of Marquette Catholic High School, Alton, to the diocese of Springfield, 1993.
Courtesy of the Ursuline Sisters, Central Province, U.S.A.

In the years since Vatican II, the sisters have worked to continue this tradition and to deepen the understanding of *Serviam* in the lay administrators and teachers who have gradually replaced the sisters at Ursuline Academy (Springfield), St. Teresa's High School (Decatur), Marquette Catholic High School (Alton) and the other schools once staffed entirely by Ursulines.

Continuity of charism can also be seen in the changes made by the Franciscan Brothers of the Holy Cross who operated St. James Trade School, Springfield, from 1930 until 1972. Training young Catholic men for blue-collar occupations was no longer a critical need. But the vision of Brother James Wirth, the founder, to serve the sick and the poor is timeless. In Germany the community had already begun their ministry to developmentally disabled men and it became clear that a similar facility in the United States would also serve a genuine need. The trade school was renamed Brother James Court and the buildings modified to meet the needs of the new endeavor.

Since 1965 the number of women religious in our diocese, as throughout the United States, has declined substantially. According to the *Official Catholic Directory* in 1966 there were approximately 1,236 sisters whose motherhouses are in this diocese. By 1985 the number had declined to 926. In 2000 the figure was 700. For men, the figures were 216 in 1966, 123 in 1985, and 84 in 2000. Among the women, many of them served in other dioceses, but the numbers reflect the trend just the same. The causes for the decrease are threefold: the withdrawal of women and men from religious life, smaller numbers of both sexes who entered religious life after Vatican II, and the death of aging members. Neither church leaders, nor the scholars who study the trends, can agree on why the decline was so drastic. Some believe that for women the combination of secularization and increased career opportunities made religious life less appealing as a voca-

Sr. Mary Ursula Diebold, O.S.U. Queen of Peace Infirmary, Alton, one of the dozens of retired sisers living in the diocese.
Courtesy of the Ursuline Sisters, Central Province, U.S.A.

tion. Others think that the institutes that adopted a more secular lifestyle—living alone or wearing secular attire, for example—fail to appeal to women who want to dedicate themselves to God. These women, it is claimed, wish to embrace a visibly counter-cultural lifestyle for the sake of the Kingdom. For both men and women, observers speculate, the materialism of American life makes a religious vocation unattractive.

Declining numbers, however, do not diminish the contributions of the sisters who continue to minister in the Diocese of Springfield in Illinois. Quite a few sisters serve in the traditional areas of education and health care. Others work as parish life coordinators, pastoral associates, parish visitors, hospital chaplains, social workers, psychotherapists, liturgists, catechists, and in other capacities. Men religious minister as pastors, professors, health care workers, and diocesan administrators. As necessary as these ministries are, an even more

important contribution of our religious is their ministry of prayer and presence.

The motherhouses and residences of retired religious are powerhouses of prayer. Many of the elderly suffer the infirmities of aging, yet their lives continue to offer witness to the dignity of human life and the mercy of God. In the ministry of presence, some religious voluntarily live and work in the poorest and most dangerous neighborhoods of the diocese. They reach out to the people others reject. By virtue of baptism and profession of the evangelical counsels of obedience, poverty, and chastity, the religious of the Diocese of Springfield in Illinois continue to be signs of the Kingdom.

Although the total number of religious in the diocese has diminished, some religious communities have begun a new presence here. Several retired members of the Franciscan men of the Sacred Heart Province live in Sherman and Riverton. The Oblates of the Virgin Mary, priests and brothers, arrived in the diocese in the early 1980s, and continue to serve in several apostolates in the Alton area. The novitiate for the Oblates of Mary Immaculate in Godfroy now serves the entire United States province. In recent years the Daughters of Divine Love from Nigeria and the Missionary Sisters of the Sacred Heart "Ad Gentes" from Mexico have come to the diocese. Futhermore, as this book goes to press, Bishop George Lucas welcomed the Sisters of the Good Shepherd to St. Katherine Drexel Parish in Springfield—the first contemplative group in the history of our diocese.

85

For the Common Good

1975-1983

Let Justice descend,
O heavens, like dew from
above, like gentle rain let the
skies drop it down
Isaiah 45: 8

A Voice for Justice

During the tenure of Bishop Joseph A. McNicholas both church and society underwent many changes. The oil embargo of 1973 adversely affected the American economy and put people in a pessimistic mood about the future. The protest movement against the war in Vietnam gained momentum and civil strife and unrest continued into the 1970s. The Watergate affair led in 1973 to President Richard M. Nixon's resignation. In the church, responding in the spirit of Vatican II, there was a greater emphasis on advocacy for a just social order. McNicholas was one of the strongest voices to speak up for people on the margins of society. He spoke forcefully and consistently on behalf of the unborn, the poor, and African-Americans. One could chronicle dozens of diocesan efforts, but three will suffice: school desegregation, pro-life advocacy, and housing for the elderly.

CHAPTER SIX

Taking a Stand on School Desegregation

Race relations continued to be a source of tension through the 1970s. The civil rights legislation and social programs of the Great Society enabled many blacks to ease into the middle class, but segregation persisted in housing and, thus, in the public schools. Within our diocese school desegregation battles erupted in Alton, Decatur, and Springfield. Each city had a sizeable African-American minority that included a few Catholic families. "White flight," the movement of white families to all-white suburbs and school districts, occurred in the wake of court ordered integration. In 1974, for example, the Springfield *State Journal-Register* reported that hundreds of families were relocating to Chatham and Riverton. Other white families wishing to avoid integration turned to private schools, including Catholic institutions. Some of the parochial schools were already filled to capacity, but others accepted the influx of both Catholic and Protestant children.

Bishop McNicholas, a long-time advocate of civil rights and desegregation, felt strongly that the Catholic schools should not become havens for those avoiding desegregation. To prevent the co-opting of the schools McNicholas issued a Notice of Nondiscriminatory Policy. The statement read:

> Schools of the Roman Catholic Diocese of Springfield-in-Illinois admit students of any race, color, national or ethnic origin to all rights, privileges, programs and activities generally accorded or made available to students at their schools. They do not discriminate on the basis of race, color, national and ethnic origin in administration of their educational policies, admissions policies, scholarship and loan programs, and athletic and other school administered programs.

The bishop expected the principals to sign the statement prior to its publication in the December 19, 1976, issue of *The Western Catholic*. He also cautioned Catholic schools against accepting transfers—Catholic or otherwise—from the public schools. African-American Catholics, as well as many others, applauded McNicholas' stand. From other quarters, however, even within the Catholic community, he suffered biting criticism, but the outspoken bishop took it in stride.

Bishop Joseph A. McNicholas

September 3, 1975 to April 17, 1983

People remember Bishop Joseph A. McNicholas as a man of tremendous energy and drive. He served less than nine years—the shortest tenure of any of our bishops—yet he accomplished a great deal before his untimely death. We best remember McNicholas for the social justice initiatives and pro-life activities of his episcopate. His compassion for the poor and disenfranchised sprang from his own experience as a child of the Depression as well as from the Gospel values instilled by his parents.

Our sixth bishop was born in St. Louis on January 13, 1923 to Joseph McNicholas and Mary Blanche Tallon McNicholas. A few years later a sister, named after her mother, joined the family. The two children developed a deep and abiding friendship. While they were still little, the family relocated to Mt. Carmel, Illinois, a small town at the confluence of the Wabash and White Rivers. The children attended St. Mary's school and at an early age Joseph expressed the desire to become a priest.

He and his sister played Mass in the family living room. He was the priest and she the server. "He always said," recalled sister Mary Blanche (Mrs. Edward Blittschau) "[that]

Joseph A. McNicholas,
first communion picture, 1930.

Courtesy of Edward F. and Mary Blanche Blittschau, St. Louis.

his religious vocation started in our home where our parents set a marvelous example." God came first and every major decision was made in the light of faith. As a family the McNicholas household

Joseph A. McNicholas on his ordination day. Mary Blanche Tallon McNicholas,
his mother, is on the left and his sister Mary Blanche is to the right, 1949.

Courtesy of Edwin F. & Mary Blanche Blittschau, St. Louis.

daily offered the rosary and night prayer. The parish church was just one block away and McNicholas often served at the altar. A maternal uncle, Monsignor Patrick W. Tallon, was a priest in St. Louis, so the future bishop found role models in the family as well as at the local parish.

Life changed dramatically with the death of McNicholas' father in 1939. Although the family had been spared the severe destitution faced by many Americans during the Great Depression, loss of the breadwinner called for additional belt-tightening. Mrs. McNicholas and

Bishop McNicholas shortly after the move to Springfield.

the two children moved back to St. Louis to be near the Tallon family. By counting pennies and living frugally McNicholas was able to attend McBride High School, one of the city's Catholic institutions for boys. He graduated in 1941. Typically, the family of a pre-seminarian paid for his educational expenses, so Mary Blanche contributed her earnings to help keep her brother in school. He completed his theological studies at Kenrick Seminary and in later years often said that without his sister's help he could not have become a priest.

Cardinal Joseph Ritter ordained McNicholas to the priesthood for the Archdiocese of St. Louis on June 7, 1949. After ordination McNicholas accumulated considerable pastoral experience. During his first assignment, at the New Cathedral, he started work toward a masters of social work at St. Louis University. Before completing the degree, McNicholas began what turned into a 14-year term as secretary of Catholic Charities for the Archdiocese of St. Louis. He also served as chaplain at the St. Joseph's Home for Boys and took up residence there from 1956 to 1970. He also served on the boards of a number of state and local welfare organizations.

In 1969, at the age of forty-six, McNicholas was ordained an auxiliary bishop of St. Louis by Cardinal John Carberry. Gradually, McNicholas let go of other commitments, but never lost the zeal for social welfare work. From 1969 until his installation as bishop of Springfield in Illinois,

In 1976 the Sons of Erin, Springfield, named Bishop McNicholas (third from left) the "Irishman of the Year." The Blittschau Family stands to the bishop's left: Benjamin Joseph (nephew), Mary Blanche (sister), Mary Genivieve (neice), Edwin F. (brother-in-law).
Courtesy of Edwin F. and Mary Blanche Blittschau, and photographer Bob Arteaga, St. Louis.

A postcard made to commemorate the sudden death of Bishop McNicholas, 1983.

McNicholas served as pastor of the Old Cathedral near the St. Louis Arch. He scheduled Masses so those attending sporting events at nearby Busch Stadium would be able to attend. He also worked with various congregations of women religious to open perpetual adoration chapels at their convents, an idea he later implemented in our diocese.

When Bishop O'Connor retired in 1975, Pope Paul VI appointed McNicholas to be the next bishop. On September 3, in sweltering heat, McNicholas was installed. His motto was "I come to serve." It did not take long for his flock to realize that a new era had begun. McNicholas was more like Bishop James A. Griffin in that he relished public speaking. Monsignor Paul Sheridan, who served as chancellor, later observed that the new bishop was "a man with tremendous energy and a talented public figure. I think he enjoyed being a bishop and his energy was just extraordinary." The new bishop continually toured the diocese where the Catholic population had reached 182,000.

McNicholas, a lifelong St. Louis Cardinals baseball fan, was horrified to find his new diocese about evenly split between fans of the Cardinals and the Chicago Cubs. The bishop devised a contest. He invited Catholics of the Diocese to predict which team would win the division championship. "It is quite likely," he wrote," that the Cardinals will win the division, the Cubs will be in the cellar. So if you are smart, and love the Cardinals as much as I do, you will have no trouble picking a winner. If you are a poor deluded Cub fan, try to explain to me why you are so off base." The friendly rivalry—carried on in *The Western Catholic*, the diocesan newspaper—"cemented many friendships in Springfield," remarked the bishop and endeared him to his people.

As often happens with a new bishop, the number of seminarians increased. Recognizing that a few men were "in the pipeline," so to speak, when McNicholas arrived, his presence nonetheless stirred excitement. During O'Connor's last five years in office, he ordained a total of ten men for the diocese. Under McNicholas the number rose and reached a peak at eight priestly ordinations in 1981, a figure yet to be equaled.

McNicholas was more active in the National Conference of Catholic Bishops than any of his predecessors. This involvement began when he was an auxiliary in St. Louis. He served in several different capacities for the National Conference of Catholic Bishops and the United States Catholic Conference (NCCB-USCC) including:

Liaison, National Office for Black Catholics (1972-1980)
Chair, Committee on Social Development and World Peace (1974-1977)
Chair, Ad Hoc Commission for the Pastoral on Marianism (1977-1980)
Liaison, Committee on Clergy, Religious, and Laity (1978-1981)
Member, Office for Missions (from 1980)
Member, Office Pro-life Activities (from 1980)
Member, Administrative Committee of the NCBB and USCC (1974-1977 and 1978-1981)

At one point McNicholas was nominated for the presidency of the NCCB. Activity at the national level gave him a keen understanding of how the church functioned and the influence it could exercise in American society. Several observers of church affairs in the United States believe that had McNicholas lived long enough he would have been transferred to a larger diocese or archdiocese.

When McNicholas arrived he had already established a reputation as a staunch civil rights advocate. One of his first acts as bishop was to help organize a Martin Luther King Day breakfast. McNicholas also took an active interest in the school desegregation cases throughout the diocese. In Springfield he served on an oversight committee monitoring the integration of the public schools.

"He worked himself to death," lamented a Dominican Sister. McNicholas had shown no signs of ill health when he died unexpectedly on April 17, 1983. The last day was much like any other. That afternoon the bishop went to St. John's Hospital to visit some patients. In one of the rooms he found his sister, Mary Blanche—her family had moved to Springfield a few years earlier—who was also visiting the sick. The bishop said good-bye and departed for Stonington for confirmations. Upon his return to the bishop's house he called his sister about 11:30 p.m. Everything seemed all right.

Bishop McNicholas' coat-of-arms. The Celtic cross symbolized the bishop's Irish heritage and the fleur-de-lis represented the Archdiocese of St. Louis.

Less than two hours later McNicholas telephoned Father John Renken, the Vice-Chancellor and the bishop's secretary, who also lived in the cathedral rectory. The bishop asked Renken to take him to St. John's Hospital because he did not feel well. While being examined in the emergency room, McNicholas suffered a massive coronary thrombosis. He was pronounced dead at 2:38 a.m. Family and colleagues were stunned. The bishop's demise came as a total shock.

In retrospect, one wonders if the bishop had a premonition of death. As usual at a confirmation, McNicholas preached about the dangers facing young people, specifically, drugs, alcohol, and pre-marital sex. He said it would be easy to have a shorter sermon—typically they lasted forty-five minutes—but that he felt bound to do everything possible for the good of their souls. McNicholas stated:

> My dear young people, just look at your Bishop. Perspiration is pouring off my forehead. The other day, someone said to me, 'Bishop, if you don't take care of yourself, you're going to die of a heart attack.' They may be right, but that doesn't really matter to me. When I die, I'm not going to be standing before the Lord wearing a mitre and carrying my crosier. It will just be me and the Lord, and He will ask me if I did everything to lead you young people to live good lives. I want to be able to say back to Him that I did everything I could for you, that I laid down my last card for Him, that I laid down my life.

The funeral Mass was held on April 21 and McNicholas became the second bishop to be interred in the cathedral. Monsignor Paul Sheridan became administrator of the diocese and under his direction confirmations and other essential tasks continued until the installation of the next bishop, Daniel L. Ryan.

Pro-Life Movement Gains Momentum

Reflecting on the tenth anniversary of *Roe v. Wade*, McNicholas wrote, "Whether or not we win or lose this fight to preserve the life of the unborn, I promise I will never stop proclaiming the sanctity of life no matter what the personal cost of the public abuse." The bishop's stance against abortion probably alienated just as many people as did his position on school desegregation.

After the 1973 *Roe v. Wade* ruling that legalized abortion, the church was almost alone in voicing disapproval. Soon others, including many evangelical Christians, rallied to the pro-life cause. Pro-life efforts initially focused on effecting a political remedy. In 1975 a handful of U.S. Senators proposed the first Human Life Amendment to the Constitution. In the thirty years since *Roe v. Wade*, Congress has yet to pass such an amendment and even if it did, it is doubtful that a sufficient number of states would ratify an amendment. The issue remains as neuralgic now as in 1973.

In our diocese McNicholas implemented a diocesan-wide pro-life program in 1976. Each pastor was required to appoint one woman and one man to be the pro-life coordinators of the parish. Their task was to rally support for political solutions as well as take steps to raise awareness about the evils of abortion. He wrote:

> [The plan] seeks to activate all the resources of the Church's agencies, institutions and people to take part in a comprehensive effort of education, moral and pastoral guidance, and social action which will restore respect for human life and establishes a system of justice in which the basic right of life is protected at every state and in every circumstance.

Catholic leaders also recognized the economic and social dynamics that drove abortion. Catholics, historically alienated from evangelical Christians, now found themselves in new partnerships to provide alternatives to abortion. In Granite City, for example, pro-life groups combined efforts to counteract the presence of the Hope Clinic for Women, an abortion service across the street from St. Elizabeth Hospital. Catholic Charities of Granite City, Lutheran Child and Family Services of Belleville, and the Baptist Children's Home of Carmi, among others, sponsored a mobile pregnancy aid center, the first of its kind in the nation. Called the PAC-VAN, the mobile center was staffed by two registered nurses. They assisted women facing crisis pregnancy in finding medical and financial assistance as well as providing referrals for pregnancy testing, and counseling, and community services. Eight years later the PAC-VAN was still in operation. One of the nurses stated, "With teenagers we are often the only ones they can turn to." Through the years the support offered through PAC-VAN and other pro-life efforts gave women a real choice, the choice to choose life.

In Springfield, since 1948, St. Monica's Center, a residential facility, has provided support for young women in difficult circumstances. Into the 1960s most unmarried mothers gave up their babies for adoption. After *Roe v. Wade* some of the residents at St. Monica's faced pressure from parents or the child's father to abort, but the existence of the center made it possible for prospective mothers to give birth and keep their babies. By the early 1980s about half of the women chose this alternative. Illegitimacy was losing its stigma and a variety of social services, many of them sustained by pro-life Catholics, made it possible for women to raise children on their own.

Pregnancy Aid Center of Granite City

2040 Iowa Street
Granite City, IL 62040
618/876-0616

"For You created my inmost being; You knit me together in my mother's womb"
Psalm 139:13

Flyer for the Pregnancy Aid Center of Granite City.

In the parishes, the pro-life coordinators raised awareness, mobilized support for the pro-life legislation, held baby showers to aid pregnancy centers, and engaged in numerous other activities for the unborn. In the Effingham Deanery, for example, the Bishop's Pro-Life Group staffed booths at the Effingham and Cumberland county fairs. Some members held prayer vigils at a Champaign abortion facility and other worked with youth.

Countless Catholic men, women, and children have participated in Walk-for-Life fundraisers, attended the annual pro-life rally at the Illinois State Capitol, joined national and local Right to Life Committees, and supported Birthright and other programs. They also prayed—and continue to pray—for an end to abortion. Many of the projects begun in the 1970s and 1980s continue today.

Bishop Victor H. Balke

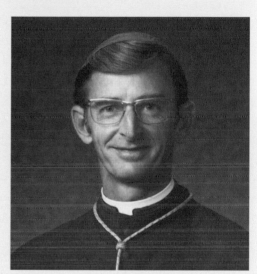

Bishop Victor Balke of Crookston, Minnesota, 1976.

Victor H. Balke, Bishop of Crookston, Minnesota was the only diocesan priest since Bishop Robert Franz to become a bishop. Balke was born September 29, 1931, in Meppen to Elizabeth Knese Balke and Bernard Balke, Sr. He attended St. Joseph School as well as the public schools in Meppen. After high school graduation in 1949 he entered the seminary. Bishop William A. O'Connor ordained Balke to the priesthood in 1958. The young priest served at the Cathedral of the Immaculate Conception and as chaplain at the St. Joseph Home in Springfield. For many years he was the rector of the Diocesan Seminary of the Immaculate Conception. Balke was involved in the charismatic renewal movement and was instrumental in organizing the first Koinonia retreat. Pope Paul VI bestowed the title Monsignor in 1974 and two years later named Balke the bishop of Crookston.

Housing for Senior Citizens

Far less controversial than civil rights or pro-life advocacy, were diocesan efforts to improve housing for low-income senior citizens. When Catholic organizations in the nineteenth century began to build homes for the aged, less than 1 percent of the population was age sixty-five or older. By 1970, senior citizens comprised about 9 percent of the total. Medical advances, in part, account for the phenomenal growth. Oftentimes, seniors were well enough to look after themselves on a day-to-day basis, but no longer capable of the rigors of home maintenance. Some were affluent enough to hire assis-

Residents of the Pope John Paul I Apartments, Springfield, return from a shopping trip, c. 1980. Note the Sister of St. Francis of the Martyr St. George assisting the shoppers. Courtesy of the Catholic Care Center, Inc., Springfield.

tance, but millions of others were not. The traditional type of "old folks home" did not address the desire of senior citizens to remain independent. Thus, an emerging social need of the 1960s and 1970s was housing for low-to-moderate income senior citizens.

Our diocese responded to this new need by forming a corporation, the Catholic Care Center, Inc., in 1976. The corporation worked with the United States Department of Housing and Urban Development (HUD), as well as state and local agencies, to build senior apartments. Borrowing money from HUD enabled the diocese to serve a larger number of people than had the diocese relied on its own resources.

The Catholic Care Center's first project was the John Paul I Apartments. In 1976, the corporation applied for, and later received, a $4,400,000 loan to be repaid over a period of forty years. The diocese contributed $50,000 in funds collected from the Campaign for Human Development. The board of the corporation decided that the eleven-story apartment building should be built on Springfield's eastside. The location was not selected on a whim. The population of this part of the city was largely African-American. McNicholas stated that building on the eastside would symbolize "our deep concern for the future welfare of the city," as well as the diocese's commitment to racial justice. Federal funding insured that the facilities would be open to senior citizens and persons with disabilities regardless of race, color, or creed.

The John Paul I Apartments opened in 1980. The building contained 150 units, most of them one bedroom apartments, but there were also a small number of two bedroom units as well as specially fitted apartments for the handicapped. Soon a wholesome family-life atmosphere developed among the residents. Two years later a similar building, the Marian Heights Apartments, opened in Alton. As in Springfield, the Catholic Care Corporation chose a site in redevelopment zone. In this case, the apartment building occupied a site on the riverfront near down-

Monsignor Frank Dirksen (1908-1994), one of the movers behind the senior housing projects.

town. Marian Heights is a seven-story building with 127 units.

For over two decades the presence of the Sisters of St. Francis of the Martyr St. George at both facilities contributed to the quality of life at Marian Heights and John Paul I. Most of the time there were two resident sisters who were nurses. They looked after the spiritual and physical needs of the residents. Their presence also fostered a Catholic atmosphere in what would otherwise have been a sterile, government-regulated project.

The story of senior housing in our diocese would not be complete without acknowledging the role played by Monsignor Frank Dirksen. This diocesan priest, ordained in 1948, served as the developer and administrator of both buildings. He worked tirelessly to transform the idea of senior housing into a reality and for many years served as chaplain at John Paul I. At the time of his death in 1994, one tribute read, "Msgr. Dirksen dedicated his life to the care and concern of others, especially the poor and aging. No request anyone made of his time went unanswered."

Architect's proposal of the Marian Heights Apartments, Alton, 1982.

125th Anniversary of the Diocese

The year 1978 marked the 125th anniversary of the diocese as well as the Diamond Jubilee of the Cathedral of the Immaculate Conception. All of the celebrations were held in Springfield. On October 15 Cardinal John Cody of Chicago presided at a jubilee Mass. Special guests included Bishop John B. Franz of Dodge City and Bishop Victor N. Balke of Crookston, Minnesota. Balke also gave the homily. Both had been priests of our diocese.

A reception for the laity followed the Mass and simultaneously the clergy attended a banquet. Although the cathedral was full most of those attending hailed from Springfield and nearby communities.

Spiritual Renewal

The interior renewal sparked by Vatican II assumed many forms. In 1982, the Sisters of St. Francis of the Martyr St. George in Alton opened the San Damiano Chapel, adjacent to Saint Anthony's Health Center, for perpetual adoration of the Blessed Sacrament. Bishop McNicholas, who never wavered in his affinity for traditional piety, readily gave the authorization to begin perpetual adoration. He also organized the Legion of One Thousand, a spiritual society without dues, meetings, or fund raising, whose members promise to visit the San Damiano Chapel at least once a week. Catholics who regularly spend time before the Blessed Sacrament find the experience enriching and edifying. Because of its proximity to the hospital, many non-Catholics also benefit from the serene atmosphere of the chapel.

From left: Sister Mary Saloma, Sr. Mary Deitharda, San Damiano Chapel, Saint Anthony's Health Center, Alton, 1996.
Courtesy of the Sisters of St. Francis of the Martyr St. George, Alton.

Charismatic Renewal

It seems a long way from the silence of perpetual adoration to the unique sounds of a charismatic prayer meeting, but the same Holy Spirit is at work. Charismatic prayer is a vehicle by which the Holy Spirit renews the gifts bestowed in baptism and confirmation. These gifts—wisdom, understanding, counsel, fortitude, knowledge, piety, and fear of the Lord—lead participants to a deeper relationship with God and the desire to build up the faith community. Developing a personal relationship with Jesus is essential in charismatic prayer and participants usually engage in bible study to help nurture the connection. Charismatics also value the gift of tongues and the interpretation of tongues.

Catholic charismatic renewal in the United States traces its origins to a small retreat of students and professors at Duquesne University in 1967. By the mid-1980s about 15 million Catholics were part of the movement. Compared to other Catholic forms of prayer, the charismatic style is more emotional. Indeed, the chance to openly manifest spiritual feelings contributed to the rapid growth of the movement.

Charismatic prayer offered an alternative to the staid litanies and ritual prayers that characterized Catholic devotion before Vatican II. Indeed, for most participants, charismatic prayer was the first time they allowed themselves to offer prayer and praise in an affective manner. "It makes everything I learned—my Catholic upbringing—come alive," said Barbara Hutter, who belonged to the St. Francis Light of Love prayer group in Springfield. The spontaneous and joyful nature of the prayer appealed to millions and brought different parts of the church together as religious, laity, and priests mingled together at the prayer services.

The Vatican and the American bishops spoke favorably of charismatic prayer, yet warned against an overemphasis on the affective. Bishop McNicholas, in 1977, about the peak of renewal in our area, issued a pastoral letter stating that charismatic prayer tended "to stress the highly emotional experience which is not reflective of the day-in and day-out struggle which is our pilgrimage here on earth." McNicholas continued that he was not aware of excesses in our diocese, but thought it prudent to appoint a priest director. Father Edward Gorman, the Viatorian pastor of St. Joseph's in Springfield, became the diocesan director of Charismatic Prayer Groups. By this time Decatur, Quincy, and Springfield were centers of charismatic renewal.

Along with the charismatic prayer meetings, the Life in the Spirit Seminars was an important component of adult faith formation. The seminars consisted of an eight-week series of classes. Along with scripture study, personal and group prayer, Catholics moved towards a deeper life in the Holy Trinity and prepared for baptism in the Spirit. In time, two additional eight-week series were offered.

One of the centers of charismatic prayer was the Franciscan Apostolic Center near Riverton. The Hospital Sisters of St. Francis had recently closed their sanitarium and a short time later, with minimal renovations, made it available to charismatic gatherings. The old sanitarium had enough room to host large groups for single sessions as well as renewal weekends.

Charismatic renewal in the diocese reached its peak in the mid-1970s. Nothing better symbolizes the height of the movement than the founding of Our Lady of the Holy Spirit Parish in Mt. Zion in 1974. About half of the parishioners were charismatic. For those who were not comfortable with the exuberance of charismatic prayer, more traditional Masses and catechetical programs were offered.

The movement, at least in terms of the number of participants, gradually diminished in the 1980s. Some charismatics simply ran out of emotional energy. Some turned to more traditional devotions. A few joined pentacostal Protestant churches. Still others found that charismatic prayer allowed them to integrate the emotional and intellectual aspects of the faith. They drifted away from the movement, but their renewal in the Holy Spirit was genuine and bore good fruit. And a few discovered that charismatic prayer fit them better than any other method. Members of the latter two categories usually remain active in parish life. They serve as liturgical ministers, catechists, visitors to shut-ins, and engage in other good works.

New Rite of Penance

The new Rite of Penance was introduced in the United States on the first Sunday of Lent, 1976. The rite became mandatory one year later. Traditionally, penitent Catholics entered a dark confessional and in two or three minutes listed their sins. The priest then pronounced the words of absolution. The new rite, stated Father Kevin B. Sullivan, diocesan director of religious education, focused on conversion of heart. "We [the priests] don't count so much the number of times a person has sinned. We are asking [the penitents] to ask themselves what is the cause of the sin. We see sin as a cancer, poison that affects a person's whole life." Many parishes also began to hold communal penance services so that the social dimension of sin, forgiveness, and reconciliation could be better understood. These services usually included the opportunity for individual confession and absolution.

Weekend Retreat Movements

Weekend retreats were yet another avenue for spiritual renewal. Teens Encounter Christ, better known as TEC, originated in Michigan in the late 1960s. The first TEC retreat in our diocese was held in Quincy in 1974. Later Monsignor Victor Balke and the late Father Richard Peradotto, along with Jim and Sue Morris of Springfield and Ursuline Sister Lorene Griffin, adapted the TEC format for adult retreat weekends. The result was Koinonia and the first retreat was held at the Franciscan Apostolic Center in September 1976. TEC and Koinonia, although distinctive from charismatic prayer, help participants to integrate the emotions and intellect in a spiritual experience. The Paschal Mystery is the focus of a Koinonia weekend. After twenty-five years 278 Koinonia weekends had been held in this diocese. The movement spread to twenty-five other states and it is estimated that approximately 25,000 persons have participated.

The Cursillo movement predates all the others discussed so far, but did not come to the Diocese of Springfield in Illinois

Koinonia # 4, held at St. Agnes, Springfield, 1981.
Courtesy of Elise Hines, Springfield.

until 1980. Cursillo, which means "short course," began in Spain in the 1940s and first appeared in the United States in 1957. In fact, Cursillo inspired TEC and Koinonia. In Cursillo men and women meet separately for three full days of prayer and study. The Cursillo begins on a Thursday evening and ends the following Sunday evening. A leadership team offers fifteen presentations and leads discussions. Participants build a sense of community over the course of three days. Cursillo remains strong in the Effingham, Quincy, and Jacksonville areas.

Cursillo, like the other spiritual movements discussed, integrates feelings and intellect. "Cursillo has deepened my love for God," wrote Mary Ellen Rauch of Montrose in the *Catholic Times*, "It has broadened my understanding of the sacraments, brought the picture of the church into clearer focus and re-sealed my commitment to her. I have come to see since Cursillo that we everyday little people too often sell ourselves short. We can be life-bringers to the church and to the world if we so choose."

Come Home for Christmas
Outreach to Non-Practicing Catholics

One of the best-remembered initiatives of Bishop McNicholas was the "Come Home for Christmas Campaign." Just before Advent in 1977, he announced this program to reconcile fallen-away Catholics with the church. The campaign called for a two-pronged approach of prayer and personal contact. There could be many reasons that an individual withdrew from the church. Some of the more common ones are:

- A hurtful situation with a priest or other representative of the institutional church
- Opposition to particular points of church teaching
- Marriage, divorce, or remarriage not sanctioned by the church
- Family break-up in which the custodial parent was non-Catholic
- A gradual indifference to the practice of faith
- Conflict with a family member

The campaign was beautifully simple. Active Catholics were asked to pray for the reunification of their non-practicing sisters and brothers. A special holy card facilitated the prayer. Some prayed as a family group. The bishop also encouraged Catholics to send in the names and addresses of the inactive so he could respond with a personal invitation. His letter read, in part:

We miss you and we want you to come back! Hopefully you also miss the Church. If I, or any of us in the Church, have hurt you, I personally extend my apologies. We can't change our Catholic faith in its essential doctrines or moral teachings. Apart from that, we will certainly walk the extra mile to reconcile you with the Church. We can help, but only you can make the decision.

COME ON HOME FOR CHRISTMAS

Will you please offer this prayer daily for those of our Faith who are presently not practicing their religion? Share these prayers with others. Additional copies are available at your nearest Catholic Church or by request from the Chancery, 524 East Lawrence Avenue, Springfield, Illinois 62705.

O, Jesus, through the Immaculate Heart of Mary, I offer You all my prayers, works, joys and sufferings of this day for all the intentions of Your Sacred Heart, in the union with the Holy Sacrifice of the Mass throughout the world in reparation for my sins and, in particular, for the return of those Catholics who are no longer practicing their faith.

Card distributed for the "Come Home for Christmas" campaign.
Courtesy of William Kessler, Sr., Alton.

"Come Home for Christmas" was a coordinated effort by laity, clergy, and diocesan officials. Radio and television advertisements attempted to reach the fallen-away. Members of the Legion of Mary accepted a special charge from the bishop to personally visit inactive Catholics. These meetings, usually in the home of the estranged individual, gave the person a chance to tell the story of his or her estrangement. Expressing feelings of rejection, anger, or emotional injury often opened the door to reconciliation.

McNicholas mailed over 1,500 letters during the first season of the campaign. The diocese made no effort to keep count of those who reconciled with the church, but from time to time, the bishop mentioned a reunion story in his column in the diocesan newspaper. An experience from Christmas eve, 1977, was typical. "At the back of the church," the bishop wrote, "a man said 'I haven't been to Mass in three years, but Bishop, I'm coming home.'"

Legion of Mary members assisted the bishop during the "Come Home for Christmas" campaign by visiting people who had fallen away from the church. Early 1980s.
Courtesy of Marie Therese Henebry, Springfield.

Hopeful Time for Black Catholics

A number of African-American Catholics in the diocese asked to meet with Bishop McNicholas shortly after he assumed office. The bishop had a long-standing reputation as a champion of civil rights. The meeting went well. The group voiced their concerns about the school desegregation battles then unfolding. McNicholas assured them that the Catholic schools would not serve as a refuge for whites attempting to avoid integration. (See above, "Taking a Stand on School Desegregation.") This meeting led to greater incorporation of black Catholics into diocesan leadership.

The Martin Luther King breakfasts, which began in 1976, mark the first time that our diocese participated in an event that specifically honored an African-American. Bishop Joseph L. Howze, auxiliary bishop of Natchez-Jackson, was the keynote speaker at the 1976 breakfast. For many black Catholics it was the first time they ever saw or met an African-American bishop. The breakfast also served as the backdrop for announcing the year's recipients of the Frontier Scholarships. These scholarships were awarded to an African-American high school student attending Ursuline Academy, Sacred Heart Academy, or Griffin High School.

In 1979, the American bishops issued a pastoral letter that set in motion a renewal of energy of the black Catholic community. *Brothers and Sisters to Us* declared that racism is a sin. In addition to addressing racism against blacks, the pastoral also raised concerns regarding Native Americans, Hispanics, and Asians. The bishops exhorted Catholics to affirm the dignity of every human person and to acknowledge our own prejudices and discriminatory behaviors.

Regarding minorities within the church, the pastoral called upon Catholics to take steps to "insure that minority representation goes beyond mere tokenism and involves authentic sharing in responsibility and decision making." The pastoral stirred hopes among those who read it, hopes that led to the National Congress of Black Catholics in 1987.

First Woman Superintendent of Catholic Schools

In the fall of 1978, Sister Mary Jeremiah Sullivan, a Springfield Dominican, became the first woman to assume charge of the diocesan schools. Sister Jeremiah had served as a teacher and administrator in Catholic schools from 1942 to 1965. Then followed twelve years as the Prioress General of the Dominican Sisters. She was well aware of the challenges facing the schools as they dealt with the transition from religious to lay faculty. In 1965 about 48 percent of the teachers were sisters. When she assumed office that figure had declined to about 28 percent. Sister Jeremiah served as Superintendent until 1984. She returned to classroom teaching for six years and then until her retirement in 1999 served as a receptionist at Sacred Heart-Griffin. High School, Springfield.

Springfield Dominican Sister Mary Jeremiah Sullivan, the first woman to head the diocesan office of Catholic schools, 1978.

Ms. Pam Michael, a lay teacher at Cathedral School, Springfield, mid-1970s. The number of lay teachers grew dramatically after Vatican II.

Courtesy of Pat Shea, Springfield.

Working Together to Build the Body of Christ

1984-1999

My grace is sufficient for you, for power is made perfect in weakness.

2 Cor. 12: 9

1985 *The Year of Learning*

Gradually, after Vatican II a more collaborative style of governance evolved at both the diocesan and parish levels. But the desire to work together did not automatically translate into the skills necessary to do so. Thus, the "Year of Learning" began in 1985. Only four parishes were involved: St. Mary (Taylorville), St. Anthony (Effingham), St. Thomas (Decatur), and St. Mary of the Assumption (Ste. Marie). Pastors, women religious working in these parishes, and laity attended a series of workshops and meetings. The techniques they learned stressed shared

responsibility for planning based in the knowledge that the Holy Spirit imparts gifts to each individual for the common good.

The bishop fully supported the ideal of shared responsibility. Bishop Daniel L. Ryan stated that when he first came to the diocese he "hoped to be a collaborator with persons who had for years dedicated their lives and energies to the service of building the Kingdom of God in this part of central and southern Illinois. We are looking together for ways to see how we can integrate our Catholic faith with the perceived pastoral needs of our area." Even if the shrinking number of priests had not necessitated change, stated the bishop, encouraging lay participation would still be essential.

The Year of Learning led to the identification of seven priorities for pastoral planning: Sacredness of Life, Spiritual Growth, Youth Ministry, Family Life, Stewardship, Adult Education, and Leadership Development. These became the building blocks for the Pastoral Plan Toward 1991. The Year of Learning also resulted in the creation of the Office for Social Concerns and the Office for Lay Ministry (renamed Office for Ministry Formation in 2001). As the Year of Learning progressed the people at Ste. Marie, in particular, came to value the experience, because soon they would become the first parish in the diocese to have a lay "parish life coordinator" instead of a resident pastor.

Sister Mary Theodora Ajagu of the Daughters of Divine Love shows the gingerbread house she made to decorate the Priests' Retirement Center for Christmas, 2001. The Divine Love community also ministers at Brother James Court and the Catholic Pastoral Center.

Bishop Daniel L. Ryan
January 18, 1984 to October 19, 1999

"Catholic Pastoral Center. How may I direct your call?" Sometimes callers to the central diocesan office are surprised to hear the voice of the retired bishop. But filling in for the receptionist is just one of the things Bishop Daniel L. Ryan has done during his retirement. A man without pretense, Ryan simply responds to the needs laid before him. He administers confirmation, substitutes for vacationing pastors and chaplains, and works in the Pastoral Care Department of St. John's Hospital, Springfield.

Daniel Leo Ryan was born on September 28, 1930, in Mankato, Minnesota to Leonard "Pat" Ryan and Irene Ruth Larson Ryan. Irene, who was of Norwegian ancestry, was a Lutheran, but entered into full communion with the Catholic Church in the 1950s. Pat ran a ladies ready-to-wear shop, but the Great Depression forced him out of business. For a while, their son and his older sister, Mary Louise, lived with a childless aunt and uncle while the Ryans reestablished themselves. Pat eventually obtained employment as a civil servant for the State of Minnesota.

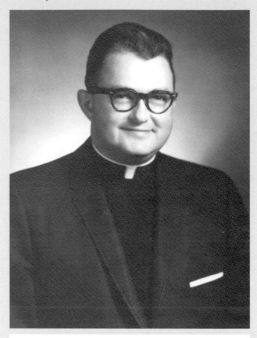

Father Daniel L. Ryan, c. 1970.
Photo by Allen Studios.

During World War II, in 1943, the family moved to Springfield, Illinois. Dan Ryan attended Blessed Sacrament School for one semester and then began his freshman year at Cathedral Boys High School. At this time the future bishop became interested in attending a minor seminary and the following year he transferred to the Passionist Preparatory High School, St. Louis. After graduation Ryan entered the novitiate, but soon discovered that life as a religious was not for him. "I really wanted to be a priest," he later recalled, "but I sure didn't like

Bishop Ryan's coat-of-arms. The griffin heads are borrowed from the Ryan family coat of arms. The wheat sheaf alludes to Wheaton, Illinois where Ryan once served as pastor.

EVERLASTING IS HIS LOVE

getting up at two o'clock in the morning for prayers." The Diocese of Joliet in Illinois accepted Ryan as a candidate for diocesan priesthood and he completed his college education in Lisle at St. Procopius College (Illinois Benedictine University) in 1952. After Ryan earned a masters degree in divinity, Bishop Martin D. McNamara ordained him to the priesthood in 1956 at the Cathedral of St. Raymond Nonnatus. During his twenty-eight years with the diocese Ryan accumulated extensive pastoral experience, but along the way, he simultaneously held various positions in the chancery including notary, assistant chancellor, chancellor, and vicar general. To facilitate the administrative work Ryan earned a degree in canon law in 1960 in Rome.

In 1981 Pope John Paul II made Ryan a bishop and assigned him as an auxiliary to Bishop Joseph L. Imesch of Joliet. The ordination occurred on September 30, 1981. Just a little over two years later, the Holy Father named Ryan to succeed Bishop Joseph A. McNicholas of Springfield. Years later, upon his retirement, an interviewer asked, "Was there ever a time when you thought to yourself that you really wanted to be a bishop?" Without hesitation,

The diocesan curia and support staff grew to meet the challenges of the late 20th century. With the support of the Annual Catholic Services Appeal (ASCA) they coordinate numerous programs and services.

Back row from left: Patrick Fitzgerald, Juanita Jeffers, Sister Chukwuma Onyekwelu (DDL), Becky Donaldson, Dan Gauwitz, Dan James, Karen Regan, Clara Fleischacker (face hidden), Cheryl Kannell, Joan Reed, Bill Callan, Eliot Kapitan, Patty Polonus, Tom Riser, Janet Westenberger, Joan Anderson, Doug Crocher, Shawn Trahan, Father Tony Theiman, Marlene Mulford, Christina Davis, Paula Ruot, Jan Griggs, Brother Joel Mark Rousseau (FFSC), Carol Muller, Martha Mayfield, Kathie Sass, Jeff Brown, Bernardine Smith, Father Donald J. Meehling, Donna Dausman, Susan Donnelly, Joe Kaufmann, Tony Claclosure, Barb Burris, Chris Malmevick, Jean Johnson, Bobbi Ozanic. Front row from left: Sister Jane Boos (SSND), Sister Susan Karina Dickey (OP), John Maxwell, Father Kevin Laughery, Father Kenneth C. Steffen, Father John A. Renken, Sheryl Spears, Father David S. Lantz

Ryan responded, "Absolutely not. I can tell you as clear as day, never. Never wanted it. I worked too long, remember, from day one as a priest at least part-time for bishops. So I saw what they were doing. I wanted no part of it. It was work." Yet work he did for the next eighteen years of his life in Joliet and Springfield.

On November 28, 1993, the Sunday following the announcement of Ryan's appointment to Springfield, the revised Code of Canon law went into effect. Ryan, like bishops of every Latin rite diocese, led the implementation of the revised code's provisions. He appointed a diocesan finance officer, a diocesan finance council, and parish priest consultors. Ryan issued statutes for the establishment of the presbyteral council (which succeeded the Priest's Senate). He centralized and restructured the diocesan curia, and expanded greatly the pastoral ministry of the diocesan tribunal. Ryan also directed that workshops on the revised code be offered throughout the diocese to familiarize the faithful with its provisions.

Ryan himself was a canon lawyer so he understood the necessity of training a new generation of experts. During his episcopate several priests obtained an advanced degree in canon law. One of them, Father John Renken, the diocese's vicar general, became president of the Canon Law Society of America in 2000. And, the diocese hosted the Midwest Canon Law Society's convention in 1991 and again in 2002.

Early in his episcopate Ryan faced a personal crisis of massive proportions. Usually, when an alcoholic decides to seek treatment it is a private matter, but when a public figure takes steps towards recovery, it becomes news. Ryan entered a rehabilitation program in the summer of 1986, an event covered in the local and national press. Anonymity, so helpful to the recovering alcoholic, was not possible. The bishop made the necessary arrangements for the functioning of the diocese in his absence. Most Catholics showered Ryan with prayers and letters of support. In fact, some later commented that the bishop's struggle inspired them to face their own difficulties with greater trust in God. Ryan returned to Springfield about three months later to take up the reins of office and carry on one day at a time.

The curia assumed its present form during the Ryan episcopate. Some of the offices were created to meet requirements of the new code while others came into existence to address the needs of the Catholic population. The Office for Social Concerns, for example, consolidated several existing programs—ministry to persons with disabilities, pro-life advocacy and education, justice and peace—under one umbrella. The Office for Family Life and Youth Ministry, begun in 1992, assumed direction of the CYO and other youth activities, marriage preparation, and other programs to promote a strong family life.

Under Ryan, the diocese devised a new way of generating revenue to operate the curia and other diocesan institutions. Previously, each parish had received two annual assessments: the "smaller" one was called the "cathedraticum," and the "larger" one was called the "Diocesan Development Fund" (DDF). The cathedraticum was simply a bill paid by each parish from its general revenue. The monies to pay the DDF were generated in a second collection each September. In addition, the bishop relied on interest income from diocesan savings to assist in running the diocese.

Following the positive recommendation of his Presbyteral Council and Diocesan Finance Council, in 1988 Ryan eliminated the cathedraticum and DDF, and implemented instead the Annual Catholic Services Appeal (ASCA). Though each parish still had its mandatory goal, determined through a formula applied equally to each parish, the ASCA involved a direct mail appeal from the bishop to each Catholic household. Also, the ASCA was designed to generate sufficient funds to operate the entire curia and other diocesan institutions; the diocese no longer relied on interest income to subsidize operations.

Increased staff required additional office space. As plans proceeded for the merger of Griffin High School and Sacred Heart Academy, completed in 1988, diocesan planners decided to renovate Griffin so it could serve as the Catholic Pastoral Center. The gymnasium and athletic fields became the West Campus of Sacred Heart-Griffin, but the classrooms were transformed into diocesan offices. The Viatorian residence became, in 1992, the Priests' Retirement Center.

The latter years of Ryan's tenure will be remembered for the beginnings of ministry to Hispanics. In some parts of the nation, church leaders have more-or-less ignored the presence of Spanish-speaking Catholics. In hindsight, it seems we might have responded a bit sooner in offering Spanish Masses and addressing the cultural conflict between the newcomers and the established parish populations. But when it became evident that the numbers of Spanish-speaking Catholics

Milestones of the Ryan Episcopate

1984 Appointed first lay directors of the Office for Rural Life

1986 Office of Finance
Office for Campus Ministry
Opened Villa Maria: Catholic Life Center

1988 Office for Stewardship and Development
Began Implementation of the Rite of Christian Initiation for Adults

1989 Appointed Gilda Fulgenzi, first woman chancellor in the Province of Chicago

1990 Catholic Pastoral Center opened in the former Griffin High School
Office for Social Concerns (absorbed Office for Rural Life and Office for Ministry to Persons with Disabilities)
Developed Pastoral Plan Toward 1991

1991 Office for Lay Ministry
Established a diocesan-wide board to oversee the allocation of monies collected for the Catholic Campaign for Human Development

1992 Priests' Retirement Center opened

1993 Diocese supplied emergency relief for victims and Catholic Churches affected by flooding along the Mississippi and Illinois Rivers

1994 Established Task Force for Racial Justice
Established Foundation for the People of the Roman Catholic Diocese of Springfield

1995 Released the Parish Pastoral Plan for parish clustering and consolidation

1996 Began ministry to Hispanic community

1997 Daughters of Divine Love arrived to minister at Brother James Court, Springfield.

1999 Missionary Sisters of the Sacred Heart "Ad Gentes" arrived to minister to Hispanics

continued to grow, Ryan made ministry to them a priority.

The people of the diocese were surprised when on October 19, 1999, the Vatican announced the retirement of Daniel L. Ryan. He stated, "I have felt for some little time that I should step aside and have an opportunity for a type of service to our Lord's people other than that of being 'where the buck stops.' My next birthday will be my 70th." The same day Ryan retired the Vatican announced that our new bishop would be George J. Lucas. After a few weeks of rest Ryan was back in the saddle performing confirmations, serving as a chaplain at St. John's Hospital and, when needed, answering the phones at the Catholic Pastoral Center.

Bishop Ryan staffing the reception desk at the Catholic Pastoral Center, Springfield, 2000.

Parish Life Coordinators

During the summer of 1986, as the Year of Learning was drawing to a close, the people at St. Mary of the Assumption in Ste. Marie learned that their beloved pastor, Father Robert Spriggs, would soon be transferred. There was no priest to replace him. Spriggs and the parish pastoral council talked over various options. The parish could merge with another or become a mission of a larger parish in a nearby town. But the second oldest Catholic community in the diocese rejected both alternatives. Many parishioners did, however, believe they could carry on with a lay leader of some sort. That person would oversee the day-to-day functioning of the parish and arrange for the sacramental services of a priest. The pastoral council held two meetings to discuss the issue and sensing support for a lay leader, asked Spriggs to approach the bishop with the idea. Ryan was willing to try the innovative arrangement.

When the people at Ste. Marie asked for a lay leader, they already had someone in mind. Dominican Sister Phyllis Schenk had been working at St.

Mary's as a pastoral associate. With that relationship already in place, it was easier for the people to choose to ask for a lay leader. "It helps that we know each other," Schenk told the *Catholic Times*. She also praised the people's sense of responsibility for the future of their parish, a feeling enhanced by participation in the Year of Learning.

On August 1, 1986, Schenk assumed her duties as a pastoral leader. A few years later the title "parish life coordinator" came into

Front page of The Catholic Times showing Dominican Sister Phyllis Schenk as Parish Life Coordinator at Ste. Marie, August 1, 1986.

use. Several factors contributed to the success of the new arrangement. First, Spriggs had prepared the people for the transition. Often he had preached on the role of the laity and the importance of collaboration. Second, the people were already comfortable with Schenk. And third, a significant number of people at St. Mary's were willing to try this new path.

There were no precedents to turn to. The first few months were rough going. One of the biggest concerns was that a priest would not be available to hear the confession of a dying parishioner or to administer anointing of the sick in an emergency. On the other hand, parishioners in crisis benefited from the steady presence of the parish life coordinator who accompanied individuals day by day in their times of trial.

Since 1986 several other parishes in the diocese have been served by a parish life coordinator, but even the presence of a full-time minister does not diminish the need for a variety of other lay leaders.

Lay Ministry Blossoms

"Ministry is service," wrote Bishop Ryan when he announced the opening of the Office for Lay Ministry in 1991. "By baptism we are called to share Christ's ministry by loving service to our sisters and brothers in the faith and to all." The creation of the office and the Lay Ministry Formation Program it administered were the culmination of several years of planning by lay, religious, and ordained leaders. Ever since Vatican II it had become apparent that many adult Catholics desired further faith formation. Parishes and other Catholic institutions needed the services of the laity. Increasingly, tasks once performed by clergy and religious were now carried out by lay women and men. Participants in the program gather together one Saturday a month for ten months, over two or three consecutive years. Topics during the first year have varied, but consistently included liturgy, spirituality, church history, scripture, morals, ecclesiology, and social teaching. During the second year participants choose to specialize in pastoral care, family life, liturgical ministry, tribunal advocacy, Rite of Christian Initiation for Adults (RCIA), or social concerns. If one chooses the three year program the participant can earn a certificate in "parish life ministry."

Catholic Youth

The Office for Family and Youth Ministry provides a number of services to promote the faith formation of youth. Among other things, high school Catholics from the diocese attended the World Youth Day in Rome for Jubilee 2000. Young people are also active in the pro-life movement.

Participants (from left) Jayne Walk (St. Mary of the Assumption, Neoga), Andrea Esker (St. Francis, Teutopolis), and Lori Kocher (Our Lady of Lourdes, Oblong), at the Christian Leadership Institute (CLI), Villa Maria, Springfield, June 24, 1999. The CLI is an annual event held to develop youth leadership.

Parish Pastoral Plan
A Response to the Dwindling Numbers of Priests

One of the hardest decisions a bishop ever has to make regards the closing of a parish. Demographic changes coupled with the declining number of priests necessitated such changes. When Bishop Ryan assumed office there were 153 diocesan priests active within our boundaries. Primarily through death and retirement, the number declined to 105 in 1995. Although several religious priests minister in our diocese as parish pastors, their numbers, too, are declining. Realizing that the corps of priests would shrink even further, the diocesan leaders began to study how to best serve the faithful ten to fifteen years in the future.

The Parish Pastoral Plan released in July of 1995 contained few surprises. The *Catholic Times* reported that the planning was a collaborative effort involving "ordained, religious and laity. It began at the parish level, progressed to the deanery level, and eventually ended with the bishop making the ultimate decisions based upon the recommendations he received." The

plan outlined the eventual merger of thirty-three parishes into sixteen. The bottom-up approach, no doubt, contributed to the acceptance of the plan. So did the fact that changes would be implemented as needed, not all at once. Father Eugene Costa, chancellor and parish planning coordinator, stated, "The plan is flexible, it will be adapted as needs and circumstances change." The plan did not mandate the selling of any church property or the closure of any school. As for adjusting to the declining number of priests, Costa said,

> I don't think the ministry is priest-centered anymore. Most of us grew up when everything depended on the priest. That is not, that should not be, the case anymore. Part of this plan is clearly a commitment on our part to invite more and more people to become involved in ministries in the church. Everybody has some gift, some role to play in the church.

After the plan was made public, reaction was muted. Not a single person wrote to the *Catholic Times* or to the bishop to express displeasure with the plan. In the western part of the diocese, Father Charles Nelson, who cares for the parishes at Winchester, Bluffs, and Murrayville, said that the people have been aware for years of the talk about consolidation. The parishes already shared resources, held an annual picnic, and offered joint confirmation and RCIA classes. They also observed Holy Week and Easter Vigil together, using each church for one of the liturgies. "I said that when the time comes [for merging] I'll let them know well in advance."

Farm Crisis

The farm crisis of the mid-1980s affected numerous families in our diocese. Nationwide, less than 3 percent of the population live on farms, but among Catholics in the Diocese of Springfield in Illinois, the figure is considerably higher. In fact, in some locales farmers are a significant majority and depend heavily on agriculture for their livelihood. Conditions varied greatly even within parishes, but generally, those who suffered the most were caught in a convergence of forces, some of them beyond the control of any individual.

A farmer from St. Louis Parish (Nokomis) told the *Catholic Times* that he had reduced acreage and that his wife had taken a job in town. He purchased

land in 1977 at $2,530 an acre. Nine years later the land was worth far less, only $1,000 an acre. His debts outstripped his assets. "I don't think it will ever turn around," he said, "I think it'll get worse."

The diocesan rural life directors, Joe and Mayme Bergschneider of Alexander, worked with the Illinois Catholic Conference, the *Catholic Times*, and other entities to aid farm families and to explain the complicated political, economic, and social dynamics to city dwellers. Rural life advocates believed that only in very rare cases could problems be blamed on an individual farmer. It was the convergence of federal agricultural and tax policies, world markets, and bad weather that swept farmers into unmanageable debt. One might think that families in crisis would turn to their local parish, but the stigma attached to financial difficulty or failure prevented many from reaching out.

Project Isidore, named in honor of the patron saint of agriculture, was one of the ways the diocese responded to the plight of the farmers. The project offered no-interest loans of up to $2,000. The bishop later commented that these loans probably did not save anyone

Bishop Ryan blesses farm equipment, livestock, seeds, and soil in the annual celebration of Saint Isidore, patron of agriculture. Photograph by Rich Saal, State Journal-Register.

from bankruptcy, but for many farm families the loan was enough to tide them over until they could restructure their debt or make a transition from farming to some other line of work.

The *Catholic Times* also encouraged rural parishes to follow the lead of their counterparts in Iowa—form teams and go door to door. "Ask farmers and their families if they would like to talk about anything. The Iowa ministers were amazed at how many asked them to come in and sit down." To be a good listener was the best ministry that one could offer.

The paper also published the phone numbers of rural crisis hotlines.

By the late 1980s the economy was improving. Many farmers had weathered the storm. Others were recovering from the loss of a way of life as they worked out an early retirement or retooled for work in other fields.

New Era Dawns for African-American Catholics

The 1987 National Congress of Black Catholics marked a turning point in the history American Catholicism as well as for the African-Americans of the diocese. The last congress had been held in 1894. African-American Catholics had co-existed, often in segregated parishes, with other Catholics, but it was not until the latter half of the twentieth century that bishops and other church leaders renewed efforts to address black concerns.

Several months before the Congress, about sixty black Catholics of our diocese met at the cathedral to select delegates for the Congress. This meeting was the first time ever that diocesan African-Americans had gathered as a distinct group.

The delegation arrived at the Congress, held at the Catholic University of America in Washington, D.C., to find themselves among hundreds of other African-American Catholics. "I never knew there were so many black Catholics," said Eunice Perry, one of the delegates. After all, the chance to pray, play, and study with other African-Americans was a rare opportunity. In the Diocese of Springfield in Illinois, black Catholics comprise about 1 percent of the faithful. Even in Alton, Decatur, and Springfield where they are most numerous, African-Americans do not comprise the majority in any parish. Thus, for

108

Black Catholics attend a gospel style Mass at St. Mary's, Alton, May 28, 1993.

some of the delegates the Congress was an opportunity to further integrate one's sense of being both black and Catholic. Renee Saunches of St. Thomas, Decatur, probably said it best when she told a *Catholic Times* reporter, "I have gone from being two people—a black person and a Catholic—to being a Catholic person who is black." She also commented on the reality of being a minority within a parish:

> Black Catholics are accustomed to being ministered to rather than with. Blacks need to assume some of the responsibility for making that change. As one of the few blacks in my parish, I have been sensitive of not forcing my blackness on people. But the congress helped me realize that I have deprived them of something. If my blackness is a spiritual gift, it is meant to be shared.

Back home in the diocese, the delegates recommended several actions. Among those to bear fruit were holding periodic gatherings of black Catholics, forming the Black Catholic Advisory Board, increasing awareness among the priests and laity of the historical contributions of black Catholics, and explaining their perspective on various social issues.

A few years later, in 1994, the conference, "Healing the Past...Creating the Future: Black and White in Illinois," tackled the subject of racism. The four-day meeting was sponsored by the Catholic Conference of Illinois. More than thirty-five persons from our diocese—black and white—attended, including clergy, religious, and laity. "Healing the Past" became the catalyst for a new round of programs designed to improve race relations within the church and society. The most popular has been the "Valuing Diversity in the Catholic Church." Another program is "Recovering from Racism." As a direct result of "Healing Our Past," the diocesan Task Force for Racial Justice was formed in 1994. This group continues to promote better race relations within our parishes and in civil society.

Front page of the Catholic Times showing diocesan delegates at the National Black Catholic Congress, April 20, 1986.

The ordination class of 1987 consisted of one man—Charles Nelson. He was the first African-American ordained for our diocese since Augustine Tolton, 101 years earlier. Nelson grew up in Springfield and had worked at Sangamo Electric, the State of Illinois, and Marine Bank before entering the seminary. Since ordination he has served in Godfrey, Jacksonsonville, White Hall, Murrayville, Winchester, and Bluffs.

Seminary graduation class of Charles T. Nelson, Pope John XXIII National Seminary, Weston, Massachusetts. From left, Rev. Mr. Peter Johnson, Rev. James DeAdder, Richard Bushee, Joseph Lutz, Ronald Gomes, Charles T. Nelson, Bishop Ryan, Stanley Kryston, Rev. Dennis Sheehan, David Adams, Richard Fitzgerald, Lawrence Walter, 1987.

Catholics on the College Campus

From the earliest days Quincy University and Springfield College in Illinois provided for the spiritual welfare of their students, but Catholics attending other institutions relied on the local parish. Students had to take the initiative to remain involved in the church. But in 1986, with the opening of the Office for Campus Ministry, the Diocese of Springfield in Illinois officially recognized the importance of adult faith formation in the college setting. The diocese operates two such ministries, one at the Southern Illinois University-Edwardsville and the other at Eastern Illinois University, Charleston. Six part-time chaplains serve Catholics at other schools, including Illinois College and MacMurray College (Jacksonville), Blackburn College (Carlinville), and the various community colleges.

The Newman Center at Eastern traces its origins to 1939, when a group of thirteen Catholic students and faculty began to meet for prayer and fellowship. The following year, Father Daniel Moriarity, the new pastor of St. Charles Borromeo in Charleston, began his long association with Catholics at the school. For the next twenty-five years Moriarity nurtured the faith. In the early years, students worshiped at St. Charles and met in private homes. The Newman Club flourished throughout the 1950s as more and more Catholics attend-

ed college. In 1964 the organization acquired its own building, formerly a Protestant church, which became the Newman Catholic Center. For Mass, the Newman members gathered at Buzzard Auditorium on the campus.

When Roy Lanham became the Newman Center director in 1986—as well as the director of the new diocesan Office for Campus Ministry—he and the chaplain, Father Robert Meyer, began to dream of a chapel and a new facility. Gradually, plans took shape. Consultation with students led to the identification of two key concepts: the building should be welcoming and it should convey a sense that healing can occur within its walls. In response to the wishes of the Newman community, the architect incorporated a Gothic arch

*Dedication of the St. Philip Neri Chapel, Newman Catholic Center,
Eastern Illinois University, Charleston, Illinois, August 22, 1999.*

into the façade so as to distinguish the structure from the secular buildings around it. In August, 1999, Bishop Ryan dedicated the Newman Catholic Center and St. Philip Neri Chapel.

At present, about 40 percent of the student body is Catholic. About 2,500 of those people participate in Newman activities and weekly Mass attendance averages about 400-450. The Newman Center is thus one of the largest communities of faith in the diocese.

Several traits distinguish the Generation X and the Millennium Generation Catholics. They are technologically literate. They are comfortable with computers and rely on them for personal communication as well as school and professional activities. The are pragmatic in faith, that is, they generously volunteer their time to support short-term projects such as Habitat for Humanity and other works of mercy. Their knowledge of doctrine and church teaching, however, is usually rudimentary—that is, they have little understanding of the theological underpinnings of the faith. Campus ministry offers a chance to grow towards an adult understanding.

The most significant characteristic of young adult Catholics—one they share with others their age—is the reluctance, perhaps for some the inability, to make long-term commitments. They are the children of a fractured society and many are the survivors of divorce. Yet, they long for connection and meaningful interaction with others. Activities at the Newman Center consist not only of service projects, but opportunities for students to worship, pray, and recreate together to build a community of faith.

Family Life

The annual diocesan anniversary celebration for couples married fifty years or more began in 1992. This popular event is sponsored by the Office for Family and Youth Ministry. Programs for marriage preparation, natural family planning, and ministry to the divorced and bereaved are among the many other services offered by the office.

Bishop Ryan with some participants on the steps of the Cathedral of the Immaculate Conception at the annual Mass for couples married 50 or more years.

Rite of Christian Initiation of Adults
RCIA

"RCIA is all about journey," said Father John Beveridge, "the journey of life, the journey of faith." Beveridge was part of the diocesan task force that implemented the Rite of Christian Initiation of Adults in 1989. Although the Second Vatican Council called for the restoration of the catechumenate, many years passed before the American bishops approved the revised rite in 1988. This text became mandatory the following year.

The Rite of Christian Initiation of Adults is the normative process to prepare adults and children of catechetical age for the sacraments of Christian Initiation in the Roman Catholic Church. Typically those desiring baptism—the catechumens—as well as those preparing to complete the sacraments of initiation and non-Catholic Christians desiring communion with the Roman Catholic Church—the candidates—meet weekly for prayer, catechesis, and community building. Sponsors also attend. Leaders usually include the pastor as well as lay or religious catechists. The catechumenal process builds upon scripture and the liturgical year, a method that integrates the intellect, emotions, and day-to-day living. Catechumens are baptized and all previously uncatechized adults complete the sacraments of initiation at the Easter Vigil.

Baptized Christians of other denominations are received into full communion either at the vigil or another suitable time during the year.

The Rite of Christian Initiation of Adults has resulted in many benefits to both participants and the local parish community. By the time catechumens and candidates are received they are already weaving themselves into the fabric of parish life. They begin to serve in various ministries and some eventually sponsor others. Accompanying the participants through the weekly liturgy and special events energizes long-time parishioners, especially in small communities. We have come a long way from the days of private instruction of "converts" by the pastor.

Baptism by immersion at the Easter Vigil became common after the implementation of the Rite of Christian Initiation of Adults. Father Mike Kuse baptizes Katie Miller. Father Thom Dennis, at right, assists, Our Saviour's, Jacksonville, April 2, 1994.

An Ending & A Beginning
Diocesan Seminary Becomes Villa Maria: Catholic Life Center

After a slight increase of priestly ordinations in the early 1980s, the number of diocesan seminarians declined. Not surprisingly, questions arose as to the wisdom of maintaining the Diocesan Seminary of the Immaculate Conception. Bishop Ryan appointed a commission to study the situation and a few months later that body recommended that the seminary be closed. Reasons included:

✓ The smaller number of seminarians

✓ There was no longer any need to master Latin

✓ Many seminarians had already completed a bachelor's degree, and those who had not could enroll at other college seminaries

Most men continued to complete their studies—as diocesan priests had for generations—at Kenrick or Mundelein. A few studied in Rome or other locations. So-called "late" or "delayed" vocations, that is, men in their forties, fifties, or beyond, went to special schools to meet their particular needs. Thus ended a chapter of our history.

What would become of the handsome edifice and other buildings on the twelve-acre seminary grounds? That very year, 1986, the main building was converted in the Villa Maria: Catholic Life Center. As a spiritual renewal center, Villa Maria began hosting Koinonia and TEC, as well as retreats for Separated, Divorced and Remarried Catholics, Kairos, and interdenominational retreats. The spacious facilities are also used for clergy meetings and twice a year hosts the diocesan seminarians for study days.

The old dining hall, dating back to the days of Camp-Star-of-the-Sea was, in 2000, renovated to accommodate meetings of sixty to seventy persons. Many secular groups also use Villa Maria. "Our ministry," stated Villa director Martina Kocher, "is one of hospitality. We seek to provide an environment where people can encounter God and themselves in nature, in the events they attend, and in their own private reflections."

Seminarians at the annual Christmas break gathering at Villa Maria, Springfield, January 2, 1986. Back row from left: Kevin Oiter, Joe Kerber, Allen Kemme, Barry Harmon, Dan La Count, Brian Garner, Tony Thiemann, Steve Janoski, Steve Stack. Middle row from left: Charles Nelson, John Titus, John Burgess, Michael Mullink. Front row from left: Bob Chalifoux, John Herndon, Mark Lewis, Ed Ohm, Kenny Balman, Carl Kemme, John Neehan.

Hispanic Ministry

The United States is sometimes compared to a mosaic in which the various ethnic groups comprise the pieces. If one steps back to admire the mosaic, colorful and intriguing patterns emerge. The newest pieces of the mosaic in the Diocese of Springfield in Illinois are the Hispanic Catholics who have moved to the towns of Beardstown, Arcola, Decatur, Effingham, and Springfield. Most of the newcomers are Mexican, either citizens of Mexico or those born in the United States. Smaller numbers trace their origins to Peru or other Latin American nations. There are also about 100 Filipino families in Springfield and Decatur who gather monthly for mass and fellowship.

Sometime before 1990 small numbers of Spanish-speakers began to come to Springfield and Decatur as part of the medical community. Then in the 1990s several Mexican and Mexican-American men arrived to take jobs at food processing plants and other facilities. Within a year or two relatives of the first arrivals began to come to central Illinois. And by the mid-1990s wives, children, and extended family members followed the pioneers. In this regard, the Hispanic influx resembles the chain migration of Italian and eastern European Catholics a century earlier. In 2000, the estimated Spanish-speaking population of the counties in our diocese had reached the neighborhood of 3,000. It is a youthful population with many children.

Like their counterparts 100 years earlier, Hispanics face prejudice and discrimination, not only from American society at large, but also from their co-religionists. None of the parishes where Hispanics now worship had recently experienced an intercultural reality. The antagonism against the Germans and Irish, the eastern Europeans and the English speaking, had long ago been put to rest.

In 1994, to facilitate better ministry to Hispanics, a program of Hispanic Ministry was established by Bishop Ryan. Efforts have been made to secure the services of more priests and lay ministers who can speak Spanish. In 1997, Sister Rene Lawless, a Springfield Dominican, became the first full-time minister to Hispanics. Lawless had been a missionary to Peru for thirty-one years so her language skills were excellent. Although she quickly learned about the cultural differences between the Hispanics in central Illinois and the Peruvians, she was able to create a ministry of presence and practical assistance. Lawless works with the newcomers for sacramental preparation as well as providing information and advice in meet-

Children celebrate the Feast of Our Lady of Guadalupe. The boy in the foreground represents Blessed Juan Diego, Our Lady of Lourdes, Decatur, late 1990s.

ing every-day needs. Sometimes that means serving as a translator between an immigrant and an employer or government official.

The membership at St. Alexius in Beardstown was caught by surprise with the large numbers of Spanish-speaking Catholics moving to the community. The pastor, Viatorian Father Eugene Weitzel, who can offer Mass in Spanish, stated that at first "I was a little remiss, a little slow, in dealing with it."

What unfolded at Beardstown—indeed, what continues to unfold—is similar to the other towns where Hispanics have taken up residence. In 1999 Hispanic ministry received a boost with the arrival of four religious of the Missionary Sisters of the Sacred Heart "Ad Gentes" from Tlaxcala, Mexico. The sisters live in Springfield near St. Agnes, but minister principally in Arcola, Decatur, and Beardstown.

The number of Spanish-speaking Catholics in our diocese will continue to increase. In fact, church officials estimate that approximately one-third of Catholics in the United States by 2025 will be Hispanic. The presence of the new Catholic immigrants is a blessing and a challenge. The Mexicans and other

"Ad Gentes" Sister Emigdia Saucedo celebrates with the Hispanic community at St. Alexis, Beardstown.

Hispanics bring the vitality of youth and a strong family-based spirituality. The challenge lies in working through the misunderstandings and feelings of discomfort that inevitably occur when two cultures come in contact with one another. The 150th anniversary story of the diocese is, in part, one of the assimilation of the European Catholic immigrants. The 200th anniversary, if present trends continue, will include a great deal more about the Hispanic Catholics of our diocese.

Catholic War Veterans

The National Association of Catholic War Veterans was organized in 1935, but the first post in our diocese was organized Springfield in 1991. Since that time posts have been established in Alton and Quincy. The Catholic War Veterans join together to promote zeal and devotion for God, country, and home. The various posts sponsor essay contests for children, scholarships for Catholic schools, visit hospitalized veterans, and participate in a memorial Mass program for deceased veterans and their spouses.

Second grader Nicole Eddington of St. Aloysius School, Springfield, accompanied by her mother, receives first place in the Safety Poster contest sponsored by the Springfield chapter of the Catholic War Veterans.
At the state level she placed second. Commander George Boehmer (left) and First Vice-Commander Harvey Page presented the award, 2001.

Beginning the 3rd Millennium of Christ

1999 to the Present

You must hold fast to faith, be firmly grounded and steadfast in it, unshaken in the hope promised you by the gospel you have heard.
(Col. 1:23)

CHAPTER EIGHT
Jubilee 2000

Each of us, all of us together, have the privilege of being alive on the eve of the third millennium. We celebrate the great jubilee of our salvation. We believe that never—not for one minute—in 2000 years has God turned away from us or withdrawn the promise of salvation in Jesus Christ.
Bishop Lucas, Evening Prayer homily, Dec. 13, 1999.

The universal church observes a holy year every twenty-five years, but the Great Jubilee of the Year 2000 was extraordinary. It marked the completion of two millennia of Christianity and beginning of a third. Prior to January 1, 2000, Catholics worldwide spent three years reflecting on the Holy Trinity in order to prepare for the celebration. Pope John Paul II identified conversion, evangelization, reconciliation, and forgiveness as prominent Jubilee themes.

The simultaneous celebration of Jubilee 2000 and the beginning of a new episcopate stirred excitement. Observances were held at the parish, deanery, and diocesan levels. Many Catholics made a pilgrimage to Rome, but recognizing that such travel was not possible for everyone, a Jubilee pilgrimage church was designated in each of the seven deaneries of our diocese. Bishop George J. Lucas presided at services in six deaneries on the Sundays of Easter: Quincy, Jacksonville, Decatur, Effingham, Alton, and Litchfield. Each observance began with the bishop preaching on the Eucharist. Because it was spring, as well as the fact that agriculture remains an economic mainstay of our diocese, the service included the blessing of soil and seed for the planting season. Exposition and adoration of the Blessed Sacrament followed the prayers. Then, about an hour later following Benediction, the afternoon concluded with the Mass.

On Pentecost Sunday, June 11, 2000, hundreds of Catholics from all over the diocese gathered at the Cathedral of the Immaculate Conception for the concluding liturgy of the Easter Pilgrimage. The bishop preached again on the Eucharist, but this time emphasized the role of the Holy Spirit. The bishop explained how the teaching and the witness of the apostles that began at Pentecost continues in us. "There is not some cathedral out there filled with super Catholics. It is up to us in the year 2000 with the power of the Holy Spirit. God has chosen us."

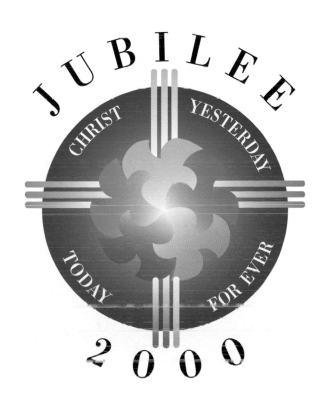

Bishop George J. Lucas
December 14, 1999 to the present

O n June 12, 1949, Mary Catherine Kelly Lucas and her husband George J. Lucas welcomed the birth of their first child. They named the baby boy after his father. Over the next few years three other children joined the family. Thus, the future bishop of Springfield became a big brother to one sister and two brothers—Catherine, James, and John.

George Jr. grew up in the Catholic Church of the 1950s. The Latin Mass and other rituals seemed timeless and immutable. Both parents were active in the local parish, St. Dominic Savio, in Affton, Missouri, and the children attended the parochial school. At home the family often prayed the rosary together and engaged in other devotions. In this atmosphere the vocation of priest began to grow. The youthful Lucas knew he wanted to be a priest and in 1963 he enrolled in a preparatory seminary in St. Louis, the year after Vatican II began. By the time of his graduation from St. Louis Preparatory Seminary-South in 1967, implementation of the council mandates had begun. During the unstable period after Vatican II many of his classmates discerned that they did not, after all, have a priestly vocation. But Lucas persevered. He completed his theological studies and on May 24, 1975, Cardinal John Joseph Carberry ordained Lucas to the priesthood.

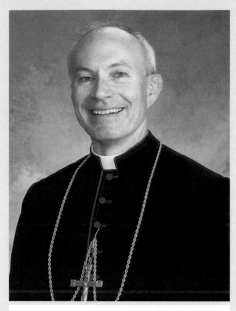

Bishop Lucas, 1999

Over the next twenty-four years, Lucas acquired a wealth of pastoral and administrative experience. First he served as associate pastor at two parishes in the Archdiocese of St. Louis. While continuing as an associate at various places throughout the 1980s, the young priest joined the faculty of St. Louis Preparatory Seminary, North. He taught history and religion and worked as vice-principal and dean. At first, Lucas was less than enthusiastic about teaching, but some years later remarked, "I found it a great opportunity for learning for myself as well as the students."

During these years at "Prep North," Lucas also earned, in 1986, a master's degree in history from St. Louis University. Showing a gift for organization and working with people, Archbishop John May named Lucas chancellor of the archdiocese in 1990. After a short stint as vicar general under Archbishop Justin Rigali in 1994-1995, Lucas assumed duties as rector of Kenrick-Glennon Seminary. Like the previous bishops of Springfield in Illinois, diocesan administration turned out to be a kind of school for becoming a bishop. Nor should the friendship and mentoring of the two archbishops be underestimated. "I learned a great deal," Lucas stated, "about service to the diocesan and universal church from both men." Lucas became an especially good friend of May and had the privilege of living with him as the archbishop was dying of brain cancer.

No one was more surprised than George Lucas himself to hear from Pope John Paul II that he was to become the next bishop of Springfield in Illinois. On October 19, 1999, the Vatican announced both the retirement of Bishop Daniel L. Ryan and the appointment of Lucas as the next bishop. Sometimes there is a delay

Bishop Lucas' installation ceremony, Cathedral of the Immaculate Conception, Springfield, 1999.

of several months between the retirement or the death of a bishop and the naming of the successor. Thus, the transition was swift and smooth. Father Virgil Mank, dean of the Alton Deanery, served as administrator of the diocese during the eight-week interim.

Lucas is the only Bishop of Springfield in Illinois to have been ordained a bishop in the Cathedral of the Immaculate Conception. On December 14, 1999, about 800 priests of our diocese and the Archdiocese of St. Louis, civic officials, family members, and friends, packed the Cathedral for the ceremony. Archbishop Justin Rigali of St. Louis preached the homily. The consecrating bishops were Cardinal Francis George, Bishop Ryan, and Archbishop Gabriel Montalvo, the Apostolic Nuncio to the United States. Near the end of the solemn ceremony Cardinal George lightened the mood when he told Lucas that in signing the various Latin documents before the installation, the new bishop had transferred his loyalty from the St. Louis Cardinals to the Chicago Cubs.

Bishop Lucas greets Catholics attending the Jubilee 2000 celebration at Litchfield, 2000.

During the Octave of Welcome, the eight days following the ordination, Lucas traveled to each deanery to celebrate a Mass and begin to meet the pastors and people of that area. He settled into his office at the Catholic Pastoral Center and plunged into the business of leading a diocese. During the first two years, after consultation with the Presbyteral Council, Lucas authorized the revival of a pastoral planning initiative begun in the mid-1990s, revamped the ministry of the Office for Vocations by appointing three part-time vocation directors, and made various changes in the assignment of priest personnel. The bishop has already confirmed scores of persons and is still completing visitations to every parish and Catholic institution of the diocese. Lucas also approved the establishment of the permanent diaconate in the diocese.

From the onset, Lucas set a tone of mutuality and collaboration. This approach was foreshadowed in a homily he gave at Solemn Evening Prayer the night before the ordination. Lucas described a statue of Mary that he particularly liked, one in which the Blessed Mother held the child Jesus out in front of her. Lucas stated:

> When I look at that statue I often think that she is offering to share Jesus with us, with me. But sometimes, it looks to me like she is accepting Jesus herself, welcoming him into HER life. I want to share Jesus with you. In my preaching, in celebrating the liturgy, in our conversations, in our work as part of the universal Church, in enjoying each other's company, I want nothing to keep you from seeing Jesus, from getting to know him more deeply in the Church. That is not all—I expect something in return. I expect you to share Jesus with me. By your prayer, your worship, your challenging me to keep my word, your patience, your forgiveness, I look forward to seeing Jesus more and more clearly.

Catholics were delighted that one of the ways Lucas shared Jesus is through a column in every issue of The *Catholic Times*. The first dealt with the Eucharist, a theme to which the bishop often returns.

As this book goes to press, Lucas has completed almost two and one-half years in office. The highlights of that short period include the celebration of Jubilee 2000, taking steps to assure the long-term financial stability of the diocese, and a greater emphasis on developing vocations to the priesthood in our diocese. Lucas approaches the ministry of leadership with energy and humility. Although conscious of his role as the principal teacher of the diocese, Lucas just as readily assumes the posture of a disciple at the feet of Jesus, someone ready to learn. In the bishop's preaching, writing, and public speaking he often refers to his desire to learn more about the matter at hand.

Throughout the history of the Diocese of Springfield in Illinois, each of our eight bishops possessed characteristics and skills that were uniquely suited to the times. In the case of George J. Lucas the story is still unfolding.

Harvest of Thanks, Springtime of Hope

Throughout our 150 years as a diocese, the generosity of the laity, religious, and priests made possible the continuation of the Catholic faith in central Illinois. At great personal sacrifice Catholics contributed time, talent, and treasure to build churches, schools, hospitals, orphanages, homes for the elderly, and offer a variety of services to the poor. But temporal needs are never met on a once-and-for-all basis. Every generation encounters new challenges and so in January 2002, Bishop Lucas and the Office for Stewardship and Development launched a capital campaign.

"Harvest of Thanks—Springtime of Hope" endeavored to raise 24 million dollars and was carried out as part of the preparation for the diocesan 150th anniversary, Jubilee 2003. The bishop stressed the importance of "assuring the long term viability of the important Catholic apostolates in our diocese." Of the 24 million, 14 million dollars would be set aside in endowments. Some of the income generated would promote Catholic education through tuition assistance, continuing education for Catholic school educators, and the formation of catechists for the parish schools of religion (PSR). Other beneficiaries of the endowment would include seminarians, retired and infirm priests, and Catholic Charities. Part of the endowment would create the Bishop's Stewardship Fund to respond to emergency relief during times of natural or civic disaster.

The remainder of the 24 million dollars would be used to cover four capital projects. For some years the Cathedral of the Immaculate Conception has been in need of restoration and repair. The scope of the project is beyond the means of the parish family. And, after all, the cathedral is the locus of the ceremonial life of the diocese. Two Catholic high schools will receive matching funds for new construction. Marquette Catholic High School (Alton) and St. Anthony High School (Effingham) will be able to serve even more families through expansion projects. "The Harvest of Thanks—Springtime of Hope" contribution will help these two schools continue to serve the Catholic community well into the twenty-first century. Other Catholic high schools in the diocese will be eligible for other kinds of assistance. Finally, in order to assist parishes, 10 percent of the funds generated in each parish will be returned to that community. Any parish that exceeds its goal will receive 50 percent of the overage.

Cultivating Priestly Vocations

As early as 1955, Bishop William A. O'Connor lamented the shortage of priests. Throughout the 1950s about six men each year enrolled at the Latin School, but only one or two—or even none—would remain by the time of ordination. In the latter half of O'Connor's episcopate, the number of ordinations dipped to zero three times between 1962 and 1975. The dearth of vocations at that time is directly related to the present challenge of offering Sunday Mass in every parish

Generous lay women and men have assumed many of the duties once performed by priests and religious sisters. Thanks to the Lay Ministry Formation Program, over 200 lay persons have acquired specialized training to help them minister. And, Bishop Lucas has accepted the Presbyteral Council's recommendation to establish the permanent diaconate in the diocese. Nonetheless, if weekly Eucharist is to continue in all areas of the diocese more priests will be needed.

It is common for Lucas during his visits to parishes to invite young men to consider a vocation to the priesthood. He has encouraged all the faithful to pray for more vocations. In Lent 2002, for example, he set aside a day on which he called upon all Catholics to pray and fast voluntarily for more vocations to priesthood and religious life from among the faithful of the diocese.

Father Michael Kuse presents the vocation basket to parishioners at Immaculate Conception, Quincy.

Some parishes, in the late 1990s, made a very deliberate effort to pray for vocations. At Immaculate Conception in Quincy parish families take turns on a weekly basis. At one of the Sunday liturgies a family receives a basket filled with sacramentals, including a rosary, a crucifix, and a statue of Mary. A vocation prayer card and some articles on vocations are also in the basket. By accepting the basket the family agrees to pray everyday that week for vocations. The next week the family hands on the basket to another family during the Mass. "Doing it at Mass," said the pastor, Father Michael Kuse (who was diocesan director of vocations from 1988 to 2000), is a good way to involve the whole parish." St. Cecilia in Glen Carbon and St. Anthony in Effingham have similar programs, but instead of a basket use a chalice. The Knights of Columbus throughout the diocese also promote vocations to the priesthood. They sponsor a monthly "Family Hour of Prayer" as well as other activities designed to foster vocations.

When Lucas arrived in the diocese, the Presbyteral Council was studying more effective means to generate priestly vocations. In the summer after his episcopal ordination, the bishop reorganized the Office for Vocations. Instead of one priest director, he appointed three priests who assumed duties on a part-time basis.

Seminarians gather with Bishop Lucas at Villa Maria for their annual holiday gathering, 2000.

In the fall of 2001 there were sixteen seminarians for the diocesan priesthood. Like most of their predecessors they study at either Kenrick-Glennon (St. Louis) or St. Mary of the Lake (Mundelein). Lucas had served as rector at Kenrick, and now sits on the advisory board of St. Mary of the Lake. Twice a year he gathers with the seminarians at Villa Maria, the former diocesan seminary, where the group socializes with one another and reflects on the priestly vocation.

The last ordinations of priests for the Diocese of Springfield in Illinois took place in 1999. About two years later Lucas ordained three men to the transitional deaconate and in May 2002 the bishop ordained two individuals to the priesthood for service to our diocese.

Support for Priests

Bishop Lucas' service as seminary rector gave him the zeal for promoting priestly vocations as well as the enthusiasm to give support to men after ordination. He serves on the Priestly Life and Ministry Committee of the United States Conference of Catholic Bishops. Lucas also takes a keen interest in the lives of our diocesan priests. On a personal level, the bishop makes himself available to meet with any priest upon request. In addition, he works closely with the Presbyteral Council and has reconstituted the Commission for Ministry to Priests. The commission's purpose is to discern and implement new and practical ways to offer support, affirmation, and on-going formation opportunities to their brother priests.

The bishop accepted the recommendation of the Presbyteral Council that each priest have a personal interview with the bishop every five years to evaluate the priest's life and ministry. Lucas also accepted the council's recommendation that priests be appointed for indefinite terms, instead of for six year periods, but added that the Priests' Personnel Board would be proactive in continually inviting priests to discern where their talents may best serve the church.

The on-going spiritual formation of priests is an obvious priority to the bishop. Lucas has encouraged priests to take part in various opportunities for spiritual renewal and growth, and invited them to receive the sacrament of penance frequently. Seldom can all of the diocesan clergy meet together, but each year before the Chrism Mass,

priests have the opportunity to spend some quiet spend time together in the presence of the Blessed Sacrament. Afterward they share a meal that precedes the Eucharistic liturgy.

Aging clergy tend to remain in active ministry long after their secular counterparts have retired. In 1998 the average age of priests in the Diocese of Springfield in Illinois was about fifty-four. Diocesan officials estimate that by 2007 over 35 percent of the priests active in 1998 could be in retirement. Lucas has also devoted himself to the pastoral care of infirm and retired priests. He has, therefore joined with two other bishops in Illinois to provide long-term nursing care for these men and has asked that every priest enroll in the social security program. The diocese is also providing annual increases in priests' pension to reflect cost-of-living adjustments.

Pastoral Planning

Bishop Lucas pledged to continue the important work of pastoral planning in the diocese which Bishop Daniel L. Ryan had begun. Just three months after his installation, in February and March of 2000, Lucas held four gatherings of priests to review the 1995 Parish Pastoral Plan. He accepted the Presbyteral Council's recommendation that each parish conduct a formal review of its mission and vitality every five years, a review which certainly will assist in future parish planning.

Together with the Presbyteral Council and the Priests' Personnel Board, he worked to provide the best possible pastoral care in parishes with a diminishing number of priests and other resources. Sadly, some parishes have been closed and other consolidated. As this history is being published, parish planning continues and it appears several other parishes will be restructured. Essential to this restructuring is exact determination of each parish's boundaries—an arduous task begun by his predecessor and completed by Lucas.

While parish pastoral planning sometimes involves consolidations of parishes, the diocese has also experienced parish growth and life. Since he became diocesan bishop, Lucas has dedicated three new churches: St. Joseph the Worker (Chatham), St. Elizabeth (Granite City), and Immaculate Conception (Shelbyville). He has also rededicated two churches which completed major renovations: St. Patrick (Decatur) and Immaculate Conception (Mattoon). A number of parishes are contemplating—or have already begun—significant building projects.

Our bishop has also engaged a professional planning group to assist the diocese in assessing its various pastoral needs and in discerning ways to meet them. He has invited a number of priests, religious, and lay persons from across the diocese to collaborate in that process. He envisions that this "think tank" will develop a "broad pastoral plan" and will lead to the eventual establishment of a viable diocesan pastoral council. The diocesan pastoral council's role will be to continue pastoral planning by discerning pastoral needs, studying them, and then making practical recommendations to meet those needs.

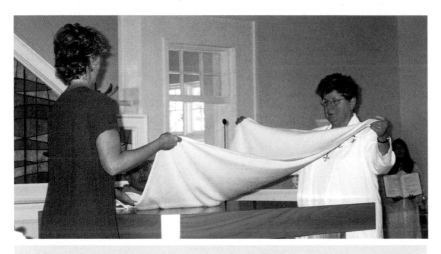

Kathy Dyher, parish secretary (left) and Sister Marie Trutter, O.P., parish life coordinator, prepare the new altar during the dedication of the new Immaculate Conception Church, Shelbyville, 2000.

Jubilee 2003

Our diocese marks its founding on July 29, 1853, when the Diocese of Quincy was established. The year 2002 is, thus, the diocese's 150th year. Bishop Lucas has designated 2003 as a year of thanksgiving and jubilee, and has announced several happenings to mark the diocesan sesquicentennial. Jubilee 2003 will begin and end on the Solemnity of the Immaculate Conception—December 9, 2002 through December 8, 2003. Events will take place in each parish and throughout the diocese.

Several diocesan celebrations are planned. The Bishop will celebrate Mass in Quincy and Alton, where the see had previously been located. There will also be special gatherings for priests, religious women and men, ecumenical leaders, and Catholics whose contribution to diocesan life merits recognition. Catholics of our diocese will also have the opportunity to go on pilgrimages to the Shrine of the Basilica of the Immaculate Conception, Washington, D.C., and to St. Peter's Basilica, Rome.

Central to the celebration of Jubilee 2003 will be the "Diocesan Jubilee Day" at the Illinois State Fairgrounds in Springfield, to be celebrated June 28, 2003. Activities for children, teens, and adults will begin in mid-morning and continue throughout the day. Spiritual renewal is an important part of Jubilee 2003 so opportunities for visits to the Blessed Sacrament and confessions will be available that day. The highpoint of the day will be concelebrated Mass with Lucas, scheduled in the late afternoon to which church and civil dignitaries will be invited.

Jubilee 2003

Catholic Diocese of Springfield in Illinois • 150 Years

Conclusion

In his apostolic letter, *Novo millennio ineunte*, Pope John Paul II invites the Church, moving into the third millennium, to *duc in altum*—"to put out into the deep." Jesus used these words when he invited Peter and the others to follow him (Lk. 5:4). But this invitation, the Holy Father remindes us, is also Christ's invitation to us. All Catholics are called to a deeper life of faith and a deeper level of Christian commitment. He concludes his letter with this reflection:

> *Duc in altum!* Let us go forward in hope! A new millennium is opening before the Church like a vast ocean upon which we shall venture, relying on the help of Christ. The Son of God, who became incarnate two thousand years ago out of love for humanity, is at work even today: we need discerning eyes to see this and, above all, a generous heart to become the instruments of his work. ... The Risen Jesus accompanies us on our way and enables us to recognize him, as the disciples of Emmaus did, "in the breaking of the bread" (Lk. 24:35). May he find us watchful, ready to recognize his face and run to our brothers and sisters with the good news: "We have seen the Lord!" (Jn. 20:25).

The Diocese of Springfield in Illinois welcomes the encouraging message of Pope John Paul II. As we celebrate 150 years of God's favor to us, we make a deeper commitment to witness the Good News of Jesus in the twenty-eight counties of south central Illinois. We thank God for the blessings of the past and with our new shepherd, Bishop George J. Lucas, our "Jubilee 2000 bishop," we move ahead with confidence, aware of God's grace and mercy.

THE 28 COUNTIES AND SEVEN DEANERIE

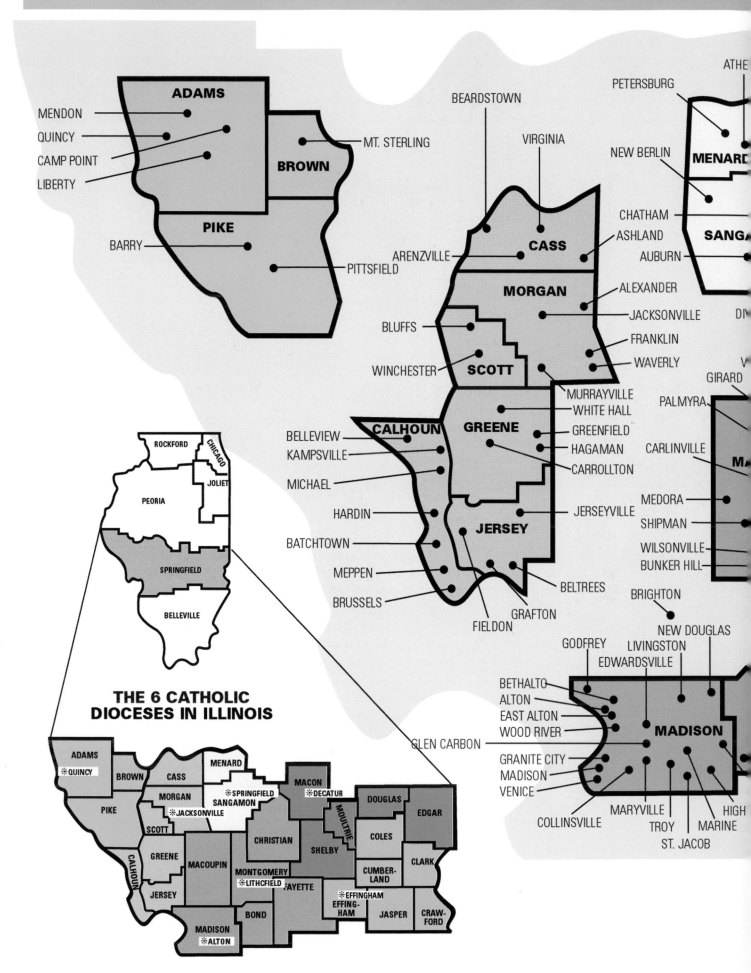

ADAMS
- MENDON
- QUINCY
- CAMP POINT
- LIBERTY

BROWN
- MT. STERLING

PIKE
- BARRY
- PITTSFIELD

BEARDSTOWN
VIRGINIA

CASS
- ARENZVILLE

MORGAN
- BLUFFS
- ASHLAND
- AUBURN
- ALEXANDER
- JACKSONVILLE
- FRANKLIN
- WAVERLY

SCOTT
- WINCHESTER

CALHOUN
- BELLEVIEW
- KAMPSVILLE
- MICHAEL
- HARDIN
- BATCHTOWN
- MEPPEN
- BRUSSELS

GREENE
- MURRAYVILLE
- WHITE HALL
- GREENFIELD
- HAGAMAN
- CARROLLTON

JERSEY
- JERSEYVILLE
- BELTREES
- GRAFTON
- FIELDON

ATHE
PETERSBURG
NEW BERLIN

MENARD

CHATHAM

SANGA

GIRARD
PALMYRA
CARLINVILLE

M
- MEDORA
- SHIPMAN
- WILSONVILLE
- BUNKER HILL

BRIGHTON
NEW DOUGLAS
GODFREY
LIVINGSTON
EDWARDSVILLE
BETHALTO
ALTON
EAST ALTON
WOOD RIVER
GLEN CARBON
GRANITE CITY
MADISON
VENICE

MADISON
- COLLINSVILLE
- MARYVILLE
- TROY
- ST. JACOB
- MARINE
- HIGH

THE 6 CATHOLIC DIOCESES IN ILLINOIS

ROCKFORD
CHICAGO
JOLIET
PEORIA
SPRINGFIELD
BELLEVILLE

ADAMS ※QUINCY
BROWN
CASS
MENARD
MACON ※DECATUR
MORGAN
SANGAMON ※SPRINGFIELD ※JACKSONVILLE
DOUGLAS
EDGAR
PIKE
SCOTT
MOULTRIE
COLES
GREENE
CHRISTIAN
SHELBY
CLARK
CALHOUN
MACOUPIN
MONTGOMERY ※LITHCFIELD
FAYETTE
CUMBERLAND
JERSEY
EFFINGHAM ※EFFINGHAM
JASPER
CRAWFORD
BOND
MADISON ※ALTON

124

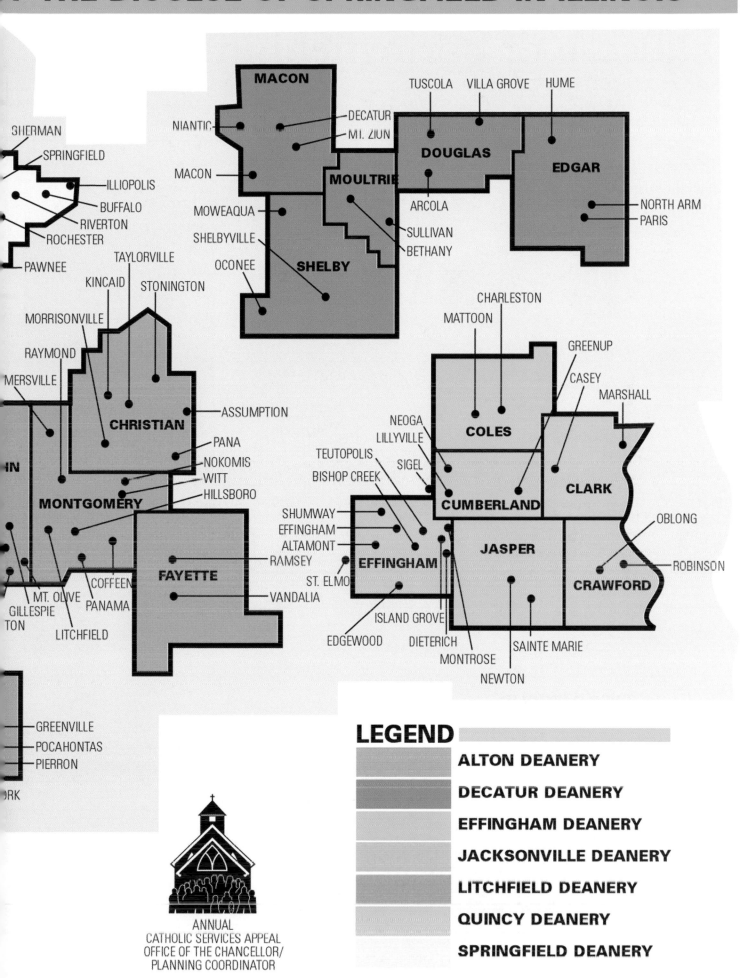

LEGEND

ALTON DEANERY

DECATUR DEANERY

EFFINGHAM DEANERY

JACKSONVILLE DEANERY

LITCHFIELD DEANERY

QUINCY DEANERY

SPRINGFIELD DEANERY

ANNUAL
CATHOLIC SERVICES APPEAL
OFFICE OF THE CHANCELLOR/
PLANNING COORDINATOR

A Timeline of the History of the Diocese of Springfield in Illinois

Current photographs of each parish church appear under the year traditionally given as the founding. What constitutes a founding is unclear. Some use the erection of the earliest church building while others use diocesan recognition or some other criteria. The dates here are based on available, but fragmentary, records. Local tradition may ascribe a different year.

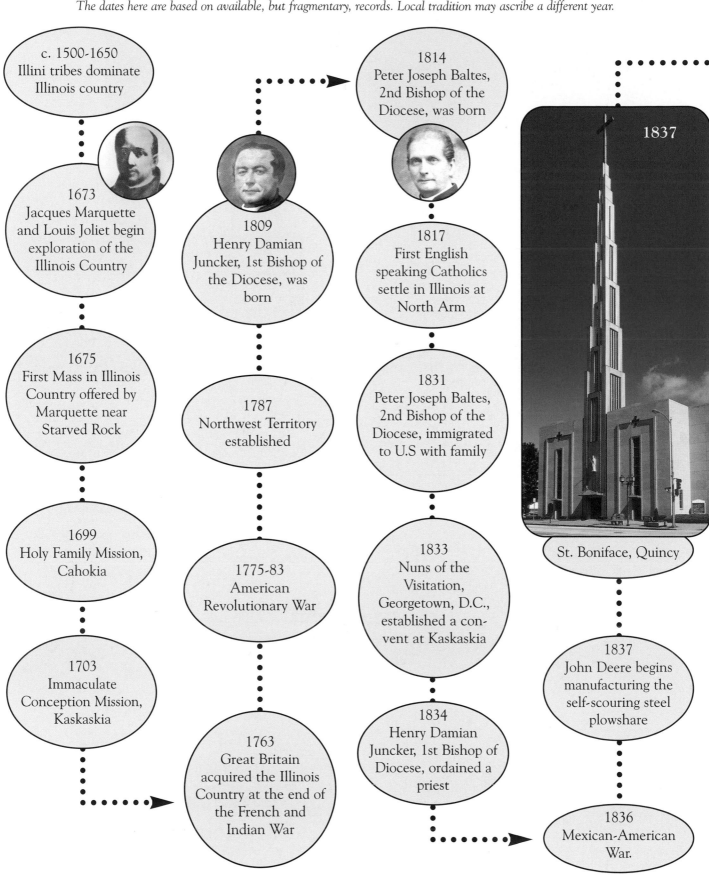

c. 1500-1650
Illini tribes dominate Illinois country

1673
Jacques Marquette and Louis Joliet begin exploration of the Illinois Country

1675
First Mass in Illinois Country offered by Marquette near Starved Rock

1699
Holy Family Mission, Cahokia

1703
Immaculate Conception Mission, Kaskaskia

1809
Henry Damian Juncker, 1st Bishop of the Diocese, was born

1787
Northwest Territory established

1775-83
American Revolutionary War

1763
Great Britain acquired the Illinois Country at the end of the French and Indian War

1814
Peter Joseph Baltes, 2nd Bishop of the Diocese, was born

1817
First English speaking Catholics settle in Illinois at North Arm

1831
Peter Joseph Baltes, 2nd Bishop of the Diocese, immigrated to U.S with family

1833
Nuns of the Visitation, Georgetown, D.C., established a convent at Kaskaskia

1834
Henry Damian Juncker, 1st Bishop of Diocese, ordained a priest

1836
Mexican-American War.

1837

St. Boniface, Quincy

1837
John Deere begins manufacturing the self-scouring steel plowshare

St. Mary, Ste. Marie

1837

1839

St. Francis of Assisi,
Teutopolis

1840
National Road reaches
Vandalia

St. Luke, Virginia

1840

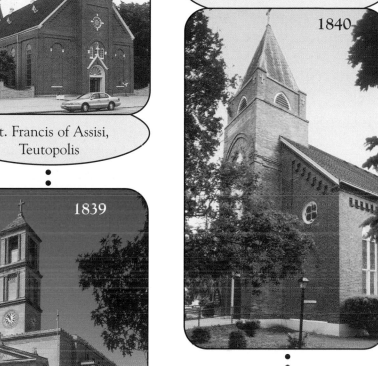

St. Mary, Alton

1837

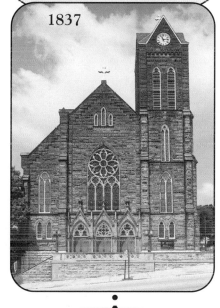

St. Alexius, Beardstown

1838

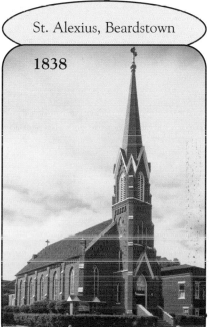

1839

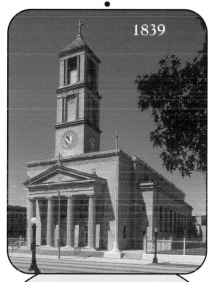

Cathedral of the
Immaculate Conception,
Springfield (Originally
called St. Mary)

1839

St. Peter, Quincy

St. Aloysius, North Arm

1840

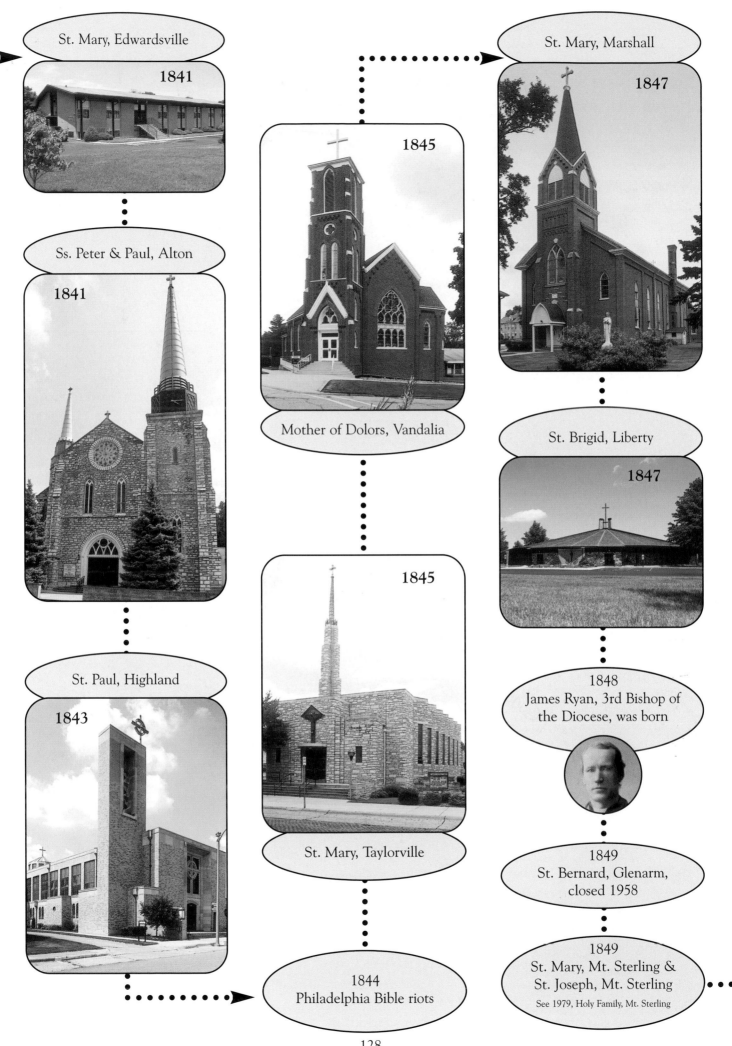

St. Mary, Edwardsville

1841

Ss. Peter & Paul, Alton

1841

St. Paul, Highland

1843

1845

Mother of Dolors, Vandalia

1845

St. Mary, Taylorville

1844
Philadelphia Bible riots

St. Mary, Marshall

1847

St. Brigid, Liberty

1847

1848
James Ryan, 3rd Bishop of
the Diocese, was born

1849
St. Bernard, Glenarm,
closed 1958

1849
St. Mary, Mt. Sterling &
St. Joseph, Mt. Sterling
See 1979, Holy Family, Mt. Sterling

1852

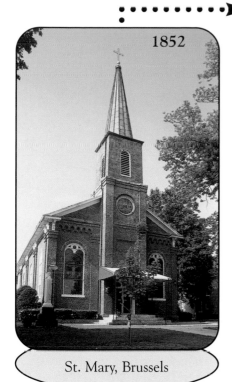

St. Mary, Brussels

1852
First Plenary Council
of Baltimore
Ancient Order of Hibernians
establish a chapter in
Springfield, the first in
the Diocese

1851

Our Saviour, Jacksonville

1850-56
Illinois Central Railroad
construction

Immaculate Conception,
Dieterich

1852

1853
*Diocese of Quincy erected,
July 29*

1853
Peter Joseph Baltes, 2nd
Bishop of the Diocese,
ordained a priest

1853
St. John, Blackjack,
closed 1992

St. Mary, Pittsfield

1853

German
Central Verein organized

1855
James Ryan, 3rd Bishop of the
Diocese, immigrated to the
U.S. with parents

1854

St. Mary, Bunker Hill

St. Patrick, Decatur

1856
Sisters of Charity of St. Vincent de Paul of Emmitsburg, Maryland, arrive in Alton

Immaculate Conception, Mattoon

1856

Ss. Peter & Paul, Collinsville

1856

St. Elizabeth, Marine

1856

1857

St. Mary, Fieldon

1857

Assumption of the Blessed Virgin Mary, Assumption

1857

St. Raymond, Raymond

1857
See transferred to Alton, January 9
Henry Damien Juncker, 1st Bishop of the Diocese, consecrated a Bishop
Ursuline Academy of St. Joseph, Springfield
St. Isidore, Farmersville, closed 1940s

1858
Pope Pius IX proclaims dogma of the Immaculate Conception of the Blessed Virgin Mary

1858
Lincoln-Douglas debates

1858
Ss. Peter & Paul, Springfield, closed 2002

St. Anthony, Quincy

1858

St. Mary Help of Christians, Effingham (Green Creek)

1858

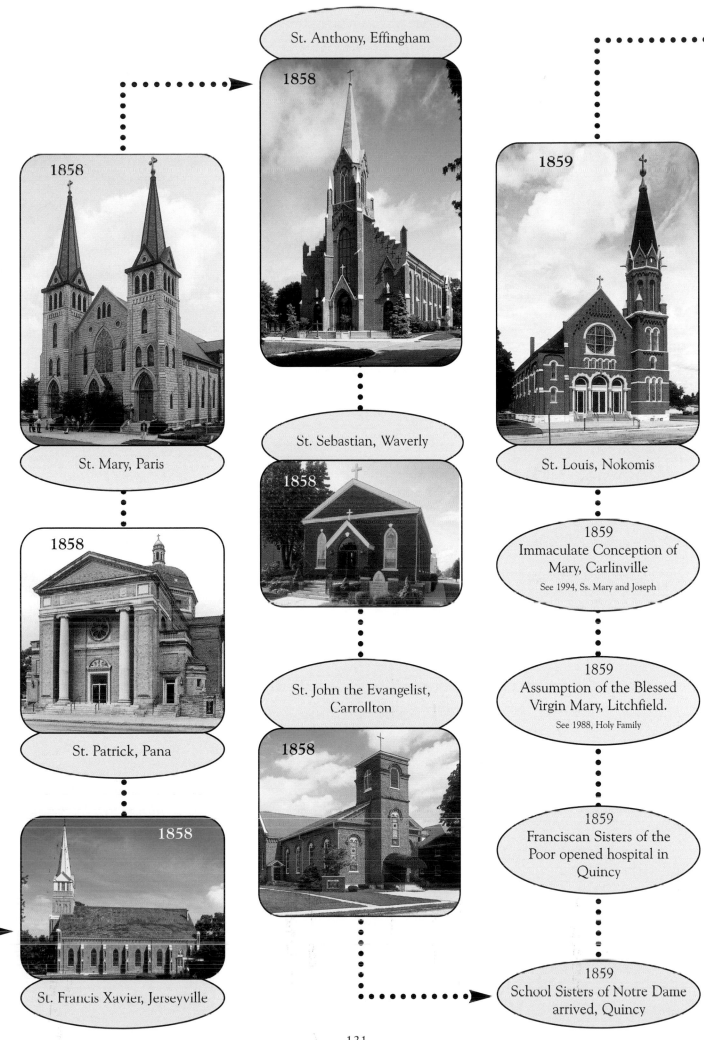

St. Anthony, Effingham

1858

1858

St. Mary, Paris

1858

St. Patrick, Pana

1858

St. Francis Xavier, Jerseyville

St. Sebastian, Waverly

1858

St. John the Evangelist, Carrollton

1858

1859

St. Louis, Nokomis

1859
Immaculate Conception of Mary, Carlinville
See 1994, Ss. Mary and Joseph

1859
Assumption of the Blessed Virgin Mary, Litchfield.
See 1988, Holy Family

1859
Franciscan Sisters of the Poor opened hospital in Quincy

1859
School Sisters of Notre Dame arrived, Quincy

St. Fidelis, Arenzville

1859

All Saints, White Hall

1859

1860
Abraham Lincoln elected
president of the U.S.

1860
Holy Cross Brothers of
Notre Dame came to Alton.

1860
St. Francis Solanus College
(Quincy University) Quincy

1860

Sacred Heart of Mary,
New Berlin

1860

St. Mark, Winchester

St. Francis Solanus, Quincy

1860

St. Michael, Greenfield

1860

St. Thomas, Camp Point

1860

1861-65
The Civil War

1864

St. Anne, Edgewood

1863
St. Patrick Trowbridge,
closed 1974

1862

Immaculate Conception,
Shelbyville

1862
St. Joseph Seminary,
Teutopolis

St. Joseph, Bloomfield,
closed 1939

St. Isidore, Bethany

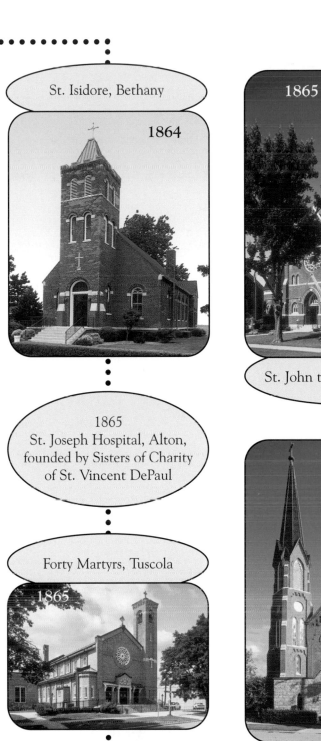

1864

1865
St. Joseph Hospital, Alton,
founded by Sisters of Charity
of St. Vincent DePaul

Forty Martyrs, Tuscola

1865

St. Denis, Shipman

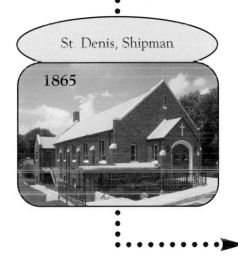

1865

1865

St. John the Baptist, Arcola

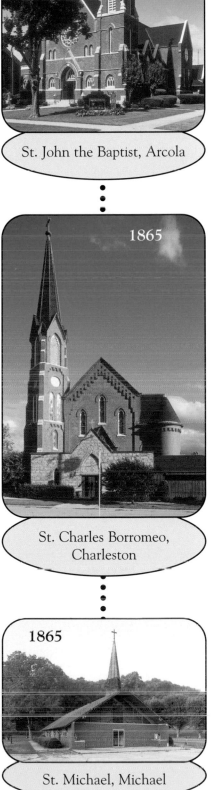

1865

St. Charles Borromeo,
Charleston

1865

St. Michael, Michael

St. Aloysius, Bishop Creek

1866

1866
St. Catherine, Virden,
Closed 1977

Visitation of the Blessed
Virgin Mary, Illiopolis

1866

1867
Notre Dame Academy
(Quincy-Notre Dame High
School.), Quincy

1867
St. Joseph, Carlinville

See 1994, Holy Family

1867

St. Joseph, Quincy

1867

St. Agnes, Hillsboro

1867

St. Joseph, Meppen

St. James, Riverton

1867

St. Michael the Archangel,
Sigel

1867

St. Mary, Quincy

1867

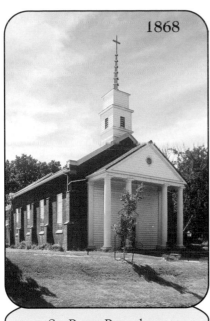

1868

St. Peter, Petersburg

1868
Henry Damian Juncker, 1st Bishop of the Diocese, died

St. Teresa Academy (St. Teresa High School), Decatur

St. Basil, Chandlerville, closed 1993

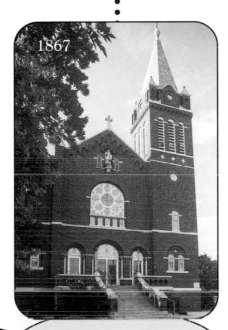

1867

St. Michael the Archangel, Staunton

St. Lawrence, Greenville

1868

St. Alphonsus, Brighton

1868

1869

St. Boniface, Edwardsville

1870

St. Maurice, Morrisonville

1870

St. Gertrude, Grantfork

1870

St. Jerome, Troy

1870
Peter Joseph Baltes, 2nd Bishop of the Diocese, consecrated a Bishop

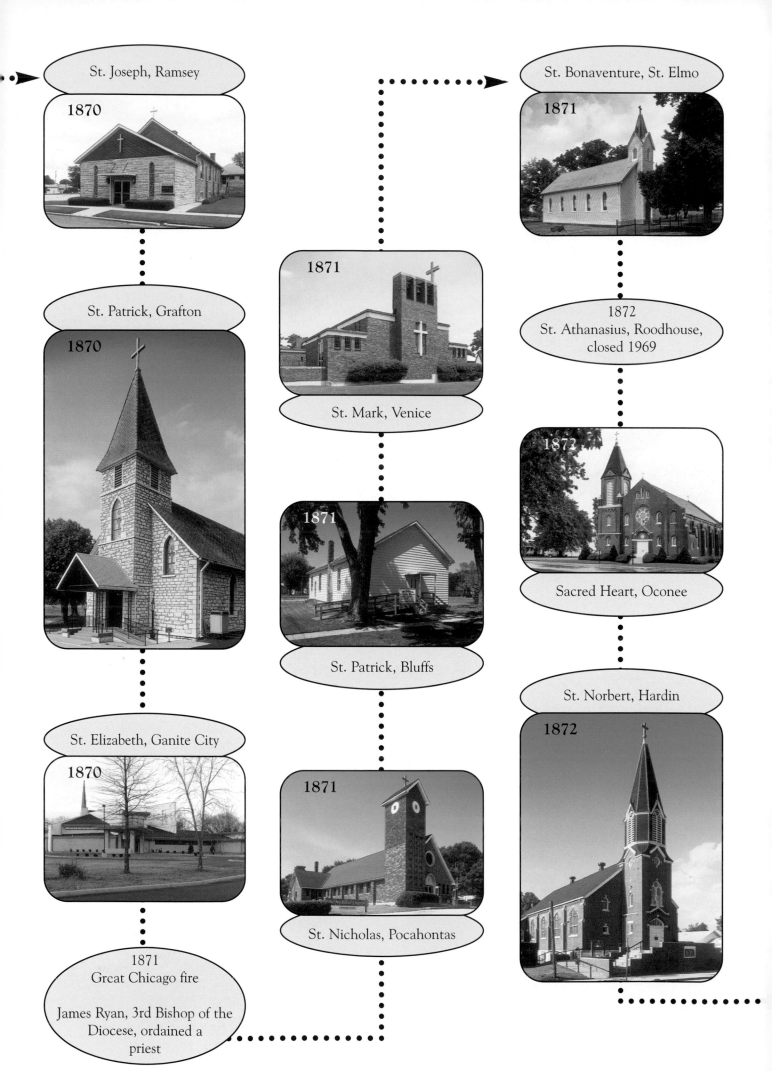

St. Joseph, Ramsey

1870

St. Patrick, Grafton

1870

St. Elizabeth, Ganite City

1870

1871
Great Chicago fire

James Ryan, 3rd Bishop of the Diocese, ordained a priest

1871

St. Mark, Venice

1871

St. Patrick, Bluffs

1871

St. Nicholas, Pocahontas

St. Bonaventure, St. Elmo

1871

1872
St. Athanasius, Roodhouse, closed 1969

1872

Sacred Heart, Oconee

St. Norbert, Hardin

1872

1873
Dominican Sisters
arrived, Jacksonville

Small Pox outbreak in
Alton

St. Thomas the Apostle,
Newton

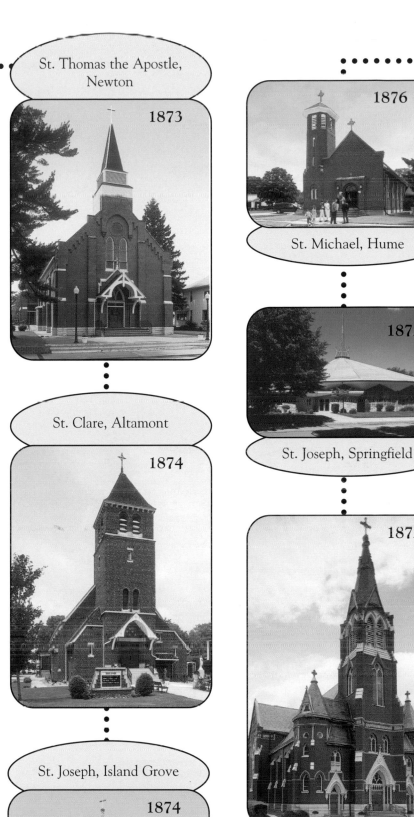

1873

1876

St. Michael, Hume

1872

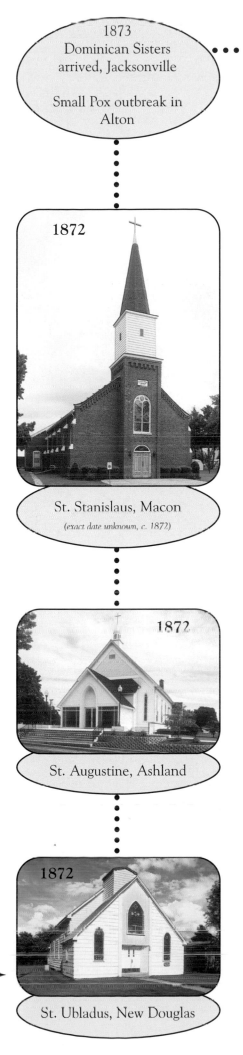

St. Stanislaus, Macon

(exact date unknown, c. 1872)

1872

St. Augustine, Ashland

1872

St. Ubladus, New Douglas

St. Clare, Altamont

1874

St. Joseph, Island Grove

1874

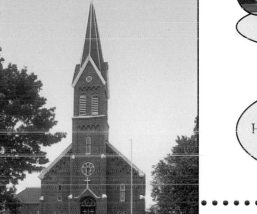

1875

St. Joseph, Springfield

1875

St. James, Decatur

1875
Hospital Sisters of St. Francis
arrived, Springfield

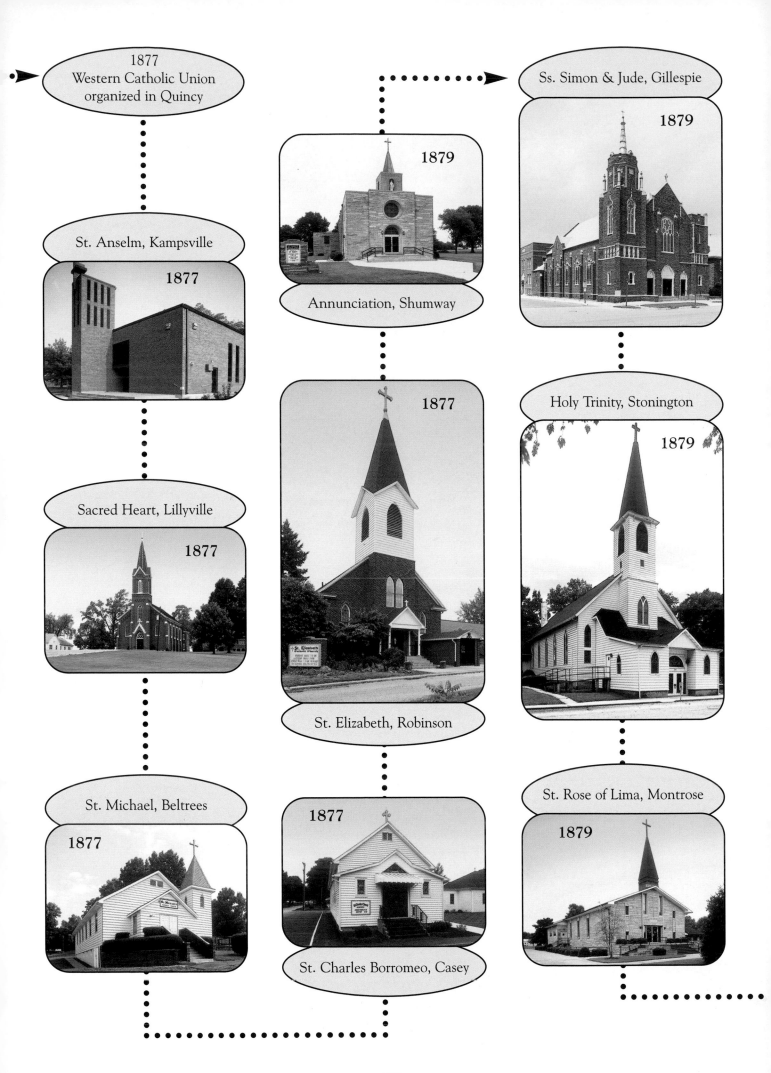

1877
Western Catholic Union
organized in Quincy

St. Anselm, Kampsville

1877

Sacred Heart, Lillyville

1877

St. Michael, Beltrees

1877

1879

Annunciation, Shumway

1877

St. Elizabeth, Robinson

1877

St. Charles Borromeo, Casey

Ss. Simon & Jude, Gillespie

1879

Holy Trinity, Stonington

1879

St. Rose of Lima, Montrose

1879

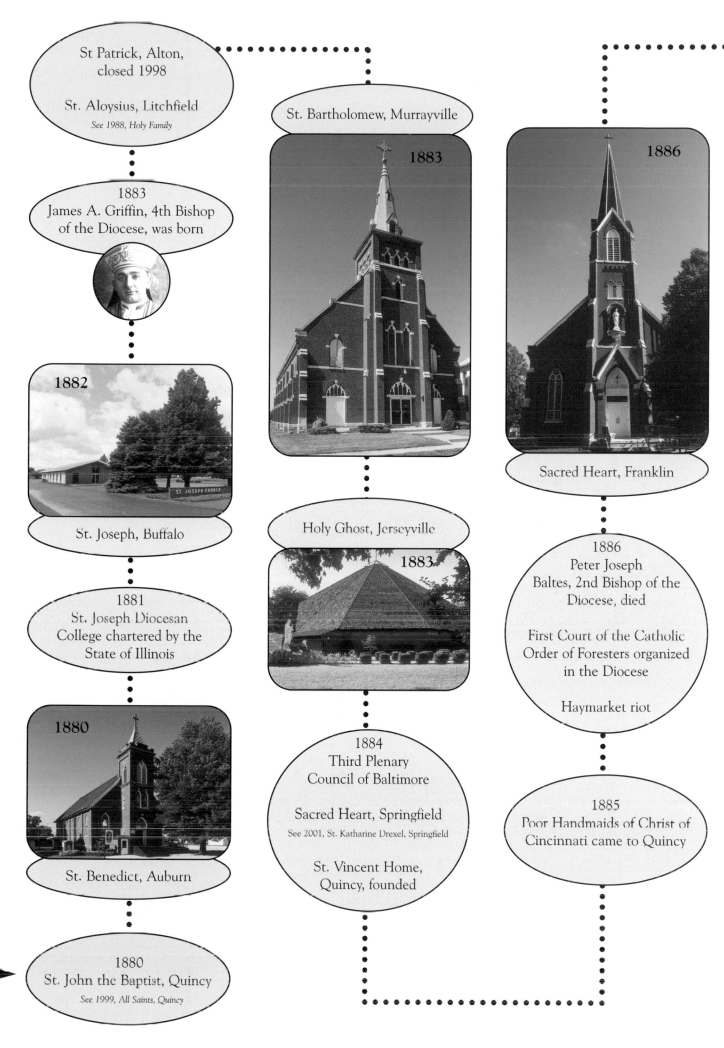

St Patrick, Alton, closed 1998

St. Aloysius, Litchfield
See 1988, Holy Family

1883
James A. Griffin, 4th Bishop of the Diocese, was born

1882

St. Joseph, Buffalo

1881
St. Joseph Diocesan College chartered by the State of Illinois

1880

St. Benedict, Auburn

1880
St. John the Baptist, Quincy
See 1999, All Saints, Quincy

St. Bartholomew, Murrayville

1883

Holy Ghost, Jerseyville

1883

1884
Third Plenary Council of Baltimore

Sacred Heart, Springfield
See 2001, St. Katharine Drexel, Springfield

St. Vincent Home, Quincy, founded

1886

Sacred Heart, Franklin

1886
Peter Joseph Baltes, 2nd Bishop of the Diocese, died

First Court of the Catholic Order of Foresters organized in the Diocese

Haymarket riot

1885
Poor Handmaids of Christ of Cincinnati came to Quincy

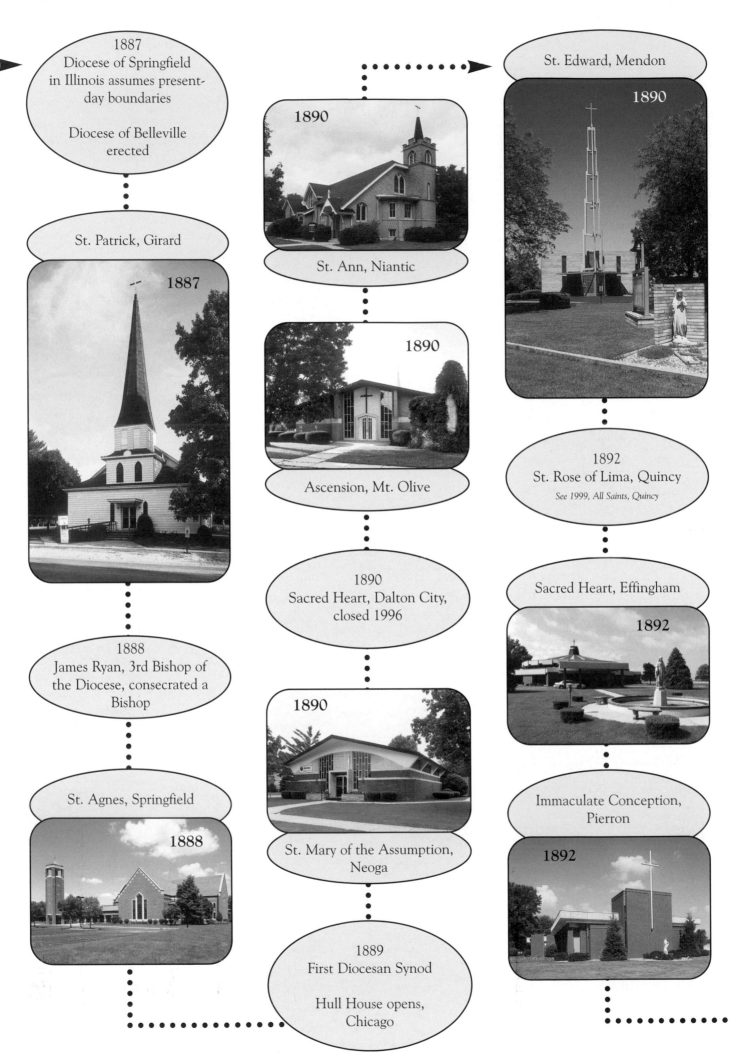

1887
Diocese of Springfield in Illinois assumes present-day boundaries

Diocese of Belleville erected

St. Patrick, Girard

1887

1888
James Ryan, 3rd Bishop of the Diocese, consecrated a Bishop

St. Agnes, Springfield

1888

1890
St. Ann, Niantic

1890
Ascension, Mt. Olive

1890
Sacred Heart, Dalton City, closed 1996

1890
St. Mary of the Assumption, Neoga

1889
First Diocesan Synod

Hull House opens, Chicago

St. Edward, Mendon

1890

1892
St. Rose of Lima, Quincy
See 1999, All Saints, Quincy

Sacred Heart, Effingham

1892

Immaculate Conception, Pierron

1892

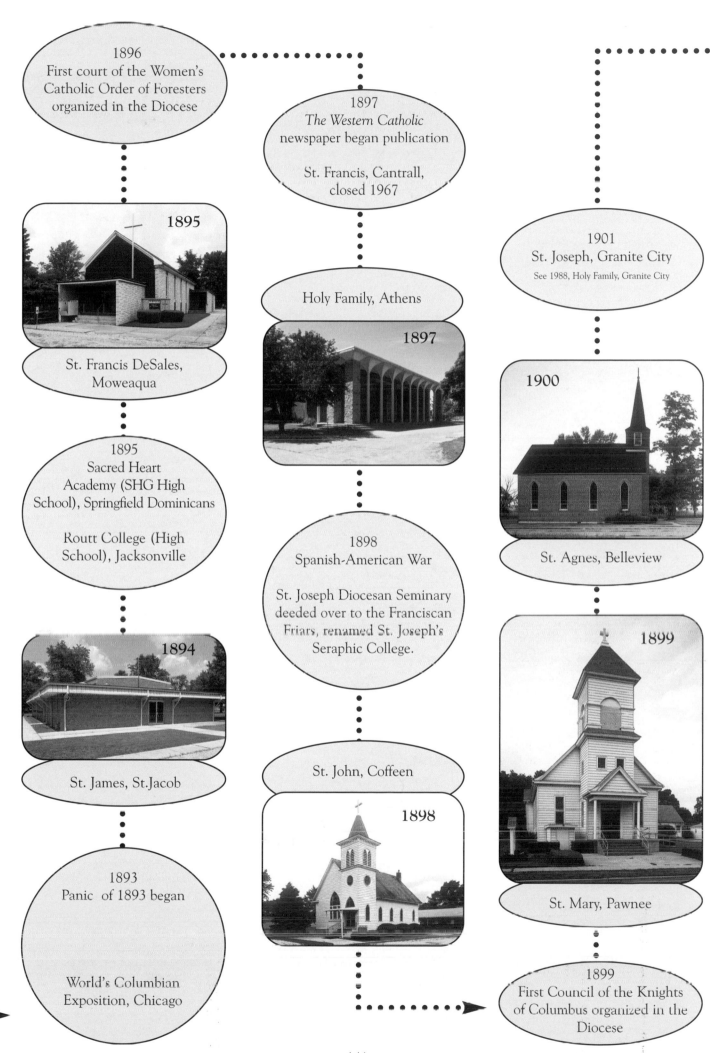

1896
First court of the Women's Catholic Order of Foresters organized in the Diocese

1897
The Western Catholic newspaper began publication

St. Francis, Cantrall, closed 1967

1901
St. Joseph, Granite City

See 1988, Holy Family, Granite City

1895
St. Francis DeSales, Moweaqua

Holy Family, Athens

1897

1900

St. Agnes, Belleview

1895
Sacred Heart Academy (SHG High School), Springfield Dominicans

Routt College (High School), Jacksonville

1898
Spanish-American War

St. Joseph Diocesan Seminary deeded over to the Franciscan Friars, renamed St. Joseph's Seraphic College.

1899

1894

St. James, St.Jacob

St. John, Coffeen

1898

St. Mary, Pawnee

1893
Panic of 1893 began

World's Columbian Exposition, Chicago

1899
First Council of the Knights of Columbus organized in the Diocese

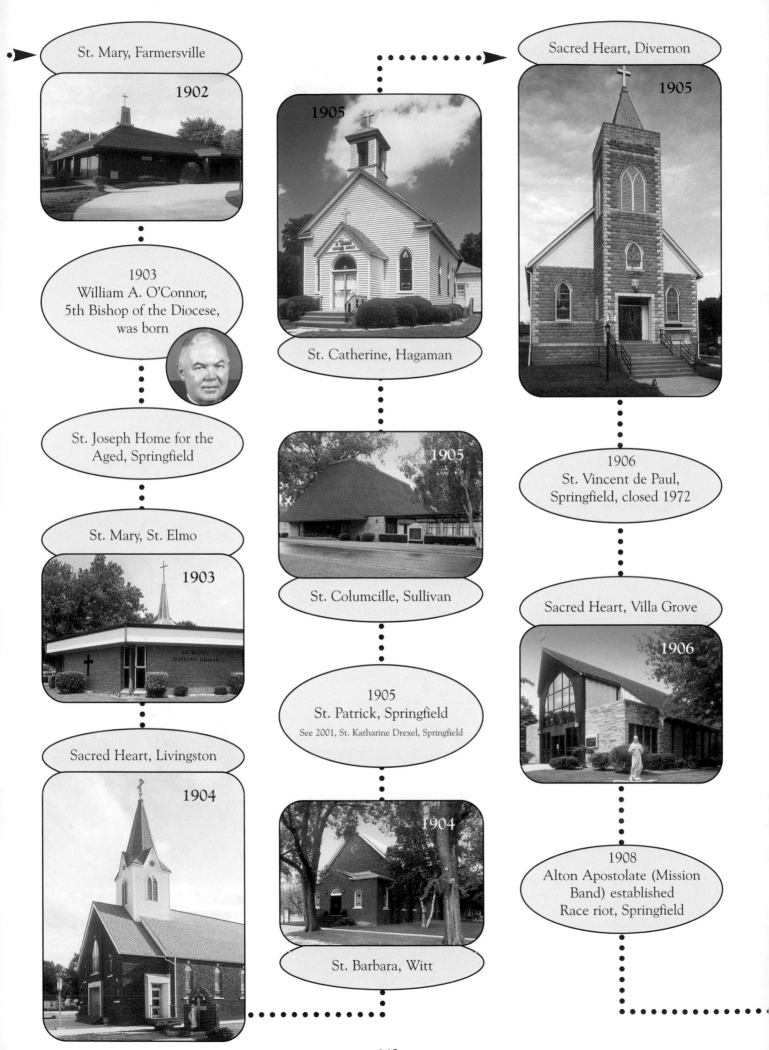

St. Mary, Farmersville

1902

1903
William A. O'Connor,
5th Bishop of the Diocese,
was born

St. Joseph Home for the
Aged, Springfield

St. Mary, St. Elmo

1903

Sacred Heart, Livingston

1904

1905

St. Catherine, Hagaman

1905

St. Columcille, Sullivan

1905
St. Patrick, Springfield
See 2001, St. Katharine Drexel, Springfield

1904

St. Barbara, Witt

Sacred Heart, Divernon

1905

1906
St. Vincent de Paul,
Springfield, closed 1972

Sacred Heart, Villa Grove

1906

1908
Alton Apostolate (Mission
Band) established
Race riot, Springfield

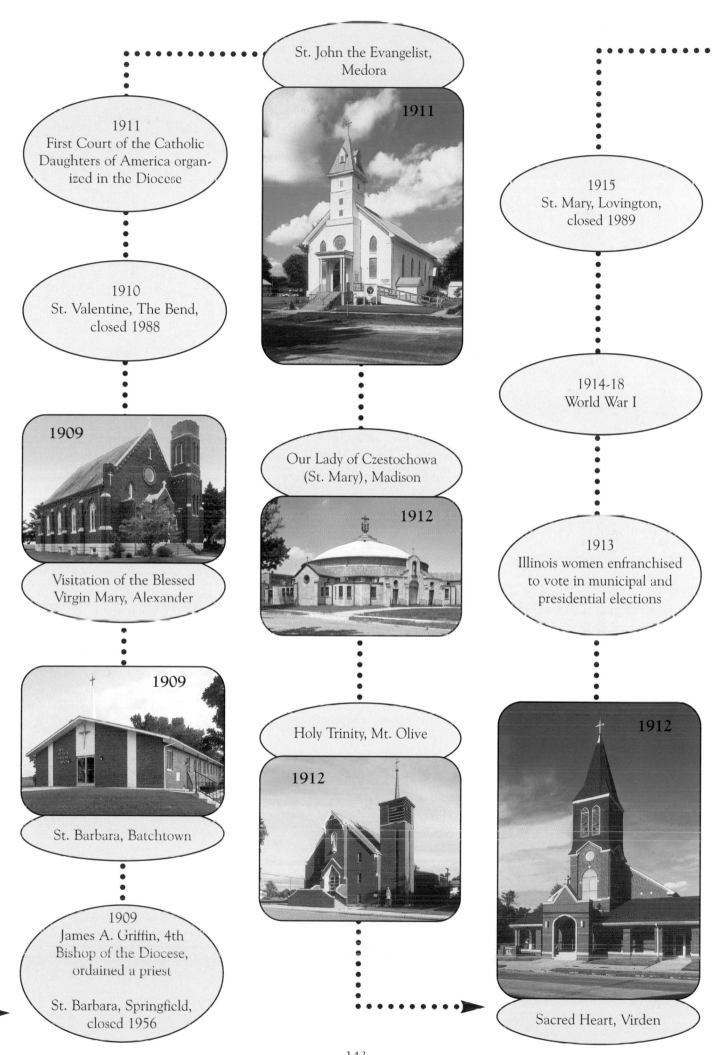

1911
First Court of the Catholic Daughters of America organized in the Diocese

1910
St. Valentine, The Bend, closed 1988

1909
Visitation of the Blessed Virgin Mary, Alexander

1909
St. Barbara, Batchtown

1909
James A. Griffin, 4th Bishop of the Diocese, ordained a priest

St. Barbara, Springfield, closed 1956

St. John the Evangelist, Medora

1911

Our Lady of Czestochowa (St. Mary), Madison

1912

Holy Trinity, Mt. Olive

1912

1915
St. Mary, Lovington, closed 1989

1914-18
World War I

1913
Illinois women enfranchised to vote in municipal and presidential elections

1912

Sacred Heart, Virden

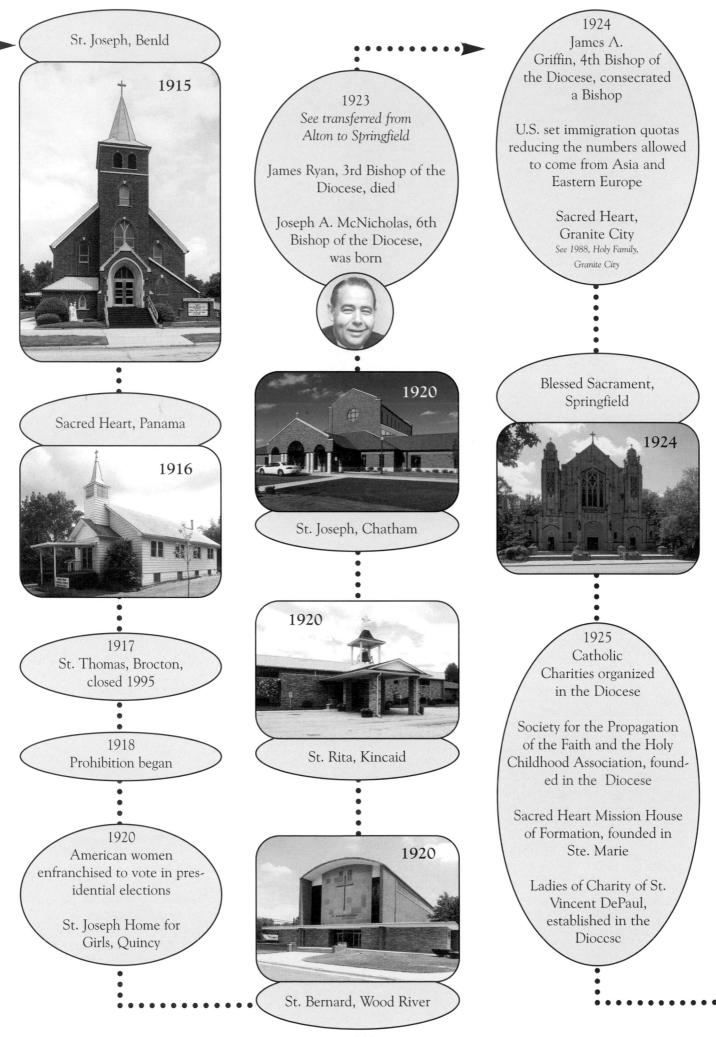

St. Joseph, Benld

1915

1923
*See transferred from
Alton to Springfield*

James Ryan, 3rd Bishop of the
Diocese, died

Joseph A. McNicholas, 6th
Bishop of the Diocese,
was born

1924
James A.
Griffin, 4th Bishop of
the Diocese, consecrated
a Bishop

U.S. set immigration quotas
reducing the numbers allowed
to come from Asia and
Eastern Europe

Sacred Heart,
Granite City
*See 1988, Holy Family,
Granite City*

Sacred Heart, Panama

1916

1920

St. Joseph, Chatham

Blessed Sacrament,
Springfield

1924

1917
St. Thomas, Brocton,
closed 1995

1918
Prohibition began

1920

St. Rita, Kincaid

1925
Catholic
Charities organized
in the Diocese

Society for the Propagation
of the Faith and the Holy
Childhood Association, founded in the Diocese

Sacred Heart Mission House
of Formation, founded in
Ste. Marie

Ladies of Charity of St.
Vincent DePaul,
established in the
Diocese

1920
American women
enfranchised to vote in presidential elections

St. Joseph Home for
Girls, Quincy

1920

St. Bernard, Wood River

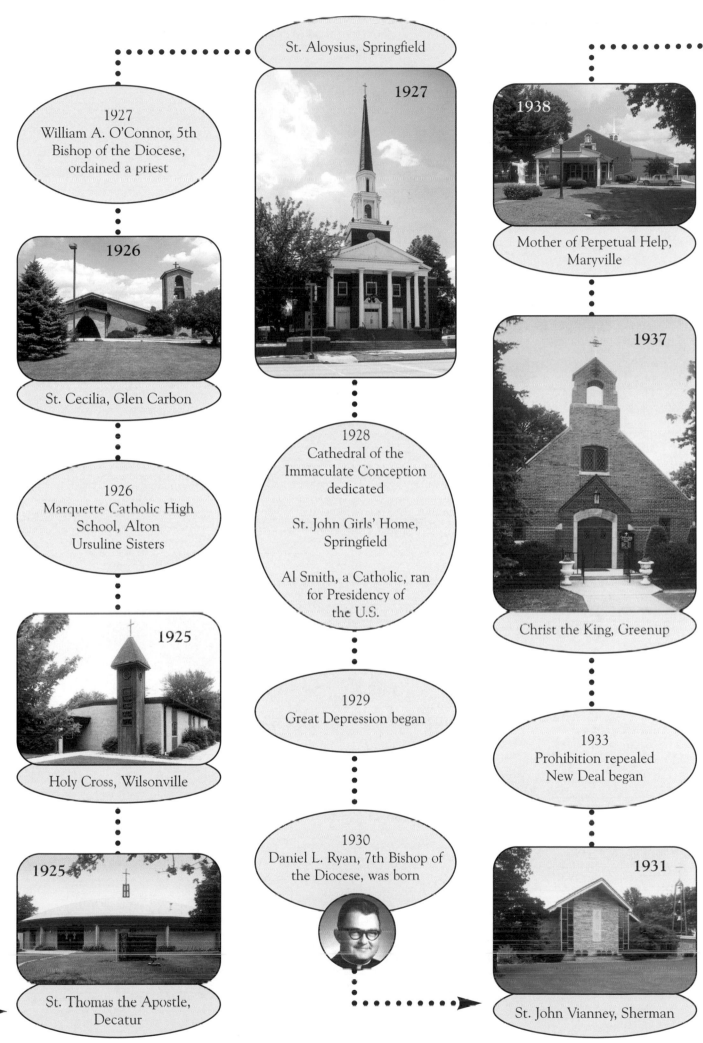

St. Aloysius, Springfield

1927

1927
William A. O'Connor, 5th Bishop of the Diocese, ordained a priest

1926
St. Cecilia, Glen Carbon

1926
Marquette Catholic High School, Alton
Ursuline Sisters

1925
Holy Cross, Wilsonville

1925
St. Thomas the Apostle, Decatur

1928
Cathedral of the Immaculate Conception dedicated

St. John Girls' Home, Springfield

Al Smith, a Catholic, ran for Presidency of the U.S.

1929
Great Depression began

1930
Daniel L. Ryan, 7th Bishop of the Diocese, was born

1938
Mother of Perpetual Help, Maryville

1937
Christ the King, Greenup

1933
Prohibition repealed
New Deal began

1931
St. John Vianney, Sherman

1941
U. S. entered World War II
Broadcast television began

Our Lady Queen Peace,
Bethalto

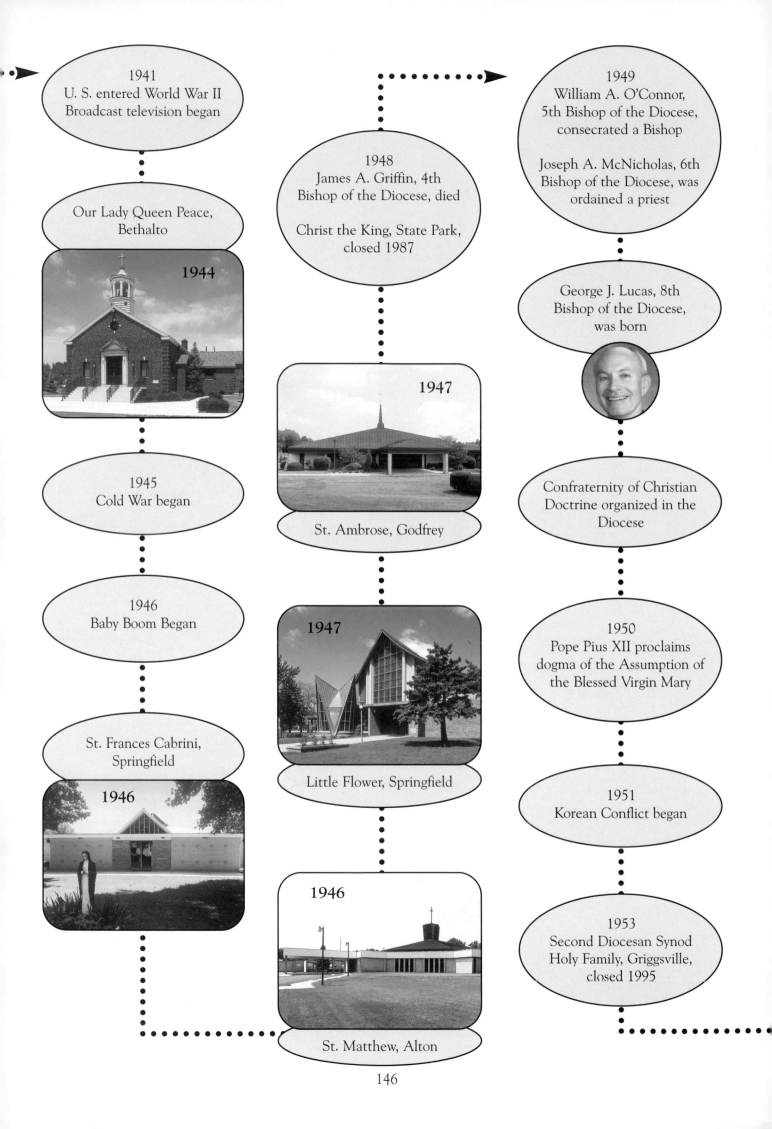

1944

1945
Cold War began

1946
Baby Boom Began

St. Frances Cabrini,
Springfield

1946

1948
James A. Griffin, 4th
Bishop of the Diocese, died

Christ the King, State Park,
closed 1987

1947

St. Ambrose, Godfrey

1947

Little Flower, Springfield

1946

St. Matthew, Alton

1949
William A. O'Connor,
5th Bishop of the Diocese,
consecrated a Bishop

Joseph A. McNicholas, 6th
Bishop of the Diocese, was
ordained a priest

George J. Lucas, 8th
Bishop of the Diocese,
was born

Confraternity of Christian
Doctrine organized in the
Diocese

1950
Pope Pius XII proclaims
dogma of the Assumption of
the Blessed Virgin Mary

1951
Korean Conflict began

1953
Second Diocesan Synod
Holy Family, Griggsville,
closed 1995

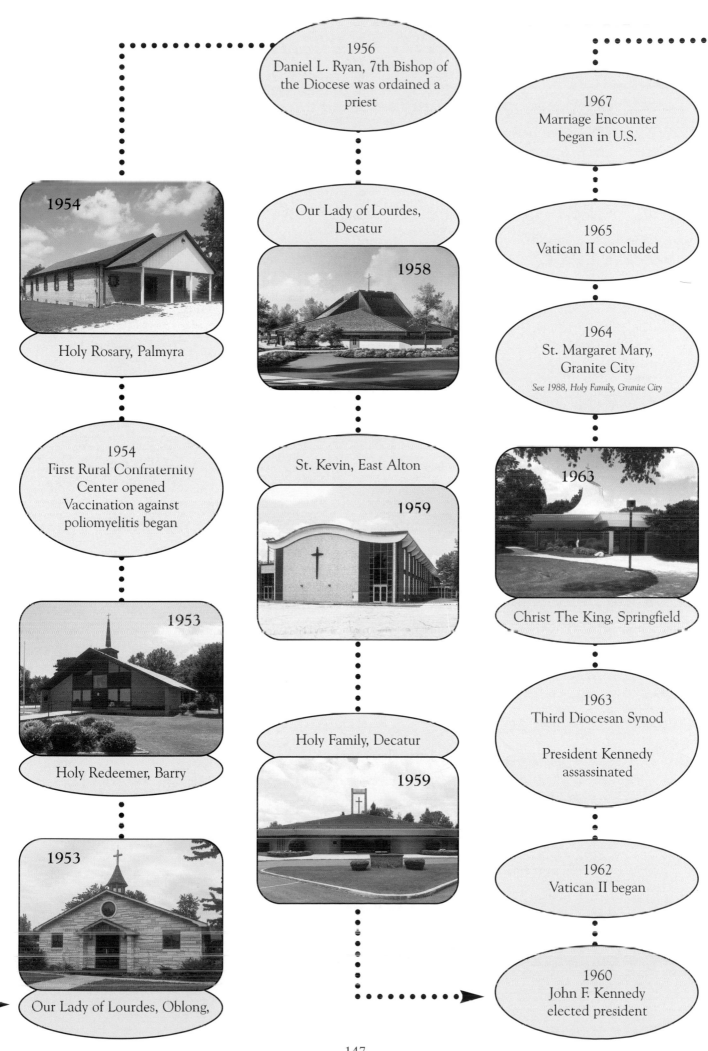

1956
Daniel L. Ryan, 7th Bishop of the Diocese was ordained a priest

1967
Marriage Encounter began in U.S.

1954

Holy Rosary, Palmyra

Our Lady of Lourdes, Decatur

1958

1965
Vatican II concluded

1964
St. Margaret Mary, Granite City

See 1988, Holy Family, Granite City

1954
First Rural Confraternity Center opened
Vaccination against poliomyelitis began

St. Kevin, East Alton

1959

1963

Christ The King, Springfield

1953

Holy Redeemer, Barry

Holy Family, Decatur

1959

1963
Third Diocesan Synod

President Kennedy assassinated

1953

Our Lady of Lourdes, Oblong,

1962
Vatican II began

1960
John F. Kennedy elected president

1968
Humanae Vitae issued by Pope Paul VI

1969
Joseph A. McNicholas, 6th Bishop of the Diocese, was ordained a Bishop (Auxiliary of St. Louis)

Diocesan Office of Catholic Education opened

Our Lady of the Holy Spirit, Mt. Zion

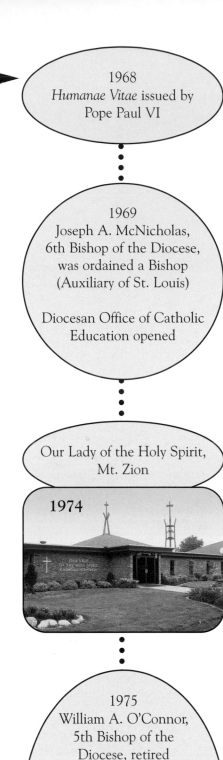

1974

1975
William A. O'Connor, 5th Bishop of the Diocese, retired

Joseph A. McNicholas, 6th Bishop of the Diocese, installed as Bishop

George J. Lucas, 8th Bishop of the Diocese was ordained a priest

1976
Call to Action holds first Congress Detroit

1979

1979
Holy Family, Mt. Sterling Merger of St. Mary and St. Joseph

1977

St. Dominic, Quincy

1977
The Western Catholic renamed *Time & Eternity*

1976

St. Jude, Rochester

1981
Daniel L. Ryan, 7th Bishop of the Diocese, was ordained a Bishop (Auxiliary of Joliet)

1983
William A. O'Connor, 5th Bishop of the Diocese, died

Joseph A. McNicholas, 6th Bishop of the Diocese, died

1984
Daniel L. Ryan , 7th Bishop of the Diocese, installed as Bishop

1985
Time & Eternity renamed *Catholic Times*

1988
Holy Family, Litchfield Merger of Assumption of the Blessed Virgin Mary and St. Aloysius

1988

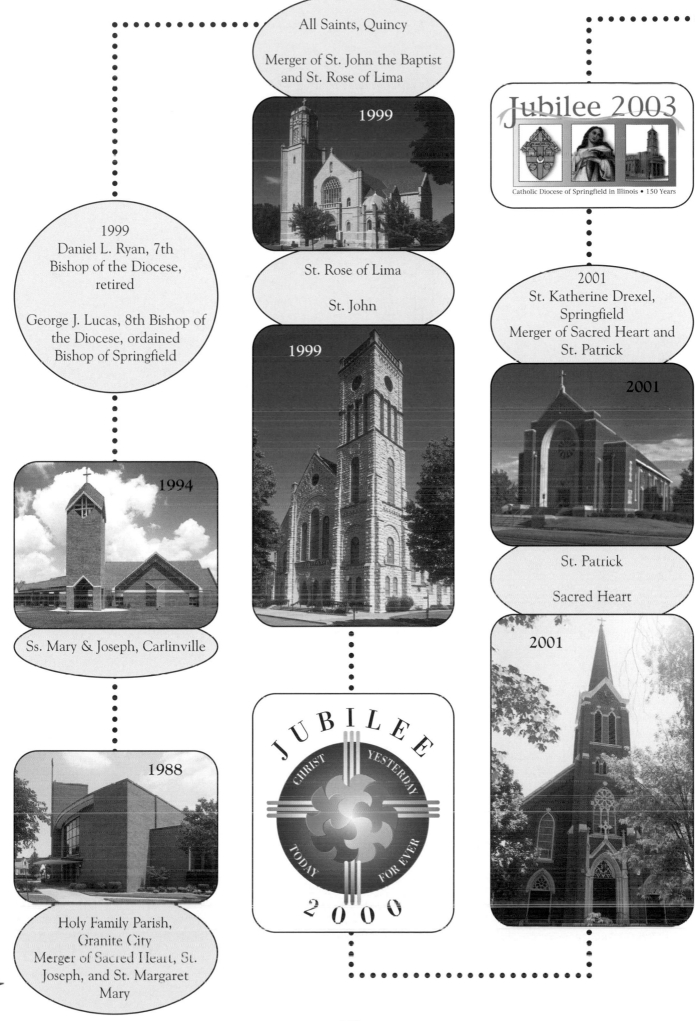

All Saints, Quincy

Merger of St. John the Baptist and St. Rose of Lima

1999

Jubilee 2003

Catholic Diocese of Springfield in Illinois • 150 Years

1999
Daniel L. Ryan, 7th Bishop of the Diocese, retired

George J. Lucas, 8th Bishop of the Diocese, ordained Bishop of Springfield

St. Rose of Lima

St. John

1999

2001
St. Katherine Drexel, Springfield
Merger of Sacred Heart and St. Patrick

2001

1994

Ss. Mary & Joseph, Carlinville

St. Patrick

Sacred Heart

2001

1988

JUBILEE
CHRIST YESTERDAY
TODAY FOR EVER
2000

Holy Family Parish, Granite City
Merger of Sacred Heart, St. Joseph, and St. Margaret Mary

Mississippi River, Calhoun County

Select Bibliography

A manuscript of this book with endnotes is available by request in the Media Resource Center,
Catholic Pastoral Center, Springfield.

Billington, Ray Allen. *The Protestant Crusade, 1800-1860: a Study of the Origins of American Nativism.* New York: Rinehart and Co., 1938.

Cooke, Mary Francis. *His Love Heals: a History of the Hospital Sisters of the Third Order of St. Francis, 1875-1975.* Chicago: Franciscan Herald Press, 1975.

Davis, Cyprian. *The History of Black Catholics in the United States.* New York: Crossroad, 1990

Davis, James E. *Frontier Illinois.* Bloomington: Indiana University Press, 1998.

Ekberg, Carl J. *French Roots in the Illinois Country: the Mississippi Frontier in Colonial Times.* Urbana: University of Illinois Press, 1998.

Faragher, John Mack. *Sugar Creek: Life on the Illinois Prairie.* New Haven: Yale University Press, 1986.

Hemesath, Caroline. *From Slave to Priest: a Biography of the Rev. Augustine Tolton, First Afro-American Priest in the United States.* Chicago: Franciscan Herald Press, 1973.

Kauffman, Christopher J. *Columbianism and the Knights of Columbus: a Quincentenary History.* New York: Simon and Shuster, 1992.

Kelly, Mary Gilbert. *Catholic Immigrant Colonization Projects in the United States, 1815- 1860.* United States Catholic Historical Society Monograph Series, vol. XVII. New York: United States Catholic Historical Society, 1939.

Kennelly, Karen, ed. *American Catholic Women: a Historical Exploration.* New York: Macmillan, 1989.

Miller, Sr. Ignatius, O.S.U., *Ursulines of the Central Province.* Crystal City, Missouri, 1983.

Sisters Adorers of the Precious Blood, anniversary book, 1938.

Thwaites, Reuben Gold., ed. *The Jesuit Relations and Allied Documents; Travels and Explorations of the Jesuit Missionaries in New France, 1610-1791;* the original French, Latin, and Italian texts, with English translations and notes. 73 volumes. Cleveland: Burrows Bros. Co., 1896-1901.

Thompson, Joseph J., ed. *Diocese of Springfield in Illinois, Diamond Jubilee History, 1853-1928.* Springfield: Hartman Printing Co. for Right Reverend James A. Griffin, D.D., 1928.

Trisco, Robert Frederick. *The Holy See and the Nascent Church in the Middle Western United States, 1826-1850.* Analecta Gregoriana, Vol. 125, Series Facultatis Historiae Ecclesiasticae sectio B, n. 21. Rome: Gregorian University Press, 1962.

Winterbauer, Thomas Aquinas. *Lest We Forget: the First Hundred Years of the Dominican Sisters, Springfield Illinois.* Chicago: Adams Press, 1973.

Zurbonsen, A[nthony]. *In Memoriam, Clerical Bead Roll of the Diocese of Alton.* 1918.

Acknowledgements

Diocesan Sesquicentennial Steering Committee

Very Reverend John A. Renken, Vicar General/Moderator of the Curia, Chair
Sister Mary Matthias Clarke, O.P., Archivist (R.I.P.)
Reverend Thom Dennis, Sacramental Minister, St. James Parish, Decatur
Sister Susan Karina Dickey, O.P., Archivist & Diocesan Historian
Patrick Fitzgerald, Executive Assistant to the Vicar General and General Counsel
Eliot Kapitan, Director, Office for Worship
Marlene Mulford, Director, Office for Stewardship and Development
Kathie Sass, Director, Office for Communications
Brother Pat Shea, O.F.M., Executive Assistant to the Vicar General, Legal Counsel
Reverend Monsignor Paul W. Sheridan, Pastor, Immaculate Conception Parish, Pierron, and St. Nicholas Parish, Pocahontas

The author wishes to thank the following individuals. She apologizes for any omissions.
(All locations are in Illinois unless otherwise indicated)

Very Reverend Lawrence Auda, V.F., Gillespie
Reverend George Auger, C.S.V., Clerics of St. Viator, Arlington Heights
Sister Ann Bailey, O.S.F., Hospital Sisters of the Third Order of St. Francis, Springfield
Reverend Robert T. Becker, Springfield
Mr. Tom Beynon, Divernon
Ms. Amy Bliefnick, St. Teresa High School, Decatur
Sister Paulette Collings, O.S.F., Hospital Sisters of the Third Order of St. Francis, Springfield
Mr. and Mrs. Joseph Eling, Quincy
Mrs. Rosemary Elsberry, Paris
Sister Mary Clare Fitchner, O.P., Parish Life Coordinator, St. Mark, Venice and Our Lady of Czestochowa, Madison
Mr. James C. Forstall, Springfield
Ms. Susan Full, Springfield College in Illinois, Springfield
Reverend Jeffery A. Grant, Greenup
Reverend Francis Jerome Gray, O.F.M., Professor Emeritus, Quincy University, Chicago
Mrs. Elise Hines, Catholic War Veterans, Springfield
Very Reverend Robert J. Jallas, V.F., Quincy
Reverend J. Michael Jenkins, Pittsfield
Sister Ella J. Kaster, C.S.J., Diocese of Green Bay, Green Bay, Wisconsin
Sister Mary Bernardine Kapusta, O.P., Springfield
Ms. Lori Large, Routt Catholic High School, Jacksonville
Reverend Kevin M. Laughery, Aubrun
Ms. Vicky Ludwig, St. Anthony High School, Effingham
Mr. Pete McCall, United Mine Workers, Fairfax, Virginia
Mrs. Freddie McEwen-Randle, Decatur
Reverend Donald J. Meehling, Springfield
Sister Anna Marie Mehigan, O.P., Springfield
Sister Rosemary Meiman, O.S.U., Ursuline Sisters, Central Province, U.S.A., Crystal City, Missouri
Ms. Nancy Merz, Midwest Jesuit Archives, St. Louis, Missouri
Ms. Mary Michaels, Illinois State Historical Library, Springfield
Sister Thomas More, O.S.U., Marquette Catholic High School, Alton
Sister Judith Morris, O.S.F., St. Joseph Home, Springfield
Reverend Charles P. Mulcrone, Springfield
Reverend William J. Overmann, Paris
Mr. and Mrs. Joseph Ozanic Jr., Mt. Olive
Ms. Regina Preston, Quincy Notre Dame High School, Quincy
Mrs. Bernice E. Probst, Island Grove
Mr. Edward Russo, Sangamon Valley Collection, Lincoln Library, Springfield
Mr. Rich Saal, *State Journal-Register*, Springfield
Sister JoAn Schullian, O.S.F., Decatur
Mr. Robert Schepers, Quincy
Ms. Clara Thies, St. Anthony High School, Effingham
Ms. Denise Thuston, Franciscans of the Sacred Heart Province, St. Louis, Missouri
Ms. Patricia Tomczak, Brenner Library, Quincy University, Quincy

Sister Mary Linda Tonellato, O.P. Dominican Sisters of Springfield, Illinois, Springfield
Mrs. Joyce Vahling, Franciscan Monastery Museum, Teutopolis
Mrs. Bonnie Weatherly, Daughters of Charity Archives, Emmitsburg, Maryland
Sister Carol Marie Wildt, S.S.N.D., School Sisters of Notre Dame, St. Louis Province, St. Louis, Missouri
Sister Mary Kenan Wolff, S.S.N.D., Diocese of Belleville, Belleville
Reverend Joseph Zimmerman, O.F.M., Quincy

Discussion Groups

St. Mary, Marshall
Our Lady of Cestochowa, St. Mary, Madison

Interviews

Reverend Roy R. Bauer, Quincy
Mrs. Edward F. Blittschau, St. Louis
Reverend Richard L. Chiola, Springfield
Ms. Mary Lou Devera, Decatur
Mrs. Rita Greenwald, Springfield
Brother Michael Groeschell, F.S.S.C., Riverton
Sister Mary Harris, O.P., New Market, Minnesota
Sister Marie Henebry, Legion of Mary, Springfield
Most Reverend George J. Lucas, Springfield
Mr. and Mrs. Jack Natterman, Springfield
Mr. Roy Lanham, Director, Office for Campus Ministry, Charleston
Mr. Henry Petrilli, Springfield
Mrs. Winifred White Howard, Alton
Most Reverend Daniel L. Ryan, retired, Springfield
Ms. Reneé Saunches, Decatur
Sister Phyllis Schenk, O.P., Springfield
Reverend Frank Westhoff, Springfield
Mother Mary Ingeborg, F.S.G.M., Alton

Diocesan Agencies and Offices

Sister Jane Boos, S.S.N.D., Office for Social Concerns
Mrs. Norma Jean Capranica, John Paul I Apartments, Springfield
Reverend Eugene Costa, Chancellor
Mrs. Donna Dausman, Office for Family and Youth Ministry
Mrs. Jana Doty, Office for Family and Youth Ministry
Mrs. Cheryl Kannall, Office of the Bishop
Mrs. Martina Kocher, Villa Maria Catholic Life Center
Mr. Leroy Jordan, Black Catholic Advisory Board
Ms. Candace Lumetta, Catholic Children's Home, Alton
Mrs. Patty Polonus, Office of the Chancellor
Mrs. Lisa Reeves, Pastoral Media Center
Very Reverend Kenneth C. Steffen, Chaplain to the Filipino Community, Springfield and Riverton
Mr. Tom Reiser, Office for Finance

Index

Index